THE
GREEN
MAGAZINE

GUIDE TO PERSONAL FINANCE

THE
GREEN
MAGAZINE

GUIDE TO PERSONAL FINANCE

*A No-B.S. Book
for Your Twenties and Thirties*

Ken Kurson

MAIN
STREET
BOOKS

D O U B L E D A Y
NEW YORK LONDON TORONTO SYDNEY AUCKLAND

A MAIN STREET BOOK
PUBLISHED BY DOUBLEDAY
a division of Bantam Doubleday Dell Publishing Group, Inc.
1540 Broadway, New York, New York 10036

MAIN STREET BOOKS, DOUBLEDAY, and the portrayal of a building with a tree are
trademarks of Doubleday, a division of Bantam Doubleday Dell Publishing Group, Inc.

Library of Congress Cataloging-in-Publication Data
Kurson, Ken.
Green magazine guide to personal finance: a no-B.S book for your
twenties and thirties / Ken Kurson. — 1st Main Street Books ed.
p.   cm.
"A Main Street book."
Includes bibliographical references and index.
1. Finance, Personal.   2. Young adults—Finance, Personal.   I. Green (Personal
finance magazine)   II. Title.   III. Title: Guide to personal finance.
HG179.K867   1998
332.024—DC21   97-48484
                                                                                                          CIP

ISBN 0-385-48759-2
Copyright © 1998 by Ken Kurson
All Rights Reserved
Printed in the United States of America
April 1998
First Main Street Books Edition
3   5   7   9   10   8   6   4   2

For Becky

Contents

Preface

This book isn't about the senseless accumulation of assets. It's about attaining the freedom to do what you want to do.

The editor of this book saw the word "freedom" in that last sentence and flinched. "Be more specific," he advised; "say '*financial* freedom.' " But it's more than just financial freedom. It's not about the ability to quit your job at any moment or to jet off to suave locales. It's about knowing that you have some control over the things that matter to you. It's about leaving time to do things that matter more to you than money. It's about working at a job because you love it, because it elevates you, instead of because you're deeply in debt, stuck with rent you can't afford or so afraid of investing you bury your savings in jars scattered around the backyard.

That kind of freedom takes planning, knowledge, discipline and all sorts of things that aren't always so fun. Most of all, it takes time. Time is the one thing most people in their twenties and thirties have in abundance. Not time to read financial books or time to pore over stock tables and credit agreements. But time to allow smart financial moves to work for them.

This isn't a book that screams "7 stocks to buy NOW!" or "How to make a million by the time you're bald!" It's not a cheerful "Gee, personal finance is so easy!" book. This book aims to help you feel a little less intimidated or bored by money matters, a little more eager to open an IRA, a little more resolute to make above-minimum credit card payments—and get you a little closer to your financial goals.

Three years ago, I started a 'zine called *Green.* I thought there was room for financial writing that wasn't breathless, intimidating, jargon-packed, humorless and boring. I thought a magazine for those new to personal finance could be funny and cool and easy on the eyes and also have a ton of useful information.

Green is for those who wince when terms like "p/e ratio" or "beta" are casually dropped in the financial press without further explanation. It's for those who cringe when headlines promise them quick fortunes from no effort. In short, *Green* is personal finance for those made nauseous by cheesy phrases like "personal finance."

Gone are the days of lifetime employment at a single company, pension plans managed by kindly and unseen managers and a Social Security system whose fiscal stability is beyond question. Gone are the days when students earned enough during a summer to pay next year's tuition and gone are the days when credit cards were issued only after careful scrutiny of a user's ability to pay the bills.

So this book was written with the idea that money matters could be interesting, compelling, maybe even cool. But underpinning it all is the idea that money is not the end, but the means. This book is designed to help you understand the financial issues for what has been condescendingly called "the real world."

Mike Royko, the late great Chicago newspaperman, once told a young reporter always to keep some "fuck-you money." Enough to know that the reason you get up every day and drag your behind into work is not that you must, but that at some level, you choose to. That doesn't mean that you have to love every minute. But a strong financial situation means more than an emergency reserve or the ability to pick up the check at a restaurant once in a while. It's the knowledge that your life is, at least to some degree, in your control. The choices you make are not dictated by starvation and eviction fears, but by your goals and dreams and hopes and the best parts of you.

This book is not for dummies. I'll assume that you haven't read a lot of finance books, but I won't assume you're an idiot. I'll explain terms that might be unfamiliar, but I won't condescend. I'll try not to use bogus young-sounding words or phony youthful expressions (please feel free to give me a wedgie if you spot "nice chunk of change" in these pages). And I'll try to give it to you straight.

This is important stuff. We're talking about your future; the issues are real and they're serious. But it doesn't have to be a drag and it doesn't have to make you crazy. In this book, you'll discover how a little smart time spent on your finances now can make a lot of difference later on. Money matters are what you make of them. It will show you how to make the most of what you have right now, so the search for what you want will be a little easier.

Introduction

Things are different today. The idea of working hard in school so that a solid American manufacturer of solid American products hires you to spend forty years earning a gold watch and a company pension is as quaint as the picket-fenced house that used to require 20 percent down to own.

Sure, there's new technology. Transactions are made over invisible wires, ledgered in laptop computers and followed by Touch-tone. But these are simply new ways of doing old things. What's truly different is not the method but the playing field itself.

Three major changes have impacted the financial horizon for young people:

1. Gone are the days when a job with AT&T or IBM meant lifetime employment and a fat pension. Today's entrant to the workforce knows that she has to fend for herself, vocationally and financially.

2. The explosion of self-directed retirement plans—IRAs, 401(k)s, etc.—means that people are more responsible for their own financial futures than ever before.

3. Lack of confidence in the long-term viability of the Social Security system means that young people must manage their dollars with greater care than their parents did.

And then there are the subtler but equally important financial shifts. Credit and loans are more readily available and widely used than ever before. Leasing has gained on buying, and investing has challenged savings, while spending has challenged both.

We'll get into all these things in detail in the chapters to follow. But the point is that there's no benevolent overseer looking out for today's young entrant to the workforce. And it's hardly just retirement and the distant future that present financial challenges. There're a million goals in between now and dentures. So the job at hand is to figure out what those goals are and how to achieve them.

This book is divided into five chapters:

- **Counting It**

Figure where your finances are and where you'd like them to be.

- **Repaying It**

Take stock of what you owe, who you owe and how to pay it back. Credit, credit ratings, student loans, bankruptcy, etc.

- **Working It**

You work hard for your cash; make it work hard for you. Stocks, bonds, mutual funds, oh my. Also: retirement, model portfolios, socially responsible investing and more.

- **Protecting It**

You realize, of course, that your financial well-being is under constant attack, from taxes, disasters, relationships, even insurance salesmen! Here's where you learn how to fight back.

- **Enjoying It**

Well, that's really the whole point, isn't it? Buying a home (or being smart about renting), traveling, car shopping and getting the most for your buck—all of these fall under the rubric of "enjoying it."

Think about your financial goals. Think about your relationship with money. Think about what you want out of life and what it'll take to make those things real. Whether you read it cover to cover, skim the sections you find useful, or are just here for the comics, this book is designed to make the sometimes scary topic of personal finance something you can conquer.

1. Counting It

NOTHIN' BUT NET: WHAT YOU'VE GOT
AND WHAT YOU OWE

YOUR PERSONAL BALANCE SHEET

WAREHOUSING YOUR MONEY

HOW TO PICK A BROKER

RECORD KEEPING

Nothin' but Net:
What You've Got and What You Owe

Every personal finance book begins with the same instructions: add up everything you've got and subtract everything you owe. This results in a number called your net worth. Usually, there's a lengthy worksheet, with spaces for the reader to write in bank account balances and credit card totals. A thorough analysis, however, reveals that no one in history has ever filled out one of those worksheets.

As it turns out, figuring your net worth is a good place to start. It's hard to argue with the good sense of knowing where you stand.

But more important than figuring where you are is figuring where you want to be. And then, of course, figuring out how to get there.

Your Personal Balance Sheet

"Keep your old love letters. Throw away your old bank statements." Mary Schmich, in a swell column falsely attributed to a speech Kurt Vonnegut never gave at MIT's commencement.

I'm not someone who believes in tracking every penny spent and earned. Money's not important enough to squander time contemplating every candy bar purchase. And I don't believe in budgeting. Preparing a list of prescribed amounts to be spent on each category each month strikes me as not only overly analytical, but somewhat dangerous. As with government budgets, you can bet that with personal budgets, every penny of resources allocated to a specific purpose will end up being spent.

But there is something to be said for taking a hard look at the gap between where your money goes and where you'd like it to go. If you consistently wonder why you're always broke, or why there's never much left over at the end of the month, or why your resolutions not to run up your credit card balance never stick, it might pay to spend some time following the footprints of your money.

Think about your finances for the last month. Estimate all the money you spent and compare it with all the money you either earned or somehow lucked into. You don't need a Nobel prize in economics to see that if the first number consistently dwarfs the second, some adjustments need to be made.

Pretty scary stuff, isn't it?

The first areas to attack are those that leap off the page like "I can't believe I spend so much on *that.*" Every time I do this exercise I'm horrified by how much money I'm wasting in at least one or two categories. For me, it's often workday lunches that throw the "dining out" category into the red. Typically, after noticing that, I start packing a lunch to work. Then my attitude slowly deteriorates from smug self-congratulations on the cash I'm not wasting to increasing resentment that I'm not hitting my favorite lunch spots enough.

But as with a lot of money decisions, there's often a middle ground that can accommodate both the need to reign in spending and the desire to enjoy whatever that spending procures. In my case, I realized that the reason I always grew to resent brown-bagging it is that I'd always eat my lunch at my desk. So I wasn't just missing the fabulous bagel joints, soup magicians and sandwich craftsmen, I was missing the time away from my desk and phone and computer. The solution was embarrassingly obvious: bring my lunch, but eat it outside the office.

It's amazing how closely frugality aligns with other values many people hold. Lots of cheaper alternatives, for example, are also better for the environment—riding the subway and reusing stuff come to mind. Borrowing books and reading magazines at the library not only saves cash, but also supports a venerable institution. Thrift-store clothes aren't just cheaper; they usually look cooler (feel free to send the author any Fred Perry striped shirts you find).

Expenses
Bank Fees .... _____
Books .... _____
Campaign Contributions .... _____
Charity .... _____
Clothes .... _____
Computer Stuff .... _____
Education .... _____
Entertainment .... _____
Food
    Dining Out .... _____
    Groceries ... + _____ = ... _____
Gifts Given .... _____
Gym/Sports stuff .... _____
Health
    Medical .... _____
    Dental .... _____
    Drugs .... _____
    Mental .... _____
    Other ... + _____ = ... _____
Hobbies
Insurance
    Auto .... _____
    Health .... _____
    Home .... _____
    Life ... + _____ = ... _____
Interest paid
    Credit card .... _____
    Student loan .... _____
    Mortgage ... + _____ = ... _____
Legal fees .... _____
Pets
    Food .... _____
    Care ... + _____ = ... _____
Repayments
    Credit card .... _____
    Student loan .... _____
    Other ... + _____ = ... _____
Subscriptions
    Print .... _____
    Internet ... + _____ = ... _____
Taxes
    Federal .... _____
    State .... _____
    Medicare .... _____
    Social Security .... _____
    Property .... _____
    Other ... + _____ = ... _____
Transportation
    Public Trans .... _____
    Auto
        Fuel .... _____
        Service ... + _____ = ... _____
Utilities
    Telephone
        Long distance .... _____
        Local .... _____
        Cellular/pager .... _____
    Cable .... _____
    Electric .... _____
    Heating oil/Gas .... _____
    Water ... + _____ = ...

Total Going Out _____

Income
Salary .... _____
Investment returns .... _____
Interest earned .... _____
Freelance .... _____
Miscellaneous .... _____
Gifts received .... _____

Total Coming in _____

There's no need to deprive yourself of things you truly believe are worthwhile. The point is not to waste money on stuff that you didn't even realize was costing such a big chunk of your monthly budget. My hobbies are important to me; I don't beat myself up for spending money on stuff for my bike or for guitar strings. But it's just as important to realize that sacrificing short-term comforts for long-term goals is worth it. As we'll learn in the "Working It" chapter, even a few dollars a week can turn into a big wad of cash over time. But even without that incentive, it's pretty easy to see that not throwing money away is a pretty good financial move. That said, we move on to . . .

Warehousing Your Money

Account inertia: The tendency of a bank account at rest to remain at rest unless acted on by an outside force.

Where you keep your money will affect you more frequently than just about any other financial decision. But because it's not a sexy decision, without the big numbers associated with choosing a credit card or a mutual fund, it's a choice often made on the basis of which bank's got the best-looking ads.

I picked my bank for the same reasons most people probably pick theirs: it was down the street and had low minimum initial and balance requirements. Actually, those aren't such bad reasons. Using a bank that's inconvenient and requires a big chunk of money just to save some fees is too smart by half. So the point is to combine as many of these elements as possible, with special emphasis on those that matter to you:

- Fees
- Service
- Convenience
- Interest rate on savings and/or checking accounts
- Manageable minimums, both to open and to maintain

All of these are worth considering when you select a place to store your cash. But of special concern are the fees banks are charging, which have been rising in the last few years. What's more irritating than bank

You Are Your Parents: Dad at Wrigley Field

What brand of peanut butter do you buy? Marketing experts will confirm that it's probably whatever brand your parents use. In fact, the more personal the item, the more likely you are to inherit the brand preference from your parents. Shaving cream and, uh, "feminine products" are even more likely to match the brands used by your p's.

When it comes to attitudes about spending, nothing is more personal than money itself. Which brings me to my dad.

My dad wasn't a cheap man. But he was in the habit of weighing all decisions, particularly financial ones, with the gravity one usually reserves for life-or-death issues. Like a lot of people his age, he had many habits that seemed annoying to those who never lived through a depression: turn off the lights, eat the heels of a loaf of bread, don't leave the faucet dripping.

There's a joke—actually, there're a million jokes, but this is the one I'm going to tell—about how a guy goes into a store for a bottle of pickles. "How much?" he asks the shopkeeper. "Ten cents for the first bottle, five for the second," comes the reply. "I'll take the second one," says the customer.

My dad loved that joke, loved any joke where illogic was evidenced in business. One time my dad and me were in a store in Toronto, buying batteries for a Lego motor he'd bought me as a present for keeping quiet during a business meeting. The batteries were kept in a big bucket. Atop the bucket was a handwritten sign: $1 EACH OR 9 FOR $10. A penalty for buying in volume was among the funniest things he'd ever heard.

People tend to appreciate a gift from a cheap person more than one from someone who's lavish with presents. It's simple economics—gifts from a tightwad are in short supply, which increases their value. The same principle applies when someone who usually prepares a cost/benefit analysis before the departure of every dime suddenly permits a mad exodus from his wallet. My dad was a serious guy. He felt things deeply and walked around with a partial but permanent sadness about the horrible stuff that happens in the world. In general, he was suspicious of fun—"What's the point?" he'd ask when you told him you'd gone parachuting or wanted a motorcycle. And he wasn't criticizing, he just truly didn't get it. So those occasions when he went wild, when a Ping-Pong table suddenly showed up in the basement, were made more special to his kids, who knew that the concept of splurge wasn't part of his instinctual character.

My dad did have one financial Achilles' heel: baseball. He'd take us to Wrigley Field or Comiskey Park in Chicago or the Old Vet in Cleveland and all of a sudden he was J. P. Morgan—pennants, Cracker Jacks, hot dogs, the works. Years later, I worked as a security guard at Wrigley. Often I'd see families come to the game loaded down like burros with warm pop and soggy sandwiches. For the middle class, the couple-times-a-year grace that is a ballpark spending spree is growing obsolete.

Today, I know that there was method to my dad's ways. He hated spoiled kids and was determined to strike a balance between providing us whatever he could afford and leaving us with the attitude that we had it coming.

And now I'll tell you about one of the worst things I ever did.

After my parents divorced, I lived alone with my dad. We were sort of poor—not poor in an eating Alpo way, but poor in that we sold our piano and I had to hand over half my Baskin-Robbins wages for the family budget. I didn't know anything about what it means to face a mortgage and a recession and a house with no furniture. And my dad, having grown up at a time when guys could both play football and sing in the glee club, didn't know anything about the pestilent shallowness of a high school that was literally the model for John Hughes's *The Breakfast Club*.

It was September, time for some new school clothes, so we headed to Marshall's. I put things in the cart, no regard for price or quantity.

We got to the counter and the mental calculator that ran in Dad's brain at all times realized he wasn't going to have enough room on his credit card to cover it. "Kenny, you're going to have to put some of these things back," he said. I rolled my eyes, embarrassed and irritated. Then, on the way out to his Chrysler, its backseat overflowing with old newspapers and limerick books, I said something: "Man, are you cheap."

My dad died a couple years ago. My brother and sister and I made a simple ceremony and bought a simple headstone. He knows how I felt about him, how I grew to admire and embrace his old-fashioned attitudes and old-world ideas, even copying some of them. It continues to amaze me how firmly one's attitudes about money are rooted in those of his or her parents. But that's not the point. The point is that it's cold in Chicago and the ground there gets hard as cement. I'm far away from him and he's far away from me. And I wonder if the simple pine box I picked out is keeping my sweet dad warm.

fees? The bank charges you for the privilege of loaning your money to others for a profit. Worse, it's a regressive system that favors rich guys— maintain a large balance at the bank and you'll escape most or all of the fees. Keep a small balance and expect to pay for everything from writing checks to using the ATM to simply falling below a prescribed minimum balance.

ATM fees are particularly grating because banks have sold America on the cash-spitting machines with promises of greater efficiency and lower costs. Now that they've nearly succeeded in eliminating tellers and other services, the banks are turning around and sticking the customers with fees for everything from out-of-network ATMs to surcharges for more than a few usages. More than 90 percent of banks and savings and loans now charge the "foreign-use fee," usually about $1 for using your card in another bank's machine. On top of that are surcharges which can put the total fees anywhere from 1 percent to a whopping 4 percent. Think about it this way: the average ATM user makes seventy-two withdrawals a year, taking an average of $87 each time, a total of $6,264. The total yearly fees a user faces: $155! That's about $2.50 for every hundred bucks you withdraw. You'd do better at those check-cashing places on the street corner that are thought of as such rip-offs—the fees there are about a buck or so per $100.

TIP

Lower Fees, Please

Here are a few tips on keeping a lid on the myriad fees banks charge:

• Try to match a bank's fee structure with the type of banking you do. If you seldom write checks but frequently withdraw cash from ATMs, be tolerant of higher checking fees if a bank has low ATM fees.

• If you keep both a savings and a checking account, see if you can link your accounts. That makes it easier to move money between accounts; it also may help you escape a low-balance charge, since the combined balance may put you over the mandated minimum.

• If you rely heavily on ATMs, pick a bank with lots of them at convenient locations; most banks don't charge for withdrawals from their own machines.

• Use direct deposit for all regular-interval deposits, such as paychecks or government benefits. Banks save a lot when they don't have to deal with paper deposits, so some offer reduced minimums or extra transactions if you save them that hassle.

Electronic Banks

With the advent of better security, banking over the Internet has recently become less Jetsonian. This can be pretty convenient for record keeping and especially for those who do lots of shopping over the Internet—users can see their balances and when their checks have cleared by simply clicking open their accounts. Besides convenience, some Internet banks pass along the savings on personnel and branch offices in the form of lower fees and better interest rates on savings and CDs.

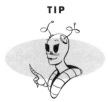

TIP

Some banks that offer electronic banking are Internet-only, while others are electronic versions of their regular banking services. When opening an account with an Internet-based bank (or any bank you don't know a lot about, for that matter), it's a good idea to check the Federal Deposit Insurance Corporation's website (*www.fdic.gov*) to make sure the bank is registered among the twelve thousand insured by the FDIC.

Credit Union

Credit unions offer all the services of banks—auto loans, mortgages, checking and savings accounts. Established in 1934 to give low-income Americans access to banking services, credit unions now number almost twelve thousand, with seventy million members. They're exempt from federal taxes, so their fees and rates are usually lower than banks'—as much as a full percentage point on car loans, for example. Credit union membership used to be restricted to those with a "common bond"—such as the same employer, church or labor union. Since 1982, the definition of "common bond" has loosened, and many credit unions have grown from part-time strongboxes to full-scale financial institutions that rival banks in assets and services offered.

Those with access to credit unions should strongly consider them as an alternative to banks. In addition to usually offering free checking and better rates, credit unions, many members feel, are the "right way" to bank—because members have something in common with other members. Call 800-358-5710 for information on CUs in your state.

Brokerage Account

This is where your stocks and bonds reside. We'll get to the distinctions between full-service, discount, deep discount and electronic brokerages later in the chapter. Some people use brokerage accounts for storing their spending and check-writing money. That's not always a good idea, though, since the day-to-day banking stuff—depositing a $35 check from your grandma, withdrawing $50 in cash—can be less convenient than at a bank with a million branches.

One particular type of brokerage account, however, is actually a terrific hybrid between bank account and a plain-vanilla brokerage account. An asset management account functions as a sort of one-stop shop for all a person's financial assets. In addition to holding securities (stocks, bonds, mutual funds, etc.), an AMA also functions as a quasi-bank. You can write checks on the account, and you get debit and ATM cards—all while your cash balance is swept into a money market fund that earns far better interest than a typical savings or checking account. Best of all, AMA holders receive one easy-to-read statement at the end of the month, detailing your credit card purchases, checks and investment performance on the same page. And AMAs are typically free of a lot of the niggling per-check and bounced-check charges with which banks nickel-and-dime their customers.

One drawback to asset management accounts is that they require pretty stiff initial deposits, from $5,000 (Schwab) to $10,000 (Fidelity) to $20,000 (Merrill Lynch). But don't automatically be scared off by that high figure. You can combine all your assets to meet that goal, so a mix of $3,000 in XYZ stock, $1,000 in cash and a $1,000 mutual fund will meet a $5,000 minimum. Additionally, unlike most banks, there's no penalty for falling below the minimum once the account is open. If you cobble together the initial minimum, you can withdraw all but $1 of it the next day.

The bigger drawback to AMAs, and all brokerage accounts, is that brokerages lack the millions of branches that the big banks operate. That means some services—depositing checks or dumb stuff like counting your loose change—can be a bigger hassle with an AMA. While paychecks can be direct-deposited, regular checks may have to be mailed if your brokerage doesn't have a branch near you. And even if there is a nearby branch, some AMAs don't even accept deposits of less than $50. Depending on your circumstances, one solution is to keep a no-frills savings account at a local bank, using it for all petty cash needs; many banks have low- or no-fee simple savings accounts that'll provide an ATM card. Then do your big stuff in an AMA—check writing, paycheck deposits and, of course, investments.

Certificates of Deposits (CDs)

You probably realize that when you deposit your money in your local savings bank, it doesn't just sit there in a drawer. It's loaned out to your neighbors, who use it to remodel homes, buy cars and start businesses. The people who borrow it pay more interest to the bank than the bank pays you to let it loan out your money. The bank keeps the difference between the rate it pays out and the rate it collects—and that narrow margin adds up to a pile of money big enough for banks to build grand headquarters and pay their executives handsomely.

The problem with regular savings accounts, though, is that the bank never knows when the depositor is going to show up demanding his money. That means the bank *does* have to keep a percentage of a depositor's money essentially sitting in a drawer, ready to be withdrawn instead of earning the bank the profits it loves.

That's why banks created CDs. Because the depositor agrees to keep his money tied up for a set period of time, the bank knows it can put that money to work without fear the depositor will come around to collect. The bank is willing to pay for that certainty, in the form of a few extra percentage points above the interest it pays on savings accounts. The longer a depositor consents to having his money tied up, the higher the rate he can expect from the bank.

The downside to this for the depositor, of course, is the loss of the use of that money. Banks charge steep penalties when depositors redeem their CDs before the term expires.

You'll hear more about whether CDs are the best place to park your money in the chapter on investing. But regardless of the wisdom of CDs as an investment vehicle, as a savings device it's clear that they're only suitable for money you're certain you won't be needing during the life of the CD.

 **WARNING!** The Internet has made buying CDs from foreign banks relatively easy. And with countries like Venezuela and Israel currently offering rates in the 11 percent range, it's tempting. Don't do it. We'll cover ways to go for the big investment returns later on, but the primary purpose of CDs is to

safely store your cash. Overseas CDs, however, expose investors to two big risks:

• Currency fluctuations. If the dollar strengthens compared with the currency of the CD's home country, then the CD loses value.

• Domestic CDs are insured by the FDIC, which means that your money's safe if the bank fails. In general, foreign banks don't provide the same peace of mind.

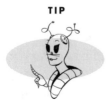

TIP

Free checking, thought to have gone the way of the dodo bird, has been staging something of a comeback. After years of standing by as bank fees rise, customers are finally beginning to vote with their feet. In response, some banks are catering to consumers who pay attention to fees. The consumer group Consumer Action does a periodic study of bank fees, including those that don't charge for checking accounts. Of course, free doesn't always mean completely free. With charges for everything from teller usage to bounced checks, ask for a "statement of fees" when you open your account. For a recent report, send an SASE to Consumer Action Free Checking, 116 New Montgomery St., Ste. 233; San Francisco, CA 94105.

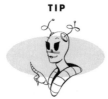

TIP

Cheap Checks

No matter where you keep your checking account—bank, credit union, brokerage—buy the actual checks on your own. That way, you'll have the chance to get checks that either advertise your support for a cause or look real cool. But you'll also save money, with self-ordered checks running about $4 to $8 for two hundred. Try these vendors:

Checks in the Mail 800-733-4443

Image 800-562-8768

Designer Checks 800-239-9222 (Usually the cheapest, although they're mostly kittens and butterflies.)

Message! 800-243-2565 (The do-gooders, with checks from the Sierra Club, Museum of Natural History, etc.)

How to Pick a Broker

I used to write a column in which wronged investors (or those who thought they'd been wronged) wrote to me asking for help. A good deal of these hassles involved brokers or brokerages—no surprise there. But when I'd ask the letter writers how they'd come to hire this guy or firm, a startling number of replies boiled down to "He cold-called me" or "I picked him out of a phone book."

You wouldn't hire a doctor or lawyer without scrutinizing credentials and demanding recommendations. So don't entrust your jackpot wad to someone you barely know. As with any professional, the best way to find a good broker is via recommendations from friends and others you trust. Remember, we're talking about your hard-earned money; finding a reliable broker is worth a little effort. Here are some things to think about before you hire anyone to shepherd your nest egg.

The Amount of Hand-Holding You Require

There are three types of broker—full-service, discount and deep discount. In general, expect a lot more attention from a full-service broker than a discounter, and a little more from a discounter than from a deep discounter.

Until pretty recently, there was no such thing as a discount broker. Full-service firms charged essentially what they felt like, which was plenty. As often as not, the broker was in charge of the client's funds, meaning he could buy and sell whatever he wanted. That's called a "discretionary" account. Unfortunately, the broker often didn't show much discretion; excessive buying and selling (aka "churning") was rampant, and putting the client's money into commission-rich but sense-poor investments funded a variety of schemes, like the limited partnership craze of the eighties.

With the advent of discount brokers, many full-service clients jumped ship. Figuring that they can manage their investments themselves and pay a lot less, many investors have gone to discounters to warehouse their portfolios. Only you can judge just how much TLC you need from a broker, but make sure you get the amount you're paying for: a full-service broker who doesn't return your calls certainly isn't worth the extra commissions. Conversely, if you don't want to spend tons of your own time and money on research and other things, you may be better off with a full-service firm.

Reputation of the Broker and the Firm

You would hope the maxim "Stay away from trouble, especially when it comes to money matters" would be so obvious that even a pretty obvious writer wouldn't need to say it. But if the years I spent writing about investors being ripped off are any indication, people often spend more time researching the purchase of refrigerators than they do where they put their life savings. If I had a dollar for every otherwise cautious and intelligent person who wrote to me after sending ten grand to someone who cold-called them with a hot stock tip, well, I'd have enough money to waste on hot stock tips.

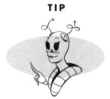

TIP

Investigate Your Broker

All brokers are required to register with the National Association of Securities Dealers. One of the easiest but most overlooked things an investor can do is to get a broker's rap sheet. Before starting with a broker (or continuing with one if you've got one already), call the NASD and ask for the broker's Central Registration Depository records. (You can also submit a records request through NASD's website.) They'll send you a form listing any "disclosable information," such as disciplinary action taken by any of the agencies under whose jurisdiction the broker may fall, any judgments he or she was involved in, and criminal convictions or indictments against the broker and/or firm. Investors may also want to check with the securities regulator in a broker's home state. Find out how to do that by contacting the national umbrella office at the address below.

• **National Association of Securities Dealers (NASD),** 1735 K Street, NW, Washington, DC 20006-1506; 800-289-9999; *http://www.nasdr.com.*

• **State Securities Regulator,** North American Securities Administrators Association, 1 Massachusetts Ave., NW, Suite 310, Washington, DC 20001, 202-737-0900

Price/Commissions

Brokers make money by charging investors a fee every time they buy or sell a stock, bond, or other security. In general, full-service brokerages charge more per trade than discounters, who charge more than the deep discounters.

As of 1997, the average discount broker charged $38.85 to buy or sell 100 shares at $50 per share (about .77 percent), while the average full-service broker charged about $150 (3.0 percent) for the same trade; deep discounters will go as low as 15 bucks a pop, regardless of the number and price of shares. If you're someone who trades a lot and you know exactly what you want to trade, saving $100 every time you deal $5,000 worth of stock is a bonus.

But it's not always so easy to calculate: some firms are cheaper for one kind of transaction and pricier for others. So even the question of price requires some introspection into what kind of trader you're going to be. Some firms are cheap for large-dollar transactions while others shine in transactions of large number of shares. If you tend to buy real cheap "penny stocks," you'll probably need a broker who cuts breaks for large-share transactions, while if you favor blue chips, you'll need the former.

Bear in mind that for the kind of buy-and-hold investing that just about all experts advise, commissions shouldn't play too big a part of the total picture. Brokerages market themselves relentlessly based on their super-low trading commissions, but I think that makes it easy to lose sight of the fact that often the best trade to make is no trade at all—and even the priciest brokerages don't charge anything for not trading.

There's no law that says you have to pay whatever commission the brokerage demands. With full-service brokers especially, the fees are almost always negotiable. They know they're at war with discounters, especially for the investing dollars of young people, who have yet to develop service-provider loyalties. Many will match or almost match the rates of the discounters (but not the deep discounters) if you simply ask.

Research
This is where the gap between full-service and discounters widens. A broker like Merrill Lynch has an army of analysts being paid millions to follow different industries and make buy/sell/hold recommendations on stocks

and bonds to Merrill clients. Schwab or Jack White can't match that kind of research depth. But there's a lot of doubt about whether the average investor is even aided by this research. A buy-and-hold long-term investor may end up paying for research he never uses.

And some discounters now offer more-than-rudimentary research and recommendations, usually including Standard & Poor's reports or Value Line's company outlooks.

TIP

It's tough to know if the research department your broker's always bragging about is actually any good. A couple places to look for insight include:

• **Institutional Investor,** 488 Madison Ave., New York, NY 10022, 212-303-3300. Every April, II runs an all-star list of the best brokerages. Single copies are a lofty $45, but it's available in most libraries.

• **Nelson's Directory of Investment Research,** Nelson Publications, 1 Gateway Plaza, Port Chester, NY 10573, 914-937-8400. Super-expensive (about $550), but carried in most libraries.

Breadth of Services
Here are a few key features you should look for in any brokerage account:

ASSET MANAGEMENT ACCOUNTS
As discussed earlier, all investors should consider asset management accounts, which organize all your financial instruments—mutual funds, IRA, individual stocks and bonds—under one umbrella. Unlike bare-bones brokerage accounts, an AMA also warehouses your savings, allows you to write checks and gives you Visa and ATM cards. Check writing is usually free, there's no monthly fee (though some charge an annual fee) and they don't nickel-and-dime you as much with annoying charges like bounced checks.

INTEREST ON CASH BALANCES
The excess cash you have in your account at just about any brokerage will usually earn interest. But there's a wide disparity in the amount and

method that you can expect, depending on the brokerage. Some discount firms pay interest only on balances above a set minimum, which is bad news for young investors who typically want to stay nearly fully invested in securities.

Also look for what's called a "sweep account," which automatically invests extra cash (from the sale of stock, for example) in a high-interest money market fund until those funds are reinvested.

AVAILABILITY OF MUTUAL FUNDS

Many discount firms sell mutual funds and you want the greatest possible variety from these "supermarkets," which are really convenient for those investors who have lots of funds from lots of fund families. But because some supermarkets charge a surcharge for buying funds through them, even on "no-load" funds, look for a brokerage that offers a variety of no-load, no-expense funds.

IRAs AND SIPC

All discount brokers these days offer IRA accounts. All have SIPC coverage, which insures the securities and cash in customer accounts up to a maximum of $500,000 per investor (CAREFUL: SIPC coverage insures against the firm going bankrupt, *not* against investment loss), and most have additional private insurance.

DIVIDEND REINVESTMENT

Young investors ought to reinvest the dividends that many stocks pay. All full-service brokers offer this service and most discount brokers do too, but be sure to ask whether there are fees and how much. Try to find a brokerage that doesn't charge anything for it, but if you have to pay, don't part with more than $2 for each reinvested dividend payment.

X-Factors
- Location and number of offices
- Availability of account information and real-time market quotes
- Electronic services

If trading and checking balances over the Internet and telephone are im-

Full Service vs. Discount vs. Deep Discount

Full Service (Merrill Lynch, Smith Barney, Prudential, et al.)

UPSIDE
- You call your very own broker when you wish to make a trade or have a question
- Research from the firm's team of analysts
- A good broker will be able to talk you out of bad ideas and recommend ideas you might not have considered. Ideally, he'll keep an eye on your portfolio and alert you to opportunities. You'll have a chance to develop a long-standing relationship with a broker, who can come to learn your tastes and get a sense of what kind of opportunities appeal to you.
- Breadth of services is excellent

DOWNSIDE
- Trades are pricey
- An untrustworthy full-service broker can be a disaster
- Minimum balances for asset-management accounts tend toward the steep

Discount Brokerage (Schwab, Fidelity, Waterhouse, Jack White, et al.)

UPSIDE
- Trades are pretty cheap
- Some research available
- Service is typically fast and knowledgeable, though impersonal
- Breadth of services is good

DOWNSIDE
- You call a general 800-number when you wish to make a trade and talk to whomever picks up
- No one monitors your portfolio
- Research is typically limited to stuff that's already available elsewhere

Deep Discount Brokerage (E*Trade, National Discount Brokers, et al.)

UPSIDE
- Trades are really cheap
- Internet-only deep discounters usually offer the best Internet-based services, compared with those who reluctantly offer Internet stuff

DOWNSIDE
- You call a general 800-number when you wish to make a trade and talk to whomever picks up
- No one monitors your portfolio
- Customer service can be horrible and disagreements are tough to resolve
- Very limited research materials
- Breadth of services is limited

portant to you—and they should be, since they're convenient and brokers usually cut you a break when you use them to trade—be sure the broker you choose is strong in these areas.

- Customer service — speediness / helpfulness / knowledgeableness of telephone reps, and all the rest

These are service firms. Don't put up with a brokerage that puts you on hold all the time or doesn't offer quick, correct answers to your questions.

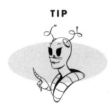

When it comes to choosing a type of brokerage, I prefer not too big and not too small. That means discount brokerages, which combine low prices and good service with decent access to research and a wide variety of available products and features. *Smart Money* magazine regularly rates discount brokers and consistently awards Waterhouse and Jack White high marks, with the more well-known discounters Schwab and Fidelity also scoring well.

As always, that doesn't mean a discounter is right for every investor. A trusted broker at a full-service firm that supplies tons of research you find useful can more than justify the higher costs, and an investor who knows exactly what he wants to do and has no need for frills may do fine with a deep discounter.

Some people think that using a full-service firm is some sort of admission that they don't know what they're doing. Not at all. In addition to my account at a major discounter, I've used the same stockbroker at a big, full-service firm ever since I had a dollar to invest. He has talked me out of several dumb trades I wanted to make, which has more than earned the extra commissions.

Arbitration Frustration: How Investment Disputes Are Settled

Among the conditions you agree to when you open a brokerage account is the promise to settle any disputes that arise by using the arbitration system instead of the courts.

Say you've got a beef with your stockbroker—you think he's churning (trading excessively to generate commissions) or he made a trade without your authorization. Your broker knows that your only recourse is arbitration. This consists of you contacting the National Association of Securities Dealers (800-289-9999 or *http://www.nasdr.com*). On the long and scary form they send, you describe in detailed plain English your version of events. After submitting the form, you'll be notified whether your case warrants a hearing by an arbitrator, who'll decide which side wins and reward compensation and/or damages and/or legal fees to the prevailing party.

It's usually a pretty equitable alternative to a clogged court system. But I'm not crazy about the fact that investors are forced, usually through a bit of small print they never even read, to accept arbitration. In a world that's become depressingly free from quick-and-easy solutions, here's a quick-and-easy solution. Next time you open a brokerage account, feel free simply to cross out the fine print that asks you to agree to settle disputes before an arbitration committee. Your broker might tell you that you've got to sign the agreement as it's presented, but chances are good he'll back down if you threaten to take your dollars elsewhere. That way, you'll be free to use the arbitration system, should you deem it appropriate—and you probably will. But you won't be limiting your options should the magnitude of your problem warrant the legal assistance and fine-toothed comb of the "real" legal system.

Record Keeping

The next step toward taking control of your finances is clearing the reams of records from your desk. It's hard enough to stay on top of your finances without being buried in documents, statements, receipts and bills.

People tend toward the extremes when it comes to hanging on to financial records—they either keep everything or ditch everything. Like Goldilocks, you should be looking for a comfortable midpoint.

You know better than to trash your Social Security card, insurance policies and passport while clinging to years-old telephone bills and last month's grocery receipts. So make it a point to create an "important papers drawer" for that stuff which obviously warrants inclusion and to dump the stuff you've been allowing to linger far past its useful life. Remember to perform this ritual every few months or so and you'll have gone a long way toward reducing the clutter and confusion that accompanies a pile of scary-looking papers.

Here are a few special cases that merit mention.

Forever Stuff

Deed to your home, receipts for IRA contributions (in case you withdraw early, you'll have tax consequences), diplomas, marriage/divorce certificates, in addition to the expected things—birth certificate, SS card, pictures of your grandparents.

Bank/Brokerage/Mutual Fund and Credit Card Statements

These monthly statements should be kept until the end of the year. When the year-end summary comes, toss the monthlies; keep the year-end statements for three years.

Insurance Policies

By definition, insurance doesn't come to mind until disaster hits. So even though they're seldom needed, insurance policies are best kept at the ready. Whenever you get a new policy, use a highlighting marker on the phone number to call to file a claim; the last thing you need when your car is stolen is a long read through your policy.

Mortgage Statements/Home Improvements/Property Tax Records

All of these should be kept for as long as you own the home; not only do they have income tax and capital gains tax implications, but mortgage lenders are notorious for miscrediting mortgage and tax payments. You'll want complete documentation of how much you've paid.

Tax Stuff

The IRS has only three years in which to launch an audit, so tax returns need to be kept at least until the fifteenth of April three years after they were due. For example, returns for tax year 1997 are due April 15, 1998, and so should be held on to until April 15, 2001. That means that all records relevant to that tax return should also be kept three years—including W-2s, receipts for deductible expenses and interest statements.

Pay Stubs

Keep stubs of salaried jobs only until the year-end summary arrives; records of freelance earnings should follow the rules of tax stuff.

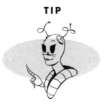

TIP Having a hard time organizing all those records? Use the "yearly shoebox" method. Get a shoebox, toss in every savable item. Each year, start a new shoebox (owing to arcane accounting principles, Keds boxes tend to work best). No sorting, no recording, no Freudian compulsions. And if you do end up needing something, it'll be there—although it'll take some digging. Plus, this method guarantees that you treat yourself to at least one pair of new shoes every year. Don't even try the "I have no room" excuse. I kept this system while living with three mammals, a lizard and five fish in a Manhattan walk-up so small that the roaches slouched.

Money Management Software

These programs, which allow the user to track one's finances in every area, are the rarest of computer applications: they're easy, do what they're supposed to and fulfill a real need. The user enters everything spent, bought and earned in a simple check-ledger interface. You can track investments, create pie charts that show where your money's going, denote expenditures that have tax implications, even print checks right from your computer. It's particularly useful for "where-does-my-paycheck-go" analysis—users may find themselves brown-bagging it when they see how quickly restaurant lunches add up, for example.

2. Repaying It

DEBT

CREDIT RATINGS

CREDIT CARDS

STUDENT LOANS

BANKRUPTCY

Debt

It's simple. Debt is compound interest in reverse. In the same way that investment returns magically grow over time, unpaid (or slowly paid) debt multiplies faster than *E. coli*. A $2,000 balance on a typical credit card, for example, will take a whopping 224 months to pay off if you make just the 2 percent minimum payment. That means you'll end up paying close to $4,000 in interest—assuming you don't charge anything else beyond that initial two grand.

And yet, it's not so simple. Many symbols of success—a college education, a home, a new car—are all but impossible for the average American without taking on substantial debt.

A totally debt-free existence is difficult at best. It can even result in long-term financial harm if opportunities are passed up that would pay for themselves many times over.

On the other hand, plenty of young people handcuff themselves by taking on more debt than they can afford. "I'll be earning large in a few years, why suffer now?" That kind of thinking can land people in a hole deeper than Jerry Springer's final thought.

So how does a body distinguish between debt that betters one's lot and debt that limits one's opportunities?

The difference lies in how the borrowed money is used.

Think of it this way. Borrowed funds used for something that will likely add long-term value is money well spent. Houses and college educations tend to benefit a borrower over the long haul. Television sets, swank lunches and concert tickets do not.

Debt can be a good thing. Suppose a promising high school grad can't afford college. She might delay attending until she's saved enough at a low-paying job to handle tuition without borrowing. But those years asking people if they want fries with their order can't be relived no matter how much debt one avoids. She may be better served by borrowing at low rates to finance a college education that results in higher-paying opportunities after graduation. (That's not to say that college automatically opens the door to Thurston Howell kind of dollars.)

Another standard when looking at different kinds of debt is whether what you purchase appreciates or depreciates in value. Houses and a college education would still pass this test, tape decks and fancy restaurants definitely would not. But what about cars and clothes? Both depreciate the instant they're bought. Yet both are necessary for certain situations that do add long-term value. Job applicants need appropriate clothes to interview. A car can be all but indispensable to a young family in a town with crummy public transportation.

There is no surefire litmus test a would-be borrower can apply to decide whether a particular liability makes sense. But don't discount the power of common sense. Buying disposable junk with money borrowed at high-interest is bad news, while doing what you have to do to get to a better place is not only justifiable but smart.

Should I Invest or Pay Down Debt?

This may be the question I'm asked more than any other. In general, the interest you're paying on debt should be weighed against the rate of return you can realistically expect from an investment. What to do with "extra" money—after minimum payments are made—boils down to measuring the particulars of your financial picture.

Let's say you owe a grand on a credit card with an annual percentage rate of 15 percent. You also are interested in a stock mutual fund that you have good reason to believe will deliver 10 percent a year. You're better off paying down the credit card. Not only will you achieve an effective interest rate of 15 percent, but you'll save on the taxes you'd owe on the investment returns. Plus, that 15 percent is a sure thing—the 10 percent you hope to get on the mutual fund isn't guaranteed.

On the other hand, there's no reason to rush to pay a 5 percent student loan if you're comfortable with an investment program likely to produce 10 percent gains. This is especially true if your investing can be done in a tax-advantaged account. Get those 10 percent gains in an IRA, for example, and you won't have to pay any taxes on the gains until you begin withdrawing when you retire. Depending on your income and other circumstances, an IRA contribution might even *lower* your tax bill, which paying down the loan can't do.

It's a closer call when the expected investment return is evenly matched with the interest rate on the debt. If your after-tax rate of return is exactly the same as the interest rate you're paying on debt, I give the edge to investing. Forming habits and building enthusiasm are critical to successful long-term investing. To me, that trumps even the lofty benefits of prompt debt repayment.

One of the worst financial moves someone can make is to slowly pay down high-interest debt while keeping a chunk of money sitting in a low-interest savings account or CD. It happens all the time, though, mostly out of inertia and laziness.

Here's an example of the havoc that such a program can cause. Say you owe $5,000 to a credit card at 19 percent interest. Meantime, you keep $5,000 in a savings account that's earning 4 percent. Making payments of $100 a month to the card, it'll take you 100 months to pay off the balance—a total of $9,971. Meanwhile, your investment will have turned into a paltry $6,978. In short, you would have saved $2,993 by using your savings to pay off your credit card. Plus, you would have had 100 months of investing $100 in something yielding better than 4 percent.

How Much Debt Is Too Much?

The old-school rule of thumb (real big thumbs in the old school) is that no more than 15 percent of your after-tax income should go toward paying debt (not counting mortgage payments). This rule, while a good place to start, doesn't reflect critical changes in the way Americans use debt. The frequent-flyer-miles addiction has people using their credit cards at grocery

stores, while online services that debit the plastic each month have to some
degree replaced subscriptions for which Americans once used checks. And
student loans are more widely available and used by even the most afflu-
ent, in greater amounts.

These changes render the 15 percent rule at least partially obsolete. The
trick is not to adhere to a magical number that represents financial holi-
ness. When considering the amount of debt you're carrying, it's better to
assess whether your spending habits are on speaking terms with your earning habits. Here are some red flags that signal a need to increase the latter
or rein in the former:

- Having to decide which bill to pay
- Chronic late payments
- Paying old creditors with loans from new ones
- Paying only the minimum to high-interest creditors
- Maxing out on all credit limits
- Using credit card advances for petty cash needs
- Lots of bounced checks
- Being denied credit or a loan

Pay the Toughest Guy First
When crafting a repayment plan, first assess the penalties charged by each
creditor. Suppose you owed four loan sharks $1,000 each. If you had only
$2,000 total, you'd have to make a choice. If you're smart, you figure out
which creditor is most likely to introduce your knees to a Louisville Slug-
ger and pay him the biggest chunk of your two grand. Then you'd probably divide the rest, paying the smallest amount to the fellow likely to do you
the least harm.

Think of all your creditors as loan sharks (usually not that great a strain
on the imagination). The one charging the highest interest rate is the
biggest thug.

Let's say you owe $1,000 each to four different creditors—a Visa card at
20 percent, a Bloomingdale's card at 15 percent, a car payment at 10 percent and a student loan at 5 percent. Assume that the minimum payment
on each of these is $50 per month. If you have $400 per month to devote

to these creditors, you might be tempted to pay each creditor $100. It's simple and has a certain symmetry—but it makes bad financial sense. A far better plan is to send Bloomingdale's, the car payment and the student loan $50 each, while cutting a check for the remaining $250 to Visa. Once Visa is paid in full, use the $400 to pay Bloomingdale's $300 a month, while continuing to pay $50 each on the car and the student loan. This strategy works regardless of how many creditors you have and how high the interest rates. So long as the highest rate gets the most cash, you'll save money.

Paying Your Bills if You're Broke

A sudden downturn in your income or an unexpected financial emergency may result in having to assess how to keep your head above water until you're back on your feet. To do this, establish the degree of discomfort each creditor is capable of inflicting.

Give first priority to secured debt—things that can be repossessed, such as cars and homes. A homeowner can expect the foreclosure process to begin after two consecutive missed payments, while just one missed payment on a car could find its driver looking at an empty parking space one harrowing morning.

Next on the list are services that can be shut off. Those who dodge their phone and electric payments will usually get up to three months of threats before service is discontinued.

Last on the list are credit cards, student loans, medical bills and loans from friends and family. These are known as unsecured debt, meaning the creditor can't do much other than cut off future service, assess penalties and sic the collection agency hounds on the debtor.

If you're in bill-payment trouble, take action before your creditors do. Contact the ones you aren't going to be able to pay. Explain your cash-flow problem and ask if they can allow any lenience. Some creditors allow temporary interest-only payments; others arrange extended-payment plans. Student loans will allow unemployed debtors to defer their payments as long as three months. Credit card companies will usually waive late fees and lower the interest rate of anyone who calls. Remember, they know you're going to pay some creditors and stiff others—it's in their interest to make a payment plan as attractive as possible.

Credit Ratings

Credit reporting agencies are to consumers as bun-wearing hall monitors are to junior high school students. These Big-Brotherly organizations, which catalog every penny you've ever borrowed and every roof you've ever slept under, are among the worst-run of all the financial world's bureaucracies.

Unfortunately, they also have the power to mess up your finances to an unbelievable degree. A bad rating can mean credit card denials, mortgage rebuff, insurance rate hikes, apartment rejections, even a cold shoulder from potential employers. Yet these agencies operate with virtually no regulation, atrocious service and an arbitrariness that borders on ridiculous. Their clients are credit providers, not credit applicants, so they really have no incentive to clean up their act.

You do have some rights, however. Under the Fair Credit Reporting Act, you have the right to learn what information about you is being distributed by credit bureaus. Contact the companies below to see what these guys are saying behind your back. Reports cost about $8 (unless you live in Colorado or Connecticut, where they're $5, or Maine, where they're $2), and getting more than one is a good idea if you've been rejected for reasons that aren't obvious from the first credit report you buy. Every consumer has the right to a free report if requested within sixty days of being denied credit. As of a subsequent strengthening of the Fair Credit Reporting Act in 1997, banks and stores that make mistakes when reporting on your credit history

are responsible for fixing those mistakes. In addition, prospective employers must get written permission from an applicant before asking for a credit
report.

Experian (formerly TRW Credit Data)
PO Box 2104
Allen, TX 75013-2104
800-682-7654

Equifax
PO Box 740241
Atlanta, GA 30374-0241
800-685-1111

Trans Union
PO Box 390
Springfield, PA 19064
800-916-8800 (800-858-8336 in California)

You can either order these over the phone with a credit card (a certain
irony there, no?) or send a check along with your full name, Social Security number, date of birth, your address and previous addresses for five
years and your spouse's first name, if you have one (a spouse, not a first
name).

When the report finally arrives (they're obligated to get it to you in thirty
days), it'll be confusing and hard to decipher. Keep at it and compare it
with things you know for sure, like where you lived last year and how
timely you paid your rent.

The biggest headache occurs when incorrect information appears on
your report. It might be a notation that accuses you of not paying (or paying late) something that you did indeed handle correctly. Even worse,
you've probably heard nightmare stories about people with names similar
to credit cheats and mistakenly transposed Social Security numbers. Mistakes must be challenged in writing. Detail in fewer than one hundred
words why you dispute the charge (it's no mean feat: I can't ask for the

ketchup in one hundred words). The rating agency, which supposedly has an obligation to verify the negative info, will simply ask the merchant or landlord if he was mistaken. If the creditor denies it, you're stuck. All you can do is append your side of the story to your report and hope future would-be creditors are compelled by your version of events. You can also request that the new version—either corrected or appended—be sent to anyone who's requested your credit report in the last six months.

Negative information stays on your credit report for up to seven years— and even longer in the case of bankruptcy. So if you've missed a few payments or had a couple utilities shut off, you're going to have to do your best to offset those blemishes with prompt payments and a clean nose.

What about those services that offer to "repair" your credit? As a personal finance writer, I've had to learn the language of hedging: some, most, hopefully, should, nearly, tends to, often, etc. So it brings me great pleasure to announce that EVERY SINGLE ONE OF THESE SERVICES IS A SCAM. Most of them simply take your money and either do nothing or send for the same report you could request yourself. Others make a perfunctory effort to dispute the charges, which you could also do yourself. But all share one technique in common: wringing money from suckers. There is no quick fix: the only remedy for a bad credit report is time and good behavior.

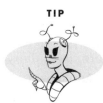

TIP

The Do-It-Yourself Credit Repair and Improvement Guide ($10 from the National Center for Financial Education, 619-239-1401) is a step-by-step guide to climbing out from under and includes template letters to send to the credit agencies—all with the good-natured finger-shaking for which NCFE is beloved.

Credit Cards

Credit card issuers are some of the shrewdest marketers around. They have come up with a splendid array of ways to disguise the basic purpose of everything they do. Which is, of course, to keep you as deeply indebted to them as possible. Cash advances, balance transfers, checks, skip-a-

Speaking of Permanent Records ...

When we were in high school, *Green*'s publisher, John P., was a straight arrow to an unprecedented degree. Not only did he do all his homework and attend all his classes, he actually liked school and respected his teachers. One day in freshman year, I convinced him to sneak out during lunch for some Asteroids and fries. As he launched into Dostoyevsky's theory of inevitable punishment, I assured him that I had sneaked out every day for the past year and that only wusses played by the rules of the Man. A few chicken noises later, John was convinced. Naturally, we were busted—John's first detention. Four years later, his guidance counselor perused John's transcripts. There among the nearly straight *A*'s, stratospheric SAT scores and AP courses, something caught the counselor's eye. In the bored voice only a bureaucrat beaten down by life can muster, the counselor had the nerve to ask about the detention John received freshman year. Just goes to show you how these things follow you around.

payment, and your alma mater's logo on the card all exist to make you poorer and the credit issuer richer.

To say that credit cards are more popular among young people than nose rings and tattoos overstates their omnipresence only slightly, and the situation is intensifying rapidly. A study in an issue of *U.S. News & World Report* found that the average credit card balance for those under age twenty-five has almost doubled from 1992 to 1997, growing from $885 to $1,721. By 1996, 67 percent of college students carried credit cards, up from 54 percent in 1990. Even more alarming is the average balance college students are carrying, which has rocketed 134 percent, from $900 in 1990 to $2,100 in 1995.

And yet, credit cards are undeniably useful and convenient. They're safer to carry than cash, accepted more universally than checks and fit in a pocket better than fishes and loaves. They represent buying power more substantial than many carry in their checking accounts and are invaluable in emergencies. They're accepted overseas and over the Internet. They aid record keeping and sometimes offer perks like damage protection and even rebates and frequent-flyer miles.

The Fine Print

In the Working It chapter, we'll see just how powerful a weapon time can be in an investing program. Well, credit card issuers also see the benefits of a long horizon, and they do whatever it takes to get users hooked at a young age. Credit cards are among the biggest advertisers in college newspapers, and student unions are littered with card offerings.

These cards often offer the worst terms of all credit cards. While just about any credit card interest is likely to be well into the double digits, cards aimed at those with little credit history are usually in the 20 percent range. They cook up charges for every little stumble—late-payment fees, over-the-limit fees, cash-advance fees. Customer service tends to be lacking—just try getting a mistaken charge removed.

Let's take a look at the information box accompanying one credit card heavily marketed to young people—the CoreStates Student card. (By the way, that little rectangle of truth-telling is called a Schumer box, named for the dapper New York congressman whose legislation made it mandatory.) It lists the introductory rate (if there is one), the annual percentage rate (and how it's calculated if it varies), the grace period, the fees and the small-print details.

As you can see, the initial—or "teaser"—rate on this card is 7.75 percent, while the rate after six months is 18.5 percent (both of these rates are subject to change, since they're tied to a moving rate), the grace period is the due date of the monthly bill (in the case of CoreStates, that's fifteen days—if the bill period closes on the first, the user has until the fifteenth to make the payment), the interest calculation method is listed (most cards use the average daily balance method) and a list of fees, including the twenty bones a user faces if he has the nerve not to use the card.

One of the most misleading credit card terms is "grace period." Here's an example to clear up this cloudy concept. Gram's credit card has a rate

---

Introductory Rate*

Variable — currently 4.9% APR — for the first six months after the account is opened.

Annual Percentage Rate*
Standard and Gold Cards

Variable — currently 14.09% APR — for CoreStates customers
(following introductory period).

Variable — currently 18.09% APR — for non-customers (following introductory period).

Skier's Rewards, The Golfer's Card, The Auto Card

Variable — currently 16.9% APR (following introductory period).

Variable Rate Information*
Standard and Gold Cards
CoreStates Customers

The rate for the first six months will be determined by subtracting .56% from the highest
1 month London Interbank Offered Rate (commonly known as LIBOR) as published in the
'Money Rates' table in *The Wall Street Journal*, on the Wednesday** prior to the first day
of each billing cycle. Thereafter it will be LIBOR plus 8.63% (minimum rate 13.25%).
LIBOR is an independent market index that we do not influence in any way, so you can be
assured that the rate on your account will be competitive based on current market conditions.

CoreStates Non-Customers

The rate for the first six months will be determined by subtracting .56% from the highest
1 month London Interbank Offered Rate (commonly known as LIBOR) as published in the
'Money Rates' table in *The Wall Street Journal*, on the Wednesday** prior to the first day
of each billing cycle. Thereafter it will be LIBOR plus 12.63% (minimum rate 17.25%).
LIBOR is an independent market index that we do not influence in any way, so you can be
assured that the rate on your account will be competitive based on current market conditions.

Skier's Rewards, The Golfer's Card, The Auto Card

The rate for the first six months will be determined by subtracting .56% from the highest
1 month London Interbank Offered Rate (commonly known as LIBOR) as published in the
'Money Rates' table in *The Wall Street Journal*, on the Wednesday** prior to the first day
of each billing cycle. Thereafter it will be LIBOR plus 11.44%. LIBOR is an independent
market index that we do not influence in any way, so you can be assured that the rate on
your account will be competitive based on current market conditions.

Grace Period for Purchases

You have until the payment due date to pay your balance in full before a finance charge on new
purchases will be imposed.

* Rates shown above are as of 7/23/96. Call us at 1-800-560-6109 for changes since that time.
** If Wednesday is a holiday, refer to the previous business day's *The Wall Street Journal*.

Balance Computation Method

Average daily balance (including new transactions).

Annual Fee

None provided the account is used for a purchase or cash advance at least once every
12 months; fee is $20 without such use.

---

of 20 percent, a grace period of twenty-five days, and he pays his bill in full when it arrives on the first of each month. If he charges a $1,000 wedding on his credit card on January 15, his bill on February 1 will include no interest, so long as he pays it in full by February 25.

What many don't realize is that carrying a balance of even $1 means that any additional purchases will start accruing interest the minute they're made. If Gram had a balance of $100 at the beginning of January, then his

February bill would reflect interest at a rate of 20 percent times his average daily balance for the entire month—meaning a finance charge of $10. (Fifteen days of $100 and fifteen days of $1,100 averages $600 a day, which at 20 percent interest for a month equals $10.)

How to Use Credit Cards

BEWARE THE MINIMUM-PAYMENT SCHEME

There's a reason the minimum payment on credit cards is so affordable, and it's not because card issuers are kindly souls. Using the CoreStates card from the example above, let's look at how a typical user would fare making only the minimum payment. (Although the required minimum payment isn't listed in the Schumer box, on this card it's the higher of $1/48$ of the balance or $20, and the minimum finance charge is 50¢.) On a balance of $2,000, it'd take 216 months—eighteen years—to pay it down, assuming you don't make additional charges on the card. Worse, you'll have paid interest totaling $3,599, on top of the $2,000 you originally borrowed.

Paying even slightly more than the minimum can save you a lot of money. In this example, the first four monthly minimum payments are $42 ($42 is $1/48$ of $2,000), the next four are $41, and so on. Let's say instead of paying the minimum, you pay $50 a month until you're paid off entirely. Instead of taking 216 months to pay off, it'll take only sixty-three. And instead of paying $3,599 in interest, you'll pay $1,134.

MATCH YOUR CREDIT TYPE

Different cards are better suited to different kinds of users. It's clearly best not to carry any credit card balance, but that's not always possible. Here's what to look for, depending on how you use credit.

• If you always pay your full balance, get a card with no annual fee and low late fees.

Some issuers that offer these are:

AFBA Industrial Bank	800-776-2265
Horizon Bank & Trust	512-419-3462
United National Bank	800-242-7600
USAA FSB	800-922-9092
Wachovia Prime No-Fee	800-842-3262

• If you often carry a balance, choose a card with a long grace period and a low interest rate—even if you have to pay an annual fee.

Some cards that fit the bill:

American Express Optima	800-467-8462
Citizens Bank	800-438-9222
Great Western	800-492-7587
Wachovia First-Year Prime	800-842-3262

• If you always carry a hefty balance, then interest rate is key, with fees and grace periods secondary. Find a card with the lowest rate you can get, and stay away from teaser-rate cards, in which the interest rate jumps substantially after a seductive introductory period.

Some cards that fit the bill:

Bank of Boston	800-252-2273
First USA Bank	800-347-7887
Wachovia Prime for Life	800-842-3262

In general, cards with good terms have the highest standards—repayment history, debt/income ratio, job stability, etc.—so many who most need favorable rates can't get them. But remember, credit issuers are in a very competitive business and users have a lot of choices. Those who are willing to do some legwork can often do themselves a big favor by shopping around. Inertia is a powerful force here, too. Because a lot of people stick with the card they've always had simply to avoid the hassle of changing, selecting a good card early on is even more important.

So where do you find these credit card diamonds in the rough?

In addition to the ones listed above, there are a couple solid sources for credit info. RAM Research, a company that is to credit cards as Bill James is to baseball, has an Internet site that lets you check current rates and other credit card details. You can even apply for some cards: go to *http://www.ramresearch.com.* You can also call the Bankcard Holders of America, a consumer advocacy group, at 540-389-5445. Their Low-Interest/No-Fee Credit Card List sells for $4.

Don't Be a Chump

Many credit pitfalls are avoidable with common sense and a little self-control.

• *Cash advances* usually trigger high fees and offer no grace period (interest begins accruing the second you get your green, even if you don't carry a balance).

• Offers to *skip a payment* are tempting but the interest keeps piling up while the user enjoys the month's respite.

• *Teaser rates* are designed to sucker users with rates that are unrealistically low. A quick look at the fine print usually reveals a big rate hike after three or six months.

• Also beware the *despicable little maneuvers* some credit issuers have implemented as they reel from record numbers of defaulters. (The fact that these defaulters are mainly people who got credit only because of the issuers' aggressive marketing doesn't seem to bother them.)

Credit issuers don't make money from those who pay their full balances on time. Some large card issuers, notably GE Capital, assess annual fees of $25 to *punctual* payers, while continuing to offer no-annual-fee cards to those who ring up $25 or more in interest charges. Other issuers, including MBNA and Citibank, have started to impose late-payment fees of as much as $20 when a payment is just five to ten days tardy, while AT&T, the country's second-largest card issuer, slaps a fine on anyone who's even one day late. Yet another scheme has rates soaring for customers who pay late just twice in one year. Then there are over-limit fees, which are ridiculous because the issuer presumably has the power simply to deny the transaction, rather than allowing it and then slapping the user with a fee. Some companies even run stealth credit checks on their cardholders. If a user's credit is faltering, the creditor might raise the interest rates, even if the user has never been late or missed a payment.

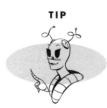

TIP

When Transfers Make Sense

If you've got a high balance on a high-interest card, it often makes sense to transfer the balance to a lower-interest card. A $2,000 balance on a 18.9 percent card will take sixty months (five years) to pay off, if you pay $50 a month. That same $50 a month on a card with a rate of 10 percent will take a full year less to pay, and you'll save over $600 in interest, too. Many cards offer low teaser rates for a short introductory period. These cards are often rip-offs, but if you're transferring a balance, some will let you continue to pay off the transferred part at the teaser rate even after the introductory period. Even if they don't advertise this feature, ask the company you're considering transferring to if they'll accommodate the transferred balance at the new rate. Transferred balances are found money to issuers, so they're usually eager to do whatever it takes to get it.

Credit Card Flavors

SECURED CREDIT CARDS

Those with spotty credit histories may find themselves rejected by regular credit cards. Secured credit cards look and function just like regular Visas and MasterCards but require a couple hundred dollars deposit as collateral for a credit limit of $1,000 or so. They tend to have high annual fees and pretty high interest rates, but since holders are using them to build credit, most shouldn't carry high balances anyway. In addition, many bank-issued secured cards will return your deposit (sometimes with interest) and switch creditworthy cardholders to unsecured cards after twelve to eighteen months of consistent on-time payments.

Secured cards are also ideal for those turned down for credit by the old catch-22, "insufficient credit history." Recent graduates, immigrants and anyone else without a history of prompt repayment should consider secured cards as a way to build a sound reputation. Secured cards generally take all comers—the fact that they've got some of your money apparently reassures them you won't run away with too much of theirs.

Some secured cards that RAM lists among the most favorable are offered by:

Amalgamated Bank of Chicago
Bank of America (Arizona)
Bank One (Arizona)
Capital One Bank

WARNING! Stick to secured cards issued by reputable banks, rather than the fly-by-night repair experts who promise "guaranteed" bank cards.

DEBIT CARDS

These look like regular Visas or MasterCards, but they actually function as a hybrid of credit cards and checking accounts. When a purchase is made with a debit card, the user just hands over the card to the merchant—no ID or other check-writing hassles at all. But instead of borrowing the money for the purchase at high rates from a credit issuer, the cost is instead deducted directly from the user's account, where it had been sitting gathering interest. Since a user has to have some money to use a debit card, they're obviously no substitute for people using credit cards strictly because they're broke. But for those simply looking for the convenience of credit cards, debit cards are often a better way to go. Many asset management accounts from brokerages offer debit cards, as do lots of regular banks.

Though they look just like regular credit cards, debit cards come up short in a couple areas:

• *Loss protection.* Regular credit cards hold a user liable for a maximum of $50 if the card is stolen, and even that is usually waived if the issuer is notified promptly. But a stolen debit card can cost the owner up to $500. Some debit cards, including all those with the MasterCard brand, are reducing the user's liability to a maximum of $50, but be sure to check how much in bogus charges your

MISCONCEPTION

issuer will stick you with if your card is stolen. Also, someone writing a check can stop a payment before the check is cashed, say if whatever was purchased turns out to be fraudulent. Most debit cards don't allow stop payments.

• *Collateral.* Some rental-car places, for example, won't accept a debit card as security for a car unless the user passes the cash-renter scrutiny—a massive cash deposit and/or advance notice of as much as thirty days with a credit check to boot.

CHARGE CARDS

American Express and Diner's Club are examples of charge cards, not credit cards. They charge no interest and must be paid in full each month. They also tend to have a higher annual fee. I don't recommend them for people without pretty substantial income because the prestige of carrying them isn't worth the fee, nor is the risk of overspending (since there's no preset limit to cap profligate charging).

REBATE/AFFINITY CARDS

Rebate cards are often associated with frequent-flyer miles, but there are cards that offer perks ranging from discounts on computers to rebates on cars to Rolling Stones merchandise (save 5 percent on a Keith Richards total transfusion kit). Affinity cards advertise affiliations of their user—colleges and political groups are biggies—and sometimes kick back a percentage of the user's charges to the group. There's even a card called the Good Citizens Visa that pays 25¢ to your favorite charity every time you use it—an amount that can later be subtracted from your taxable income if you itemize your deductions.

In general, these cards carry high interest rates and annual fees. What's more, they sometimes change the deal midcourse, as Ford and Apple recently did when they simply canceled their rebate programs, leaving those owed rebates no choice other than to keep using the card until they were ready to cash in the dough accumulated before the cutoff date. Unless you don't carry a balance and are positive you'll be using more of the perks or earning the group more than the cost of the annual fee, you're better off with a plain-vanilla card.

GASOLINE/DEPARTMENT STORE CARDS

You know what these are—don't use them. They are virtually always at very high rates and provide no advantages over using a general-purpose card. And who needs the extra paperwork?

 **WARNING!** NO PAYMENTS TILL NEXT YEAR! You've seen the ads—computer stores, carpet shops, appliance giants—tempting you with buy now, pay later schemes. Lest you need reminding that deals that sound too good to be true invariably are, here goes again.

Deferred payment plans typically allow the consumer from ninety days to a year before the first payment on a purchase is due. A clever and well-heeled consumer could view this as an interest-free loan—investing that money, then paying the entire balance before the first payment is due provides free use of the money owed the store. More often, however, shoppers take the bait and worry about how they'll pay for it later.

Big mistake. Those who buy on deferred payment plans face some of the highest rates around—often between 20 and 25 percent. But what a lot of buyers don't realize is that the interest is accumulating the entire time—even during the no-payment period. Let's say you buy a $2,000 computer on a one-year deferred payment plan, with a 25 percent APR. On day 366, when the first payment is due, you owe $2,500. In other words, the interest clock's ticking the whole time you're playing Tetris on your new computer.

Naturally, all the rates and payment schedules are included in the million-word credit application you're given, but by then you're so desperate to own the computer you wouldn't read the pamphlet even if it was the only printed material in a long bathroom visit. So this is one of those kindergarten proverbs that's more easily written than obeyed: Don't buy things you can't afford. If you simply must, you're probably better off with a regular credit card than with the store's in-house deal.

PRECIOUS METAL CARDS

These are gold and platinum cards. They usually feature credit limits of at least $25,000 and a bunch of goofy features like accident insurance, emergency legal aid and "cancel all your cards at once if wallet's stolen" non-sense. They also usually have steep annual fees. High limits are great but don't let a card's color blind you to the basics: its rate and fees.

Credit Limit

Some personal finance types recommend intentionally keeping a low credit limit to avoid the temptation to overspend. I disagree.

We're not infants here and I think that most little tricks designed to rein in destructive behavior end up backfiring. One of the unsung benefits of credit cards is their usefulness in an emergency. You never know when a trip to Europe or to the bail bondsman is going to be critically important.

Having the ability to indulge is not the same as actually doing so, however. Debt is a temptation far too powerful for many, awash in second mortgages and personal bankruptcies (over a million a year). It's clearly not a good idea to have access to more credit than a user could ever hope to repay. So I recommend a happy medium. Carry just one credit card—no gas cards or store cards. But get as high a limit as you can on the card you carry, being careful to keep your balance as small as possible.

 **WARNING!** You've seen credit cards for every sort of group—GreenPeace, sports teams, colleges, airlines. Well, now there are credit cards for a new class: brain donors.

Heavily marketed in Sunday newspapers (Cross Country is one brand name), these cards actually brag about their absurd terms. "Processing fee of $100, along with the annual fee, will be billed to your account after your card has been approved and issued." *Processing fee?*

And how about that annual fee? An astronomic $50. That's 150 percent higher than the standard $20 and infinity times more than the $0 you'll pay if you shop around even a little. All this for a card that guarantees a *minimum* interest rate of 20.99 percent. Somewhere Charles Dickens is taking notes for an updated Fagin.

What makes this larceny more despicable is that the offer clearly targets people who probably ought to run the other direction at the very sight of a credit card. "If you meet the following requirements, you will be approved!" goes the pitch, including such toughies as "phone number at your residence" and "no credit problems in the past six months."

Consumers with credit histories shoddy enough for scams like this are better off with a secured credit card or no credit at all.

Doing Without?

Despite my mixed feelings toward credit, I don't think it's smart to try to get by without at least one card. I used to edit a newspaper column by radio chatterbox Bruce "I wish you well, my friend" Williams. He was constantly getting letters from people who refused to carry credit cards. Whether they were Depression-era cash-only types or off-the-grid commandos, all were incensed that they'd have to do back flips to avoid plastic for certain things—reserving hotel rooms, ordering from catalogs over the phone (not to mention Internet stuff, which all but requires a card for both access charges and online purchases). Some were proud of the avoidance tactics they'd invented, but if you don't routinely carry the $500 in cash car rental agencies require of non-credit-card customers, you're going to have to bite the bullet.

If you're credit-averse or recovering from credit trouble, total withdrawal might not be the answer. Consider keeping one no-annual-fee card with a low credit limit, for use exclusively in credit-only situations. This will not only save you some headaches but, if promptly paid in full each month, will keep your credit record in good shape for when you really need it, such as for a car loan or mortgage.

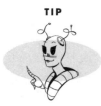

TIP Credit cards also come in handy for overseas travel. Charging purchases frees a traveler from the hassle and potential danger of carrying lots of various currencies. Also, because the credit issuers trade currency in large volume, credit-card users usually get pretty good exchange rates.

Student Loans

In today's enlightened America, there are no debtor's prisons. For college students, they've been replaced by dungeons from which escape is equally improbable: student loans.

Since 1980, the cost of a college education has more than tripled. Government grants have failed to keep up, and more students require debt to cover the gap. According to the Department of Education, student loans have doubled in the past five years alone—not counting money borrowed from credit cards and relatives. In fact, American college students have borrowed more money in the 1990s than in the '60s, '70s and '80s combined; and in 1996, the average undergraduate's total debt load under the government's Stafford loan program crossed the $10,000 mark for the first time. And it's increasingly common for graduate students to find themselves entering the real world six figures in the hole.

Consider the fate of Steve, who borrowed $100,000 from a variety of lenders to put himself through college and grad school. After graduation, he was lucky enough to find work he considered noble at a starting salary of thirty-five grand.

Student loans typically require repayment over a ten-year schedule. At 8 percent, Steve would end up paying $1,213 a month, for a total of $145,593—over $45,000 in interest. But since that monthly nut is well over half his take-home pay, Steve had his back against the wall. He opted to extend the repayment period of his loan from ten years to fifteen. Banks are often very willing to renegotiate student loan terms. And why not—in Steve's case, those extra five years will mean an additional $26,424 in interest. But his monthly payment is reduced to a more manageable $956. When he starts making better money later on, he can pay down his balance early.

Other tips:

• Rates are everything. The difference between 9 percent and 7 percent on a $20,000 student loan is $2,536 over the life of the loan. Refinance at lower rates, if you can get 'em. If your student loan is at 9 percent and a different lender will take a gamble on you at 7 percent, go ahead and borrow from Peter to pay Paul. By the same token, if your loan is really cheap (say 5 percent or so), consider paying only the minimum and putting whatever extra money you'd otherwise apply into something likely to yield better than 5 percent (or, of course, other higher-interest debt).

• Don't jump the gun on the grace period. Unlike the bogus grace period of credit cards, student loans don't start charging interest until the student is out of school for six months. So paying early is cheating yourself out of the use of that money, which could be earning interest or paying down high-interest credit card debt.

• Be punctual. The last place you want your hard-earned cash going is to late-payment fees. In addition, if your loan is serviced by Sallie Mae, the quasi-government agency that administers student loans (call 800-524-9100), you can shave one percentage point off your interest rate by making the first forty-eight payments on time. If you make payments via automatic deduction from your checking account, Sallie Mae will pass along the paperwork savings by deducting another quarter point off your loan. That quarter point can add up: on a $20,000 loan, it's a total savings of $316—not to mention late fees and 120 first-class stamps.

• Sallie Mae operates a decent website. Online access to account information, a helpful-but-preachy downloadable debt counselor and an improved repayment calculator are provided: *www.salliemae.com.*

• Consider consolidating. Many students borrow from a variety of sources to finance the four-year (or five- or six-) money toilet known as higher learning. Balling all your payments into one can save paperwork headaches, and sometimes money as well. Find out who holds each of your loans and the payment terms for each. Sallie Mae (800-524-9100) and the Department of Education (800-557-7392) both operate consolidation programs that allow for a variety of repayment schedules. Consolidation is well suited to those newly out of college who aren't yet making a lot of money. Both Sallie Mae and the DOE offer plans that allow interest-only payments toward the beginning of the loan term, as well as payment schedules adjusted for income. Obviously, the more you can pay early in the term, the less you'll end up paying over the long haul. But if you're broke, it's more convenient to negotiate terms with one lender than several.

Consolidation is best when you can get a rate on a consolidated loan that's comparable to the mean interest rate of all the money you've borrowed. (For example, if you've borrowed $10,000 at 8 percent and $20,000 at 6 percent, a consolidated loan makes sense only if its rate is near or below 6.67 percent.) Sallie Mae, the largest consolidator of loans, rounds the mean rate to the next whole percent. For those planning to return to school, consolidation might not be a good idea. Not all consolidated loans will suspend payments for returning students, so ask about that if further schooling is a possibility.

If you've forgotten who your lenders are, call the Federal Aid Information Center at 800-4FED-AID. They can tell you who holds the loans, though you'll have to contact the lender to find out the balance and payment they expect. For a printout of your loan history, write to:

National Student Loan Data System Division
U.S. Dept. of Education
600 Independence Ave. SW
ROB-3 Rm. 4640
Washington, DC 20202

Include your full name, Social Security number, date of birth and a signed, dated note that says "I'd like a record of my loan history."

• As of 1998, interest on student loans is tax deductible—up to $1,000 in 1998 and increasing $500 a year until maxing out at $2,500 in 2001. That's big news for those with big balances; for a more thorough explanation of tax deductibility, consult the taxes section in "Protecting It."

• Call them before they call you. If you're having trouble making payments, contact your lender as soon as possible. Many will be willing to make arrangements to lighten your load—either extending the term or accepting reduced or interest-only payments for a few months. But it usually takes at least thirty days for such a program to kick in. With the federal government cracking down on defaulters, failure to make arrangements can result in all sorts of stormtrooper techniques, including garnisheed wages and a hijacked tax refund.

Grad School = Money Sink?

Many graduate school students now finish their education over $100,000 in debt. That's a hell of a burden for someone beginning "real life." Yet for some reason, the decision to attend graduate school often escapes the cost/benefit analysis to which Americans subject nearly every other choice.

Would-be lawyers, doctors and other professionals aren't allowed entry to their fields without graduate degrees. But it seems that plenty of college graduates head to grad school after a quick stroll through the real world fails to result in satisfying, easy, meaningful work that also pays real well.

Unfortunately, a graduate degree is no guarantee of an easier career path. Fields that don't have an established apprentice and recruiting structure—history, English, psychology, etc.—offer particularly bleak prospects for graduate students. Many turn to teaching, but with funds dwindling for humanities programs at universities, the competition for teaching jobs has reached a cutthroat level.

Of course, money isn't everything. Far be it for me to discourage tomorrow's poets and historians from pursuing education to their heart's content. I've met quite a few humanities-type grad school survivors who benefited spiritually and even financially from MFAs and such. (Heck, I even married one.) But plenty of people who use grad school essentially as a stalling tactic are horrified to discover that their post-school options are severely limited now that they have to find work that pays enough to cover the cost of all that book learnin'.

The decision whether to attend grad school should be studied with at least as much care as the GREs. I know that job-market analysis and student loan amortization aren't as fun to think about as Victorian heroines in post-Pynchon pornography. But leaving your options open is pretty fun, too.

Bankruptcy

Bankruptcy is one of the more vexing financial issues a person can face. When you're staring at a pile of debt that grows bigger every time the mailman comes, it can be a tempting option. But don't assume that you'll be completely off the hook. For one thing, not all debt is created equal.

If you're in deep enough trouble even to be considering it, the first thing you need to do is assess your situation. Take a deep breath, sharpen a pencil and figure out exactly where you stand.

Assemble the most recent statements from each of your creditors (not counting your mortgage). Add the total monthly payments owed to all of them. If that amount is more than half your monthly salary, and you've got no backup savings or emergency money, bankruptcy might be an option to consider.

The Plus Side

- Wipes the slate clean

Bankruptcy entirely cancels certain types of debt, including back rent, utility and medical bills, and of course that three-toed sloth of personal debt, credit card balances.

- Puts an end to harassment from collectors

Supposedly, there are rules about how often and at what times creditors can call you. But when I last moved, my new phone number was apparently the old phone number of a guy who'd run out on some pretty substantial debts. For more than six months, I was getting at least half a dozen calls a day—from early morning to late evening—demanding repayment of debts, return of videos (like I'd really rent *Home Alone*—as if!) and reexamination of character. The more insistently I explained that I was not the guy they were looking for, the more they assured me that they knew I *was* the guy.

- Allows a fresh start

Obviously, the point of a bankruptcy is to learn from one's mistakes and get on with one's life. Gotta feel pretty good to wake up debt-free after dodging phone calls and ignoring the mail.

- The court can't confiscate everything

Most states allow bankruptcy filers to keep certain property, such as furniture, IRAs, 401(k) money and clothes. Many states even let the filer keep his swanky home, if he's got one.

The Minus Side

- Pummels your credit rating

If you're considering bankruptcy, your credit rating is probably pretty battered already. But a bankruptcy is the blackest mark of all. Other derogatory information—such as garnishees, late payments, liens and repossessions—can linger on your credit report for a maximum of seven years. But a bankruptcy haunts your credit report for up to ten years, with a mandatory minimum stay of seven years. Anyone planning a major purchase or access to extensive credit (say, to start a business) will face a much costlier scenario with a bankruptcy on his record.

This is not the threat it once was. Some credit card companies, increasingly desperate for customers, specialize in offering credit to people who've declared bankruptcy, reasoning that those folks are going to work hard to rebuild their credit, and also knowing that people cannot file another bankruptcy for six years.

Adding insult to injury, however, is the fact that many employers now routinely ask applicants for permission to check their credit reports. A bankruptcy doesn't look too good to prospective employers, which is double-plus bad news if the reason you declared bankruptcy is that you needed a higher-paying job.

- Ineffectual for certain debts

All taxes and judgments ordered by a court, such as alimony or personal-injury liability, are not dischargeable. Student loans whose first payment came due within the last seven years are also not dischargeable.

- Expensive

Simply filing the paperwork can run you about $1,000. And if you've got significant assets to protect—such as a house in those states that don't protect homes from seizure by creditors—you should hire a lawyer, which will likely run you another grand. If you have a less complicated case, you can probably do much of the paperwork yourself or hire a paralegal to prepare the documents.

- Not quickly repeatable

A person who has declared bankruptcy cannot do so again for six years. If you've already declared bankruptcy once and find yourself in trouble soon after, there will be very little you can do to alleviate pressure from

Where to Turn

• Nolo Press is an invaluable resource when tangling with any aspect of the law, including bankruptcy. Their *How to File for Bankruptcy* (Elias, Renauer, Leonard, $26.95) walks you through the process of deciding whether bankruptcy is a good option for you, and provides all the proper forms if you decide you need them. If you're already positive and just need the forms, save a few bucks by ordering Nolo's *Law Form Kit: Personal Bankruptcy,* a more spartan version of its how-to sister. Nolo Press: 800-992-6656.

• The National Foundation for Consumer Credit runs Consumer Credit Counseling Service, a branch of which is available in most cities nationwide. Funded by credit-card issuers, this is not the place if you're certain that bankruptcy is the route you want to take. But if you're wavering, CCCS makes a pretty convincing case against bankruptcy. If you're swayed, they'll help you negotiate a repayment schedule with better rates than you'd likely get on your own.

The fact that you're there lets them know that you're serious about getting out of the hole, and if you mention that you're considering bankruptcy they'll make it a priority to cut a good deal on your behalf. While there's an undeniable twelve-steps feel to the program—their debt management program involves a ceremonial cutting of your credit cards—they've dealt with every kind of reprobate and are pretty skilled at not making you feel like a loser for needing their help. Call 800-388-2227 to locate the CCCS office nearest you.

creditors. And since they know you can't file again, you've lost even the threat of bankruptcy as a way to get them off your back.

• Loss of independence

It takes as long as a year for a personal bankruptcy filing to be completed. During that time, your entire financial life is exposed to the scrutiny of a trustee who administers the seizure and sale of your property. Not fun.

Chapter and Curse

The kind of bankruptcy discussed here is Chapter 7, which allows for the canceling of debt. But you've probably heard Chapter 11 and Chapter 13 tossed around, and no doubt can't take another breath until you know what they mean.

Chapter 13 doesn't eliminate debt—it simply establishes a court-sanctioned repayment schedule, usually over three to five years, which gets creditors off your back. It's better suited to individuals whose debt mostly consists of the kinds that cannot be discharged under Chapter 7. Those who have debt with co-signers may prefer Chapter 13, since it bars creditors from going after the co-signer's assets as long as the payment plan is followed. Chapter 13 also stains the credit report for a shorter time—six years, versus Chapter 7's ten years.

Chapter 11 provides time for a debtor to reorganize finances while maintaining day-to-day control unimpeded by creditors. Until 1994, it applied only to companies rather than individuals, and is still primarily associated with fallen stars such as TWA, The Sizzler and Burt Reynolds.

- Feels bad

Emotional fallout from a bankruptcy can be pretty severe. Most people sign their name to debt with every intention of repaying it. It just plain feels bad to fail at that obligation.

Don't Reaffirm

If you file for bankruptcy, some creditors may ask you to "reaffirm" your obligation to pay them. Say you owe company XYZ a lot for charges you made on their credit card. When you file for bankruptcy, XYZ knows its going to have to kiss the money you owe them good-bye. So immediately following the bankruptcy, they "ask" you to sign an agreement to pay them all the money you owed them, sometimes threatening to repossess whatever you bought if you do not sign. (Sears made this threat recently to many credit card holders.)

Don't do it. The creditor is extremely unlikely to repossess used household goods that would be difficult to sell. More important, the whole point of bankruptcy is to begin looking forward, not spending whatever cash you have on debt that's behind you.

3. Working It

Investing. When it works right, it's hard to beat the premise: something you buy either earns you money every so often or increases in value during the time you own it. Or both.

It's not possible to exaggerate the importance of investing. Whether working toward a down payment on a bungalow or a retirement not spent asking people whether they'd care to "supersize it," being smart with the money you're able to squirrel away is essential. But you probably wouldn't be reading this book if you didn't already realize that investing is not just a good idea, but an absolute must. Beyond whether to invest, however, lie the tricky questions of why, how and how much to invest.

This chapter's about how to manage that portion of your resources that has eluded the jaws of debt and withstood the temptations of Ikea and Nobody Beats the Wiz. Whether that's a couple hundred or a couple hundred thousand, there are issues to consider both when you get started and as your circumstances, income and goals change throughout your life.

Investment Basics

An investment is anything bought for the purpose of producing income or increasing in value. That can include CDs (Certificates of Deposits), bonds, stocks and mutual funds, but also art, a home or starting one's own business. Some of the same principles apply to all of these investments. But in this book we're going to stick to those investments that don't require an eye for color, a picket fence or every waking hour of your time. Nevertheless, don't assume that stocks and bonds and traditional investments are the only acceptable choices for you. Personal satisfaction and the ability to sleep at night are just as important as annual returns.

Here's a quick look at the basic workings of the investments you're most likely to encounter.

Stock

In a word, ownership. A share of stock represents equity in the company that issued it, which is why stocks are also known as *equities*. If you hold a share of McDonald's, then you own a tiny sliver of all its assets—its brand name, company-owned restaurants, special sauce recipe.

When a company wants to raise money, it can sell a piece of itself to investors. Investors buy shares of the company and the company gets their cash to use for expansion, product development, lining the pockets of its founders and so on. When a company wants to go public, it sells shares of itself in a process known as an *initial public offering* (IPO); if a company needs more cash later on, it can sell more of itself in a *secondary offering*. After it's public, the stock is then traded on an *exchange,* such as the New York Stock Exchange, the biggest exchange in the world, the American Stock Exchange or one of the several regional exchanges, like those in Chicago, Philadelphia or Vancouver, British Columbia. Brokers *make a market* in the stock at the exchanges by matching those who want to buy a particular stock with those who already have it and are looking to sell. People who want to buy the stock offer a certain price for it, called a *bid.* The price that sellers want is called the *ask,* and when those prices meet, a sale is made. (Actually, they don't quite meet—the buyer often pays just a sliver more than the seller gets; the difference is called the *spread* and the market maker keeps it for his trouble.) Many stocks aren't traded in a physical exchange but are traded via NASDAQ, a network of computers operated by the National Association of Securities Dealers. The NASDAQ lists more companies than its two older brothers, the NYSE and the AmEx, and is where some of America's biggest companies (Intel and Microsoft, for example) are traded.

As owners, shareholders are entitled to participate in the running of the company. They vote on the appointments to the company's board of directors and can attend yearly shareholder meetings, where they can grill the bigwigs about the company's performance.

More important, shareholders are entitled to participate in a company's profits. Many companies periodically pay a percentage of their profits to their shareholders. These payments are called *dividends* and are usually paid on a quarterly basis. A $50 stock that pays a dollar a share in dividends is said to *yield* 2 percent—someone with one hundred shares can expect a dividend payment of $25 every three months (four quarterly payments of $25 = $100 a year, or a dollar per share). Investors can either pocket the cash or use it to buy additional shares of the stock. Some companies tend to pay very small or no dividends—such as those that are recently public or those in quickly growing industries (like high-tech companies) or, of course, companies that don't have any profits. Other companies reliably pay relatively large dividends—including many utilities and big, old companies like automakers.

Dividends are just one way that stock investors make money. The more talked-about way is for an investor to buy a stock at one price and sell it later for a higher price, the old "buy low, sell high." That's where the majority of the individual investor's attention is focused—trying to buy stocks that will rise in value. Any time an investor sells a stock (or any asset) for more than it cost, the profit is called a *capital gain.*

The stock you're most likely to encounter is *common stock.* That's what they're talking about when they say on TV, "Coca-Cola's up a dollar"—the common stock. *Preferred stock* is similar in that it also represents ownership in the company, but there are a couple key differences. The dividend payments of preferred stock are guaranteed, and preferred holders come before common holders if the company fails and its assets are liquidated. These perks, however, carry a price. Preferred shares usually appreciate less quickly than common shares. Then there are stocks that have different classes. Some companies might issue stock that's slightly different from the rest of its stock. Maybe a conglomerate will call them B shares and they'll more closely track the performance of one of the company's subsidiaries.

Or maybe the C shares will carry ten votes per share, which gives a share-holder, often a founding family member, the ability to control the company's direction even without owning much of the stock.

Bond

A bond is an IOU. Whoever issues the bond gets the use of an investor's money. In exchange, the issuer makes regular interest payments, which is why bonds are also called *fixed income investments.* At the end of the bond's life, or *term,* the issuer pays the investor back the original loan amount. The date the bond expires is called the *maturity date* and the loan amount is called *par value.* The interest payments are called the *coupon*—a $10,000 bond with a coupon of 9 percent will pay its holder $900 every year, usually dividing the yearly payout into two semiannual payments.

Bonds are issued by both companies and governments, either to raise funds or to finance a specific project, like the building of an airport. They can be for any length of time, ranging from short (a year or less) to inter-mediate (one to ten years) to long (more than ten years).

Bonds issued by the U.S. government are called *Treasury bonds* if their maturity is over ten years, *Treasury notes* if it's one to ten years and *Treasury bills* (T-bills) if the maturity is a year or less. Bonds that pay no interest during the life of the bond are called *zero-coupon* bonds; they sell at a big discount to the par value that the investor will collect when the bond matures. For example, the perennial birthday and graduation gift, *U.S. savings bonds,* are zero-coupons—they pay no periodic interest, but the $100 bond that your gramps gave you only set him back $50. Savings bonds are unlike other bonds, however, in that they can't be traded—they can only be cashed by the person in whose name they were registered when they were purchased.

Corporate bonds are usually backed by the issuer, who promises to make good on the loan when the term is up. These bonds are called *debentures.* Some companies, particularly those with shaky credit, have to back their bonds with more than their word. *Asset-backed bonds* are secured by specific property owned by the issuer—a factory or real estate, for example, or even the future royalties from songs, which David Bowie packaged as a bond in 1997. When the assets backing a bond are a group of home loans, the bonds are called *mortgage-backed bonds.*

Mutual Fund

An investment company that takes a lot of money from a lot of individuals and buys a lot of different stocks or bonds or other securities with it is a mutual fund. Its holdings are managed by a professional money manager, who decides what to buy and sell, and when.

As with individual stocks or bonds, fund investors make money both from the dividends or yields paid by the fund's holdings, and by appreciation in value of those holdings. Mutual funds are sold in shares, and the price of a share is called the *net asset value* (NAV).

The *fund manager* has wide discretion to do what she thinks is best for the fund, although many funds do have to stick within certain guidelines. Those parameters, which may include stuff like avoiding overseas securities or keeping the percentage of bonds below a certain number, are spelled out in a document called a *prospectus* that the fund sends all investors. The prospectus includes information on the fund's investment style and goals, its past performance and information on how to purchase and redeem shares. The prospectus also details the myriad charges investors will face.

There are mutual funds for virtually every style of investor. Stock investors can select from a multitude of funds that invest only in stocks, also called *equity funds.* There are equity funds that are named for the size, or capitalization, of the companies in which they invest. *Small-cap* or *aggressive* funds invest mostly in small companies, *mid-cap funds* invest in medium-sized companies, while *large-cap* or *blue-chip funds* stick mostly to corporate giants. Other equity funds are named for their investing style. *Growth funds* buy companies thought to be growing quickly; *value funds* buy companies the manager believes are underpriced; *income funds* buy companies that pay large dividends. Equity *index funds* seek to replicate the performance of a stock index; they contain only the stocks of a particular index, such as the S&P 500, in weightings that copy the index. Funds that invest only in companies in one area, such as utilities or computer makers, are called *sector funds.* Then there are *international funds,* which invest only in foreign companies, and *global funds,* which invest at least a quarter of their assets in foreign companies. There are *country funds* that invest solely in the funds of one country, as well as *regional funds,* like those for the Pacific Rim or Europe. Funds that invest only in companies that pass screens for various ethical, environmental or even religious practices are called *socially responsible funds.*

Bond funds are equally diverse. There are funds that invest exclusively in the various types of bonds. That means *high-quality funds, corporate-bond funds, high-yield funds* (aka junk-bond funds), *government-bond funds, municipal-bond funds* and funds that invest only in bonds that are backed by a pool of mortgages. Bonds also have index funds of their own, which seek to replicate the performance of an index, such as the Lehman Brothers Aggregate Bond index.

Just as many investors seek diversity by investing in both stocks and bonds, investors often hold both stock funds and bond funds. Some mutual funds, called *balanced funds,* buy both bonds and stocks to achieve that blend within one fund. *Asset allocation funds* give a fund manager even more discretion to move into different classes—the manager weights the fund with stocks, bonds or cash, based on his or her feelings about which way the economy is headed.

Money Market

Money market accounts function like savings accounts—you put your money in and then get your money back, plus interest. But what's actually at work behind the scenes more closely resembles a mutual fund.

The manager of a money market fund buys mostly ultrasafe short-term government and corporate bonds. That safety means that money market funds are virtually risk free. But it also means that the interest rate money markets pay is less than what you'd expect to earn from longer-term bonds. Unlike a mutual fund, money market funds are not priced with a net asset value. Instead, one share is always worth $1, with interest being paid in the form of additional shares. Thus, when you take $100 out of your money market fund, you're actually selling one hundred shares. This also means that you pay no capital gains tax (though you do pay regular income tax on the additional shares).

Money market accounts typically pay at least a couple percentage points higher than a savings account. And they're way more liquid than mutual funds, meaning you can access your money in small amounts far more frequently than by selling shares of a stock or bond mutual fund. And many money market accounts offer traditional banking conveniences, like check writing, ATM cards and a debit card that draws against your money market fund.

Money market accounts are offered both by banks and brokerages, as well as some companies that specialize in money market funds. If you open an asset management account at a brokerage, in which to hold your stocks, bonds and mutual funds, any uninvested money is automatically swept into a money market account. That way, your dough can earn good interest instead of just sitting there.

Investment Strategies and Concepts: The Basics

You've already selected a broker (back in Counting It) and now you know the basic terms. But where the fudge are you supposed to come up with any money to invest? And what portion of the dollars you manage to scrape together should you dedicate to investing?

Getting Started: The 10 Percent Solution

Americans aren't great at saving money. We average only $.31 saved for every $10 of personal disposable income. Compare that with Canada and Italy, where it's over $.50, Germany, where it's almost $1.50, and Japan, where it approaches $2. On the other hand, Americans have proven to be remarkably effective investors.

In "Repaying It," we discussed how to determine when to direct money toward repayment of debt and when to invest it (quick recap: put the dough wherever the rate—or expected rate—is higher). So here we'll assume we're talking about whatever money you're able to commit toward an investment program.

But how much should that be? Short answer: 10 percent of your take-home pay.

You hear a lot about this topic, usually in the form of clichés like "Pay yourself first." Well, sayings usually don't get to be clichés without at least a germ of good sense behind them and this one's got more than a germ. We're about to see how important time is for the young investor and how it can turn even modest deposits early on into large sums. The old "Pay yourself first" saw is simple—you consider that 10 percent as your most important bill each month, the one that you're least willing to delay or ignore. No, that doesn't mean you should shiver in the dark so that your mutual fund account gets its 10 percent. But it does mean that you should view your obligation to yourself at least as seriously as you view your obligation to the electric company.

Time to talk about some of the concepts at the core of any investment program.

Compound Interest: Investing's Silver Bullet

> "A man has three great friends: an old wife, an old dog and compound interest."—Benjamin Franklin

Its definition is deceptively simple: compound interest is the accumulation of interest on interest. If you have $100 in an account that pays 10 percent interest per year, at the end of the year you'll have $110—the $100 that you started with plus $10 in interest (10 percent of $100 is $10—duh-hay-nu). You may decide to blow that $10 on video poker and Kit Kats. But if you let that interest ride a second year, you'll finish with $121—$110 + $11 = $121. That extra dollar—the one that turned year one's $10 into year two's $11—is the most powerful force in investing.

Sounds too simple to be true? Let's look at a couple more examples to see how compound interest really makes a difference.

1. Take the scenario above a few steps further. Start with a measly $100, invested in something that pays 10 percent annually. If you do nothing for thirty years—no deposits, no withdrawals—you'll end up with $1,745—a total return of better than 1,600 percent!

2. Where compounding really starts to kick in, however, is when you add extra dollars at regular intervals, as in an IRA or 401(k) plan. Let's take a typical IRA. Suppose you warehouse the maximum yearly contribution of $2,000 in an investment that earns 10 percent a year. Keep it up for thirty

years, and you'll have over $375,000—not a bad return on a $60,000 investment.

The two critical variables of compound interest are the rate of return and the time period that an investment is allowed to grow. As you'll learn from the discussion of investment classes, the rate you attain is as much a product of chance and your personal tolerance for risk as it is skillful investing.

But you're in full control of the second variable—time. The longer you keep your money invested, the more powerful the effects of compounding, even if you stop adding fresh capital to the pile. This period—known as your "time horizon"—levels the playing field for many young investors, who can compensate for the fact that they don't have much money to start with by getting started earlier.

Let's take a look at two more examples that demonstrate the power of compound interest and the importance of starting to invest as early as possible.

• Two sisters, Laurie and Tracy, begin selling their poetry with great success in 1968. Laurie, her father's lessons still burning her ears, diligently puts $2,000 a year in a mutual fund that returns an average of 10 percent a year. Tracy, on the other hand, blows her discretionary dough on Donovan and clove cigarettes.

By 1978, Laurie has broken free of her buttoned-down lifestyle and decided not to invest another cent. Tracy, however, has settled down and decided to mend her spendthrift ways. Starting that year, she puts $2,000 annually in the same fund in which Laurie's money still resides.

Cut to 1998. Tracy has deposited a total of $40,000, which has grown to a little more than $125,000. Not bad. But Laurie, who contributed only a total of $20,000 and hasn't added a cent in twenty years, now has about $230,000. Why? Because compound interest had longer to work its magic with Laurie's money. What's more, Tracy will never catch Laurie, even if she continues to contribute another two grand every year.

• It's June 1978, and Velma and Daphne are graduated from State U. They've heard whispers of a foolproof investment that guarantees a 10 percent return. Velma immediately sinks $75 into the scheme and continues to do so every month. Daphne, eager to enjoy every penny of her newfound freedom, holds off. "There'll always be time to catch up," she reassures herself, as she savors the Slurpees and Pet Rocks to which she feels entitled.

As 1988 rolls around like Dukakis in a tank, Daphne suddenly grasps the lyrical force of the Ant and the Grasshopper. Beginning June 1988, Daphne plays catch-up, investing $200 each month in the same reliable fund that Velma continues to favor with $75 a month.

Cut to 1998. Velma has invested a total of $18,000; Daphne's ponied up $24,000. Yet Velma sits on a pile of $56,952, almost fifteen grand more than Daphne's kitty of $40,969.

What happened? Two words: compound interest. The point is that it's far better to make a relatively small sacrifice now than to try to play catch-up later.

Risk vs. Return: A Struggle

In investing, the relationship between risk and return is simple: the less risk one assumes, the lower potential reward one can expect. The risk/return relationship usually works both ways—the greater the risk, the greater the potential reward one should be entitled to expect.

In other words, an investor should be compensated better for assuming more risk. Let's look at bonds, for example. If you lend your money to a company that may not pay any or all of it back, you're taking a risk. In exchange for that risk, you're entitled to expect a better rate of return. On the other hand, if a safe and secure entity such as the U.S. government wants to borrow your money, you're virtually assured of getting your money back. Since you assume very little risk, the government doesn't have to pay you as much in return.

With stock, there's no promise that you'll be paid back, because you're not loaning the company your money; you're becoming a part owner. That means you benefit when the company does well and suffer when it falters. That's why stocks, in general, are riskier than bonds. So why would anyone invest in stocks? Because they typically provide higher returns than bonds.

Not every individual stock provides better returns than every individual bond. Stocks as a whole will not necessarily have a better year or even ten years than bonds. If that was guaranteed, they could hardly be said to be riskier. But it does mean that stocks, in general, provide greater *potential* payoff than bonds. You may have a blue-chip corporate bond that reliably pays 7 percent interest. Unless interest rates do something crazy, you're not going to do much better than that. Had you bought stock in the company, however, you would have the chance to do 10 percent or better. But you also have a pretty decent chance of earning less than 7 percent, or even losing some of your money. In other words, the bond investor in this example is willing to give up the chance to do substantially better than 7 percent in exchange for the stability of an investment that, failing bankruptcy or other disaster, is very unlikely to do worse than 7 percent.

The same concept works for different types of stocks as well. Since smaller, lesser-known companies are more likely to vanish or go belly-up than larger blue-chips, they're riskier. But investors who take a chance on the occasional small company that triples its stock price in a year are well compensated for that risk.

What about money market funds and other cash investments? Since they're supersafe, they can be relied upon to pay rates lower, on average, than bonds and stocks. How about Broadway shows, microcap stocks or opening a restaurant? Since the chances to make a killing is there, you can bet the chances of losing everything are woefully high.

Simple as it sounds, risk is actually one of the hardest things for investors to grasp. For one thing, many investors, author included, sometimes neglect to consider risk when making investment decisions. Those charts that show stocks returning better than 10 percent over time make it easy to forget that plenty of stocks have returned 0 percent and plenty more have returned below that and lost all an investor's money. Even stocks that have kept pace with the averages more often than not do their gaining in short bursts rather than steady climbs. If you buy a stock just after one of those bursts, you may be looking at a long ride before the stock lives up to your expectations.

Then there are countless schemes that violate the risk/return relationship by providing very high risk with very little potential for reward. Out-and-out scams fit into this category, of course. But so do firms that charge high fees or loads for badly performing investments. Paying a high fee increases the chances that you'll lose money on your investment. So if the investment has little chance of outperforming its lower-fee peers, its buyers overpaid for the risk they're assuming.

The magic potion all investors search for is a high-return/low-risk investment. But so far no one has found one that's repeatable, long-term and legal. It is impossible to create a precise guideline to determine when a dollar's worth of risk is worth a dollar's worth of potential return. So much of the decision to tolerate risk in search of higher returns depends on an individual's financial circumstances and psychological comfort with risk. Investors who simply cannot relax without knowing their money is absolutely out of harm's way should invest differently from those who spend more time obsessing over the opportunities for profit they'd be missing if their dough were parked in a savings account.

Even strictly from an investment point of view, this difference in style makes sense. The point is to assume only as much risk as necessary to justify the return on the investment. Let's say a worrier and a risk-taker both invest in a stock fund they're hoping will return 10 percent. If you think of risk as the price one pays for a chance at financial gain, the worrier gnashing teeth over the investment is actually assuming *more* risk than his daredevil counterpart. His worry and discomfort are making the investment more expensive than it is for the other guy.

Then there's the financial circumstances. An investor who's hoping to retire in two years has a very different set of concerns from an investor who won't be needing a nest egg for forty years. Since a catastrophe within two years would hurt the first investor a lot more than the second, they're assuming different risk, even when they buy the same investment. That's why younger investors are often advised to assume greater risk than those with fewer earning years ahead of them. While it's generally correct that younger investors can and should assume more risk than older investors, age and time horizon are just one piece of a complex puzzle.

That doesn't mean that risk-averse types, or those investing for a near-term goal (retirement, grad school, buying a house), automatically should seek the shelter of low-risk/low-return investments. Putting one's money under the mattress (or in CDs or a savings account) skews the risk/reward relationship in another way. Since inflation will wither its buying power year after year, money that does not earn interest will actually decline in value over the years. There are other risks to playing it too safe. Lost chances to benefit from the strong performance of other investments can be said to hurt those who take no chances. A lost chance to gain, called an opportunity cost, is why sometimes the riskiest thing is to assume too little risk.

MISCONCEPTION

Past Is Not Always Prologue

My friend Nabs the screenwriter is talented in a lot of areas, but math isn't one of them. He used to play poker a lot, and one time he explained his betting strategy to me. "Whenever I lose a hand, I always bet twice as much on the next hand. I figure I'm not likely to lose two in a row."

Without getting into a big discussion of probabilities, suffice it to say that the reason this is incorrect is that, in poker, the past doesn't influence the future. (Before the degenerate gamblers out there write me smarty-pants letters, I'll concede that those who study the patterns of their opponents can of course eke out an edge as the game progresses, and counting cards in blackjack of course aids the counter.)

Let's say you were going to flip a coin five times. If you placed your bet before the coin was tossed at all, you'd feel pretty sure of getting at least one tails (the odds of getting five heads are only one in thirty-two). But let's say you had already tossed it four times and gotten four heads. Assuming it wasn't a trick coin, would you still feel confident betting the ranch that you would see tails on the fifth toss? I didn't think so. The odds of any given toss coming up tails are fifty-fifty, no matter how the preceding tosses turned out.

So how does all this apply to investing? Well, a lot of investors who have bet wrong a few times in a row figure they're due for a big score. Unfortunately, the market doesn't know how an investor's last several stocks have performed. It doesn't owe a break to the guy who's had a patch of rotten luck. So that's why you keep your bets spread out from the beginning. And remember, your odds of disaster are reduced if you understand that good fortune is more often the product of hard work and sticking to the investment principles you so firmly embraced after reading this chapter.

Diversity: Spreading the Risk Smooths the Bumps

The concept is as simple as a Don Quixote moral: don't venture all your eggs in one basket. But its application is too often overlooked by investors eager to cash in on whatever strategy is the flavor of the month.

A portfolio that includes many stocks is less susceptible to the wild swings that a single stock faces. But simply making several investments instead of one doesn't really diversify a portfolio. Many similar investments and investment classes move in lockstep. Investing in the stocks of Chrysler, Ford and GM provides more diversity than betting your wad on just one of them, but it doesn't really do the trick, because all three will likely get hit if, say, there's a recession, or if the dollar rises against the yen.

A mutual fund, in which one purchase nets you anywhere from twenty to five hundred stocks at a time, offers instant diversification—if one stock heads south, others hopefully will rise. Or at least sink less. Even buying a single mutual fund won't adequately spread your money around, although it goes a lot farther than buying a single stock. If you buy a high-tech fund, you shouldn't be surprised if the whole thing is just as volatile as a single tech stock—companies in a similar industry often tend to move as a group.

In fact, stocks on the whole often move as a group. In any given year, there are only a handful of funds that zig when the market zags. The correlation isn't exact, but there are few large stock funds that are going to be plus or minus even 20 percent from what the market does in most years. That's good news—if you're in a U.S. stock fund when domestic stocks are rolling, as they have been throughout the 1990s. But if you were exclusively in stocks in a period like the early eighties, when the market lost 16.9 percent over nineteen months, you'd have wished you'd scattered your dollars more widely.

Investors new to the market should diversify in stages. Someone who's got a single big U.S. stock should think about adding a stock in a different industry. Someone with just a few stocks could get a large-cap domestic stock mutual fund, and then add a fund that invests in small companies. Someone with domestic stock funds might add a foreign fund. Someone with stock exposure worldwide should consider other asset classes, especially those that have a low correlation to the majority of their investments, such as real estate investment trusts (REITs).

Redistribution is another part of diversification. Say you create a $10,000 portfolio by investing $1,000 in each of ten different stocks. Over the course of a decade, one of the stocks has gained 1,000 percent while the others are flat. Your portfolio is now worth $20,000; it has $11,000 of one stock and nine worth $1,000 each. Without doing anything, your portfolio suddenly has more than half its dollars in one stock.

Every year or so, reassess your entire portfolio and consider flattening out overweightings like the one in the example above. (You should also think about getting out of the stock-picking business if nine-tenths of your picks went nowhere in a decade.)

Diversification can be taken too far. Someone with a small amount of money shouldn't spread their dollars so thin that transaction costs and paperwork hassles outweigh the benefits. The line between overweighted and scattered is imprecise, but novice investors with portfolios under $100,000 will do well to keep any single investment above $2,000 and below $10,000. This range works for a variety of reasons. The lower limit means that each year's maximum IRA contribution ($2,000) can be placed in one investment with the ease of use that retirement investing ought to have. The upper limit means that an investor can buy a round lot (one hundred shares) of all but the priciest stocks.

If all this sounds like a lot of work, remember that your basic style of investing doesn't have to change. You're still looking for solid long-term investments that you don't have to check every hour. In fact, a diverse portfolio actually allows its owner to sleep easier than a big bet on one stock or fund because the chance of a wipe-out is much less. So the concept applies across the board, regardless of portfolio value—lots of baskets means safer eggs.

Actual Investing: Getting Started

The past is not necessarily an accurate predictor of the future. It's entirely possible that corporate bonds will outperform stocks over the next ten years or that stocks will earn even less than ultrasafe short-term government bonds. And it goes without saying that not every individual small-company stock has outperformed every individual T-bill. These disclaimers are real, and too often ignored by investors who seem to think the Constitution promises them yearly returns from the stock market of 10 percent or better.

Nevertheless, history is the single best gauge there is for comparing how different asset classes can be expected to behave. There are good reasons behind these historical returns. These reasons, mostly a function of compensating investors for assuming risk, will be dealt with in the following sections on investing in different types of assets. But keep in mind that just about all investing advice, here and everywhere, is based on the notion that stocks as a whole will continue to outperform corporate bonds, which in turn continue to outperform government bonds.

Asset Allocation: The Weighting Is the Hardest Part

Before you begin selecting specific investments, there's a big-picture question to ask yourself: What kind of investments do I want and in what proportion?

I don't wanna get all touchy-feely here, but the fact is that there is no simple, one-size-fits-all way to approach this question. What's right for one twenty-seven-year-old with $10,000 isn't always right for another twenty-seven-year-old with $10,000. There's no formula that allows you to plug in your age, financial status and risk tolerance while spitting out a recipe that guarantees lofty returns and low blood pressure. No personal finance book can reach into your head and heart to determine what's best for you. Those kinds of gut checks require a little bit of introspection and some experience.

Investment Classes

Different investments have produced different returns over time. Here's a look at how investors would have fared over the last seven decades, and since 1970.

Investment Classes

Different investments have produced different returns over time. Here's a look at how investors would have fared over the last seven decades, and since 1970.

Asset Class	Jan. 1926–Dec. 1996
Large Stocks (S&P 500)	10.7 percent
Small Stocks	12.6
Long-Term Corp. Bonds (20-year maturity)	5.6
Long-Term Govt. Bonds (20-year maturity)	5.1
Intermediate-Term Govt. Bonds (5-year maturity)	5.2
30-Day Treasury Bills	3.7
Inflation	3.1
Foreign equities	N/A

Asset Class	Jan. 1970–Dec. 1996
Large Stocks (S&P 500)	12.3 percent
Small Stocks	14.2
Long-Term Corp. Bonds (20-year maturity)	9.6
Long-Term Govt. Bonds (20-year maturity)	9.3
Intermediate-Term Govt. Bonds (5-year maturity)	9.0
30-Day Treasury Bills	6.9
Inflation	5.5
Foreign equities	12.9

There are, however, some general guidelines that help steer a beginning investor in the right direction. The longer you let the invested money work, the more time compound interest and the historical upswing of the stock and bond markets have to do their thing. Conversely, if you're nearing the time when the investment is needed—a down payment, college expenses— you'll be more affected by a market crash than someone who doesn't need the money for a long time. This is especially true for those nearing retirement. Not only will a market crash take a chunk out of the nest egg that they'll soon need, but their ability to replenish it will be hampered by the reduced time they have to earn back the loss. Obviously, that goes double for those already on fixed incomes or living off their investments.

But for a young investor, time is a loyal friend. We've seen the role that compound interest plays and how even small differences in the rate an investment returns can quickly add up. But here's a thrilling and dramatic look at just how important time horizon is.

The three variables to any investment are *principal* (the money you put in), *rate* (the interest rate it earns) and *time* (time).

These four scenarios demonstrate that time is often more important than rate:

In scenarios 1 and 2, the same $20,000 invested buys the long-term guy more than $13,000 in returns. True, it took twice as long to get there and inflation will have eroded some of the value of that twelve large. But it's also a heck of a lot easier to come up with $1,000 every year than $2,000.

Or look at what the same $10,000 outlay in scenarios 3 and 4 buys an investor. Even though number 4 copped only half the rate of return the talented number 3 enjoyed, their returns were essentially the same. Again, inflation will have eroded some of number 4's returns. But inflation cuts both ways: number 4 needed to come up with only $500 each year. The extra $500 he didn't spend in those first ten years when number 3 had to pony up $1,000 went a lot farther in those early years.

Okay, so you get the point: investors who start early will enjoy the benefits of compound interest.

The second part of the equation is risk: in general, younger investors can and should assume more risk. But exactly how much and in what ways is

Rate=Important. Time=Real Important.

The three variables to any investment are **principal** (the money you put in), rate (the interest rate it earns), and **time** (time). These four scenarios demonstrate that time is often more important than rate.

SCENARIO #1		
Yearly deposit	$1,000	low
Rate of return	7 percent	low
Time (in years)	20 years	high
Total: $40,995 (principal invested: $20,000)		

SCENARIO #2		
Yearly deposit	$2,000	high
Rate of return	7 percent	low
Time (in years)	10 years	low
Total: $27,632 (principal invested: $20,000)		

SCENARIO #3		
Yearly deposit	$1,000	low
Rate of return	14 percent	high
Time (in years)	10 years	low
Total: $19,337 (principal invested: $10,000)		

SCENARIO #4		
Yearly deposit	$500	real low
Rate of return	7 percent	low
Time (in years)	20 years	high
Total: $20,497 (principal invested: $10,000)		

trickier. We already know from the asset class table that different investments tend to produce different rates of return. And we know from the risk section that the loftier returning classes carry a price—namely, an increased chance that they'll gain less than their historic returns or even decline in value.

Some direction is clearly in order.

One popular rule of thumb is to subtract your age from 100 and then invest that percentage in stocks, with the rest going into bonds and cash. For a twenty-five-year-old, that means a portfolio of 75 percent stocks and 25 percent bonds and cash.

That's not a bad place to begin, but it's clearly not going to work for all young investors, some of whom are inherently risk-averse, others of whom are investing for very near-term goals. We've already recognized the limitations of applying a single standard to individuals and sets of circumstances that may be very different. Here are three models that suit investors of different personalities and risk-tolerance.

But first, a few assumptions:

• A time horizon of at least ten years. This doesn't mean that you can't get at your money if you really need it, only that you have no foreseeable need for it.

• The portion of money invested in equities is in well-chosen, diverse stocks that are primarily chosen by a professional (such as a mutual fund manager); we'll talk about picking stocks on your own, but for now, when you see "stocks," assume that most of that exposure comes from stock mutual funds.

• You're keeping your emergency cash in a money market fund. In other words, don't fund the expansion of your portfolio into stocks and bonds with the money you're keeping on reserve, but feel free to consider that money part of your portfolio.

Stock Investing

We already know that a share of stock represents a sliver of ownership in a company. Whoever holds that share gets to participate in the company's successes—a dividend payment, perhaps, or operations with increased profitability. These successes will hopefully make the stock more attractive to other investors, causing them to pay more for your shares than you paid for them.

We already know how we buy a stock—it's as easy as calling the broker we've carefully selected and placing an order to buy, say, one hundred shares of Coca-Cola or fifty shares of Intel. Furthermore, we already know the rationale behind buying stocks—as a group, they've outperformed other asset classes by a good margin.

But all this doesn't help select a particular stock. Why buy Ford instead of GM, GM instead of GE, GE instead of some tiny start-up no one's ever heard of?

The mission is clear enough: you're hoping to buy a stock that will be worth more later on than it is now. But you also want one that's not riskier

AGGRESSIVE
(Pretty Risky)

Almost entirely invested in stocks, including substantial
exposure to overseas stocks and small-company stocks.

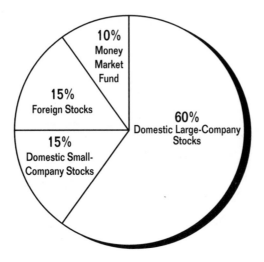

10%
Money
Market
Fund

15%
Foreign Stocks

60%
Domestic Large-Company
Stocks

15%
Domestic Small-
Company Stocks

MODERATE
(Sort of Risky)

Primarily invested in stocks, including a taste of
overseas stocks; supplemented by a chunk of bonds.

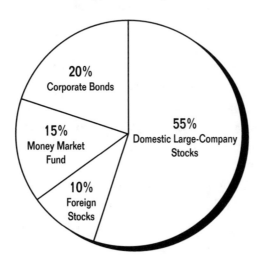

20%
Corporate Bonds

15%
Money Market
Fund

55%
Domestic Large-Company
Stocks

10%
Foreign
Stocks

TIMID
(Not Real Risky)

Almost half invested in stocks, including a sliver of overseas
stocks; a substantial cash portion and chunks of both corporate and
government bonds comprise the rest of the portfolio.

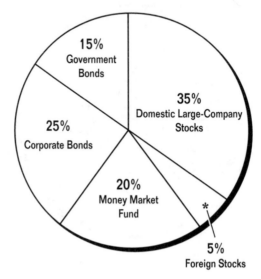

15%
Government
Bonds

35%
Domestic Large-Company
Stocks

25%
Corporate Bonds

20%
Money Market
Fund

*

5%
Foreign Stocks

than others that are appreciating at a similar rate, and you wouldn't mind
one that sent you money to reinvest every so often.

The price of a stock is not like the price of a box of Cheez-Its on the su-
permarket shelf. The store charges Cheez-It buyers a fixed price, established by what the store needs to make a profit on what it had to pay the
distributor, which charges whatever it can get above what it pays the manufacturer. There's a little slack built in—a store may lower its Cheez-It
price in order to compete with a store down the block; it may even take a
loss on a certain product in order to get people in the store. In the end,
though, the store's got to make enough profit on its stuff to keep the bag-
gers paid, the shelves stocked, the lights on and something extra for whoever owns the place.

A stock, on the other hand, has no such fixed price. Its price is established only by what people who want it are willing to pay (called the *bid*)
and what people who have it are willing to take (called the *ask*). So when
your broker or newspaper or online service gives you a stock quote, it just

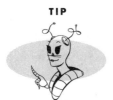

TIP

means that's the last price at which a stock was traded. The price is constantly in flux because the perception of what a stock is worth is constantly in flux.

How to Think About Stock Price

The clearest description of what a stock investor is actually buying comes from Andy Tobias's first book, *The Funny Money Game,* so I'm just going to paraphrase that here.

Imagine a wallet that was empty when you got it but gave birth to a dollar after every year of ownership. How much would you pay for this magic wallet? If you got it for $5, you'd have made a good deal—after five years you'd have recouped your investment and every year after that you'd have a dollar of profit.

Stocks are like that wallet. But instead of guaranteeing the amount they produce, you take a chance on how big that yearly payout will be. So a stock that has always paid a dollar and looks like it always will would attract a higher price than a stock that looks as though it'll never be able to pay a dollar. And a wallet that can't pay anything now but looks like it may be paying $2 or $3 a year in the future would probably go for more than the dollar-a-year wallet.

In general, stocks rise in price because investors perceive that the prospects for the company are improving, and a million factors contribute to that perception. Primary among them are:

- How quickly (or slowly) a company's profits are growing (or dwindling)
- Prospects for whatever the company sells or provides
- Outlook for the industry of the company
- Outlook for the economy as a whole
- How much room for growth there is (Are there new markets that haven't been tapped? Is the trend that's driving sales gathering steam or coming to an end?)
- Stability and smarts of the company's management
- Talent and productivity of the company's workforce

It's tough to get a good read on all this stuff. But that's not even the hardest part. Even if you did assimilate and analyze all this information, that only puts you on the same level with all the other investors who have done the same. That phenomenon—the idea that all investors have access to roughly the same information—is why big, active markets like the New York Stock Exchange are called "efficient" markets. In other words, there's a constant tug-of-war over the price of each stock. Based on the information at every investor's disposal, a stock moves up and down. If it gets lower than where investors think it should be, they pile in and drive the price up; if it gets too expensive, people start to sell and the price falls.

With this constant back-and-forth, the prices of the stocks you can buy are pretty darn near "what they should be" at any given moment. It's extremely tough for the novice investor to find a stock that's selling for $10 but is actually worth $20 and will be at its "correct" price soon.

Don't despair. While it's true that it's very tough to pick a stock that's soon going to shoot skyward, it's also true that time has been a friend to the investor who buys good stocks and holds them. Holding a stock for many years greatly diminishes the importance of buying it at the "right time." Buying a stock the day before it loses $5 feels cruddy. But if you were right about whatever attracted you to the stock in the first place, over the long haul that $5 loss will be compensated for by plenty of gains.

Stock picking is hard work. One hears a lot of idle chatter about some stock that tripled in value and made someone a pile of money, but verified, consistent performance that outshines the overall market is rarer than a steak from a broken oven. That's why individual stocks that you've picked yourself shouldn't consume more than a small portion of your time or your portfolio. But as a fun way to learn about the markets and try to make some money besides, picking stocks has a lot to recommend it.

Dividends vs. Appreciation

Stock investors are looking to make money in two ways: from the cash dividends that many companies pay shareholders and from the increase in the value of shares that they hold. A stock that paid a 5 percent dividend and appreciated in value 5 percent in one year is said to have a 10 percent total return for that year.

It'd be great to find a stock that pays a fat dividend and also raises in price a lot, but there's a reason stocks like that are just about impossible to find.

In general, the higher a stock's dividend, the less of its profits are being poured into growing the company. That's why high dividend payers tend to be stocks that don't have a lot of growing left to do, like electric utilities and established industry leaders. These are known as income stocks since they produce income for the shareholder, but investors generally don't expect their share prices to skyrocket. They also don't expect the share price to plummet, which is why safe stocks with a long history of high dividends are called "widow and orphan" stocks.

On the other hand are young and quickly growing companies. These companies need to spend every dollar of profit expanding operations—hire more people, build more plants, whatever. Paying dividends would be shortsighted.

In general, investors with a long time horizon should concentrate more on share price appreciation than on dividends. That doesn't mean that dividends should be shunned or that only hot-growth companies should be bought. Only that, as a general rule, a long-term stock investor ought to look to share prices as the way to make money. Investors looking to their investments for consistent income would probably do better in bonds rather than high-yielding stocks.

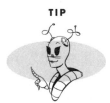

TIP

Dogs of the Dow
This stock-picking theory, which is also known as the Dow dividend theory, has become quite popular of late, and its historic return is pretty impressive. On the first trading day of the year, you invest an equal amount in the ten members of the Dow Jones Industrial Average that have the highest dividend yield. After holding for a year, you sell those ten and buy equal portions of the ten new highest yielding (some of which will undoubtedly be the same stocks).

Dividend payment is expressed as a percentage of a stock's share price (i.e., a stock at $20 that yields $1 per share per year is said to yield 5 percent, since $1 is 5 percent of $20). That means yield moves in the opposite direction of share price—a stock whose price doubles while it still pays the same dividend yields half as much. That's why the highest-yielding stocks are called *dogs*—because their share prices have either gone down or stayed level.

Unless you're sinking quite a bit of money into this theory, the commissions on ten yearly trades can eat into returns. Even with a discount broker at $25 a trade, that's $250 every year, or 2.5 percent if you put $1,000 into each stock. Since the theory has become so popular, some brokerages have begun to sell all ten of the stocks in a basket called a unit trust, which means you have to pay only one commission. Alternatively, you might consider the puppies of the Dow, in which you figure the ten highest-yielding Dow stocks but only buy the five with the lowest share price.

Stock Investing Tools

There are a million things that an investor can consider when buying or selling a stock. But the average investor doesn't have the time to agonize over every number in a company's balance sheet. That's why the bulk of an investor's stock exposure ought to come through stock mutual funds, especially for beginner's. But it doesn't mean you've got to avoid buying stocks altogether.

Take heart, stock buyers of the world. There are a few tools that are powerful enough and easy enough to assist the small investor. Let's look at four things any investor ought to consider when buying or selling a stock.

EARNINGS

Earnings, or profits, are the bottom line in stock investing. It's good news for investors when a company is making more money than it spends, because the company can invest that money in things that make it more valuable to its shareholders. That may mean acquiring other companies, more research and development spending, salaries that will attract better workers or higher dividend payments.

Companies announce their earnings every quarter, an event closely followed by eager investors. Earnings of major companies are covered in the business section of most newspapers, and *The Wall Street Journal* releases

A Stock Is Born:
How a Company "Goes Public"

The journey from good idea owned by a few people to giant corporation owned by thousands is one of the great adventures of American business. The nexus between public stock buyers and private company owners is an investment banker or a brokerage, which underwrites the sale in what is called an initial public offering (IPO).

It's the underwriter's job to drum up interest in the offering. This is a tricky process because the SEC, the agency that regulates the sale and trading of stocks, prohibits flashy ads and hype from the company's officers. That's why company founders are reticent during the "quiet period" before the stock hits the market and also why the offering is listed only in boring black-and-white, text-only ads, which are known as "tombstones." The broker helps the company create the prospectus that the SEC requires companies to make available to those who wish to buy its stock in an IPO. The prospectus contains the company's vital statistics—its revenues, profits (or losses), foreseeable pitfalls, officers, and so on.

Having gauged the demand for the stock, the underwriter then establishes a share price that will provide the capital the company needs and be attractive to the public. It then actually buys the shares from the company and lines up customers from its ranks of institutional clients (like mutual funds or big money managers) or fat-cat individual clients, to whom it resells the stock on the day of the IPO. If any shares are left over, the little guys in the general public get a shot at it.

When real big companies go public (like Lucent in September 1996, which was the biggest IPO in history), they often hire several underwriters; with access to more customers, the company has a better chance of creating more demand and unloading all the shares.

A couple newfangled ways are emerging for companies to access public capital. Electronic public offerings (EPOs) are when a company sells shares of itself via the Internet, making its prospectus and financials available to anyone with a browser. Spring Street Brewery and others have tried to sell shares this way. But question marks remain about the potential for rip-offs. Then there are direct stock offerings, in which the company goes right to the public and bypasses an underwriter.

From an investing point of view, IPOs are a tough game. Quite often they come out of the gate strong, amid an intoxicating burst of energy ("Wow, this company makes a search engine that purrs like a Harley!"). Then they often dart back down to earth as the hangover hits ("They think they're going to sell *how many* banner ads?").

It's tough for the little guy even to buy the shares. Unless you have an account with the broker underwriting the offering, you can forget it. And even if you do, underwriters save shares of "hot" IPOs for their biggest clients. When Netscape went public in 1995, I called my broker right away, noticing that his firm was way up there on the tombstone. The price was set for $14. Then all the preoffering interest took it to $28 before it even opened. By the time the shares actually went on sale, I was locked out. When shares finally became available to the little people later in the day of the IPO, they were far too expensive.

Those interested in newly public companies might do well to wait until the fat cats have had their digs. The price will eventually calm down as the momentum players and buy-dear types have moved on to other stocks. Alternatively, investors can look to the aggressive mutual funds that sometimes invest in IPOs. The Kaufmann Fund (800-237-0132, minimum initial purchase $1,500), for one, invests in lots of IPOs and has the clout to get in at the actual offering price, rather than on the way down.

its comprehensive "Digest of Earnings Reports" every quarter, which includes year-to-year comparisons and tons of other useful info.

Say you're following the stock of General Motors. First Call (on AOL, keyword: *firstcall;* on the Web, *www1.firstcall.com)* or another analyst-reporting service will survey all the analysts who follow GM. They'll say something like, "For this quarter, I expect GM to earn $2.12 in profit for every share of its stock." Then those analysts' estimates will be averaged and a consensus estimate will emerge. If the consensus is $2 and GM announces that it in fact earned $2.50 for the quarter, expect the stock to soar. By the same token, companies that fail to meet the estimates will usually suffer a big hit in stock price.

You might wonder why the stock of a company that's expected to earn 25¢ per share but actually earns 30¢ will rise while a company that's expected to earn $1.30 but actually earns $1.00 will tumble. Isn't $1 in earnings still better than 30¢? Well, yes—but only if you paid the same price for that dollar as you did for the 30¢. Remember, the expected earnings of a company is already built into the price an investor pays for its stock. So if both companies were "fairly priced," the one that earns more than expected will have given its buyer a better deal than the one that earns less. It's like seeing two different movies, one at the cheapie theater and one for which you wait in line for and pay full price. Unless you like the second one a lot better, you probably got a better deal at the cheapie flick, simply because you invested less in it.

P/E RATIO

Listed in any good newspaper, a stock's price/earnings ratio is among the most useful tools for evaluating whether a stock is a good buy. In many ways, it's the single quickest clue to how the market as a whole views the prospects of a company's stock.

Also referred to as a stock's "multiple," p/e ratio is simply the price of a stock divided by its yearly earnings (profit). So if a share of company XYZ costs $40 and the company earned $4 per share over the last four quarters, its p/e is 10. Hot companies (i.e., anything prefixed "cyber") that have little or no earnings history but high expectations will have very high p/e's,

Asset Allocation Chart

Time Horizon	Risk Tolerance	Traits to Look For in Investments	Drawbacks	Investments to Consider
Short-term (0-5 years)	Low/Conservative	• Investments that change very little in price • Maturities of less than 5 years (bonds and CDs) • Regular, reliable income payments • Easy withdrawal	• Low returns • Vulnerable to inflation	• Money Market • CDs • Short-term gov. bonds (t-bills)
Medium-term (6-10 years)	Medium/Moderate	• Regular, reliable income payments • Prices that don't deviate much from month to month • Maturities of less than 10 years (bonds)	• Slightly vulnerable to inflation • Moderate Returns	• High-dividend blue chip stocks • Growth and Income stock mutual funds • High-rated corporate bonds • Mid-term gov. bonds (t-notes) • Bond mutual funds
Long-term 10 years or more	High/Aggressive	• History of strong returns • Potential for big capital gains • Maturities of more than 10 years (bonds)	• Big price fluctuations/volatility • Potentially less liquidity	• U.S. equities, including both small- and large-company stocks • Growth stock mutual funds • Foreign stock mutual funds • Medium- and low-rated corporate bonds • Long-term bonds (gov. and corp.

while stodgy, dependable companies tend to have low p/e's because no one expects their earnings suddenly to shoot skyward.

Suppose you want to evaluate whether a stock is a bargain or not. Comparing its p/e with those of other companies in its industry will provide an insight into the market's perception of the company's future. In general, the higher a stock's p/e, the more brightly the market regards that company's potential for growth. Suppose the p/e ratios of Chrysler and GM are 10 and 9 respectively. Investors apparently think that Chrysler's earnings per share will increase faster than those of GM.

Even if that turns out to be true, it doesn't mean Chrysler is a better buy than GM. That's because the difference in expectation is already built into the price. In other words, you have to pay only $9 for a dollar of GM earnings, compared with $10 for a dollar of Chrysler earnings. So if both Chrysler's and GM's earnings per share this year are exactly what they were last year, investors in GM got the better value because they paid less for their dollar of earnings than did Chrysler investors.

Price/earnings ratio is just one piece of a complicated puzzle. A high p/e does not always signal danger, and a low p/e does not automatically indicate value.

P/E Ratio ÷ Growth Rate = Big Fun (PEG)

While a company's p/e ratio is among the most important measures of whether its stock is a good value, the fact that it is only a backward-looking indicator hampers its usefulness somewhat. After all, investors are more interested in what a stock will do than what it has done.

One tool, known simply as PEG, looks forward and has proven quite useful. PEG means the ratio of a stock's p/e value to its expected earnings growth rate. If a company's stock is trading at twenty times its last year's earnings, it has a p/e of 20. If the earnings of that company are expected by the analysts who follow it to grow 20 percent a year for the next several years (or however long the analysts have projected its earnings), then its PEG is 1 (20 divided by 20 is 1).

A stock with a PEG of 1 is thought to be a better bargain than a stock PEGed at 2 but more expensive than a stock with a PEG of .5. Remember, what stock investors hope to buy is a company that's growing its profits faster than other companies of similar risk. Paying $10 for a dollar of earnings expected to grow 10 percent a year is a better deal than paying $20 for that same dollar of earnings at the same expected growth rate. And a stock that's selling a dollar's worth of earnings with an expected growth rate of 10 percent a year for only $5 is, comparatively, a real bargain.

Because it relies on correct growth projections, PEG is better suited to valuing companies that are growing quickly. Stolid, stable companies don't typically enjoy big spurts in earnings growth, so the differences between one conglomerate's PEG and another's isn't so meaningful.

Keep in mind, of course, that when you're dealing with expectations, there's an inherent margin for error—earnings forecasts are only slightly more reliable than weather forecasts. And also remember that there is no "magic indicator"—lots of other investors have access to the same information as you and if they're not pouncing on that .5 PEG stock, there might be a good reason you shouldn't either.

Nevertheless, PEG remains an excellent tool for comparing the value of one stock with another. Despite its growing popularity as a valuation tool, a stock's PEG is hard to come by—it's not printed in the newspaper stock tables, nor does it show up when an investor calls up a quote on most on-line services. But its components—the p/e ratio, which *is* in the newspaper, and the expected earnings, which are available from First Call and else-where—are easily accessible. Even a die-hard math hater can divide one number into another—for a stock you're hoping to stick with for a while, it's worth the effort.

Your Eyes and Ears

Hey, don't laugh. Peter Lynch, who managed the mammoth Magellan fund with amazing skill, swears by the power of the perceptive regular Joe. And Warren Buffett, the country's most successful investor, buys companies that make products he uses, likes and understands.

The method is simple enough: if one of your favorite restaurants is al-ways crowded and seems to have staying power, it's not reckless to buy some of its stock. True, the fact that you know about it probably means that others also know and have already bought the stock. But unless you're the absolute last person to hear about it (the "greatest fool," as Keynes might say) there's good reason to think interest will continue to build. Same goes for a product that you love and rely on—chances are there are others who will come to feel the same.

This doesn't mean you should pour your cash into every trend that comes down the pipe. But it also doesn't mean that investing in stocks is some sort of bizarre guesswork. In the end, stocks do well when the com-panies behind them make products and services that people like. Yes, a product that gets hot often sees its stock price soar to levels that can't last, even if the product's as good as everyone says it is (hello, Zip Drive). That's why it's important to use the other tools—p/e ratio, PEG, etc. But when these all line up, don't be scared to take a little chance on a company that you use, like and understand.

Growth and Value

There are two basic styles of investing in stock—growth and value. Obvi-ously, both methods are expected by their fans to result in higher share prices, but they have different thinking behind them.

Growth investors buy shares in companies with quickly growing revenues and earnings. This usually means relatively young companies or companies in industries that are expanding rapidly—in short, "hot" companies, which make products or services for which demand is growing. Growth in demand will allow a company to sell more of whatever it sells and/or charge more for it and/or make the product or service available more cheaply. All of these things will hopefully mean more profits for the company. More profits for the company means more dough can be paid to the shareholders in the form of dividends, or the company may use those profits to make the products and services even more appealing, both of which should increase the price other investors are willing to pay for the stock.

Value investors, on the other hand, look for stocks that are cheaper than their earnings ability and the worth of their assets would suggest they should be—in short, "bargain" companies, which have fallen out of favor for one reason or another. Value investors believe that the stock market is efficient, meaning that the "true value" of the company will eventually be noticed by other investors, who will then drive up the price of the stock. Value investors are often called "contrarians" because they buy stocks that are cheap because they have been passed over by most other investors. Think of them as the thrift store shoppers of the stock market—that bell-bottom stock that everyone else couldn't sell fast enough might come to be worth something someday. The same companies that attract value investors also sometimes attract takeover offers, since the value of the company is not fully reflected in the stock. Value investors hope to make out like bandits from owning stock in companies that are taken over by an acquirer who pays more per share than the stock had been at before.

Growth investors tend to pay more attention to a stock's growth rate than to how "expensive" its p/e ratio is. They also tend to flee from stocks that report disappointing earnings results, which makes growth stocks in general somewhat volatile. Value investors pay more attention to stocks with low p/e ratios than to earnings reports.

The historic p/e ratio for the market as a whole is around 14. During gloomy times, it can drop to as low as 6 or so, and during booms, expect to see it around 22. Stock mutual funds also have p/e ratios, derived by averaging the p/e's of all the stocks held in the fund and adjusting for the weight of the stock the portfolio holds. This info is available from fund

What the Hell Is Beta?

Beta measures a stock's volatility, or tendency to rise and fall in value. Here's how it works. The S&P 500 is assigned a beta coefficient of 1. Any stock that rises and falls more sharply than the market as a whole has a beta greater than 1; a stock whose peaks and valleys are less dramatic than the market's has a beta lower than one. So a stock that experiences wide and frequent shifts in price compared with the S&P 500 (e.g. many small-cap technology stocks) will have a high beta, while large, stable blue chips tend to have a low beta.

Beta is a good place to look for a quick reference point on how sharply a stock's ups and downs have occurred. But remember, all it measures is the volatility compared with that of the market as a whole. So don't automatically associate beta (or volatility) with risk or assume that a low beta means a low chance of losing money. If the stock market is headed down, then a low beta probably means the company is going down with it. Also bear in mind that beta reflects past performance, not future. A stock with a high beta can, for a variety of reasons, suddenly start mirroring the index. That's why the beta numbers most often shown in the paper and elsewhere reflect the stock's performance over the past three years.

Companies like Morningstar calculate betas for mutual funds as well, based on how closely they track the performance of an index such as the S&P 500 or Lehman Brothers Aggregate Bond Index. A stock fund with a beta of 1.5 is expected to outperform the market by 50 percent during an upswing and sink 50 percent more during a down period. A fund with a beta of .5 is expected to drop half as much as its index during a downswing and rise only half as much during a climb.

raters like Morningstar and ValueLine. A value fund can be expected to have a much lower p/e ratio than an aggressive growth fund. Both may be excellent funds, but their p/e's offer a clue to their investment styles.

More Stock Stuff

Penny stocks—generally, any stock whose share price is less than $1—are usually far riskier than blue chips. These stocks, also called *microcaps,* sometimes carry a greater potential for reward—I'd have loved to ride Iomega up from 50¢ to $50. But for every Iomega there's a hundred bizarro companies and elaborate shell games that seduce investors with hot prospects and cold returns.

Because of the increased risk and volatility, penny stocks need to be followed more closely than their bigger brethren. Unfortunately, finding information on really small stocks—many of which don't even trade on a major exchange—can be a challenge. One excellent data source is *The Red Chip Review* (800-721-1972). Investors who gamble on penny stocks should invest no more than they can comfortably afford to lose on a learning experience.

MISCONCEPTION

Investors sometimes justify buying penny stocks by saying "It's at 35¢—how much lower can it go?" The answer is the same as any stock: it can lose up to 100 percent of its value. Investing $3,500 to buy ten thousand shares of a 35¢ stock that goes to 15¢ is no different from buying one hundred shares of a $35 stock that tumbles to $15—either way you lose $2,000.

TIP

A Little Security?

Bonds and stocks (and options and warrants, too) were originally called securities because the certificates issued for them proved, or "secured," that the holder owned a piece or has lent money to the company. Nowadays, certificates are seldom issued to investors. Rather, people store their investments at the brokerage, which is known as "holding in street name." This method is nearly always preferable, as it eliminates the chance of losing the certificate and speeds the redemption or sale. Some stock certificates, like those of Disney, are actually quite pretty; Disney holders may choose to certificate a share or two just for the heck of it, but they should expect their broker to be annoyed and charge a fee.

Points vs. Percent

MISCONCEPTION

It's tough to ignore a 100-point move in the Dow Jones Industrial Average. But investors should bear in mind that a 100-point move in a market at 8,000 means a lot less than it did when the market was at 2,250 or so. When the Dow crashed on October 19, 1987, its 508-point drop meant a loss of 22.6 percent—the worst one-day hit in the Dow's history. But a 508-point loss when the Dow is at 8,000 means a dip of 6 percent and change—nothing to sneeze at, but not worth calling the doctor, either. Investor habits change slowly, as they should. So it's common for financial types to trumpet 100-point moves more loudly than they might have mentioned 25-point moves ten years ago, even though the relative significance of the two events is similar.

DRIPs

Dividend Reinvestment Plans (DRIPs) take the quarterly dividend payments of a stock and reinvest them in more shares of the same stock, using compound interest to build a larger position in the stock over time. Most brokerages now offer automatic reinvestment, so just about any dividend-paying stock can be converted to a dividend-reinvestment plan in a regular brokerage account. But what DRIPs refer to are companies that operate their own dividend reinvestment program.

DRIP programs often allow investors to get started investing in a participating company's stock with as little as one share. They also allow additional purchases of stock, with many companies offering services that rival discount brokerages, such as automatic monthly deductions from your bank and IRA accounts. In addition to saving on commissions, DRIPs also give investors greater control over future purchases. While an investor would never have his broker buy $10 worth of stock in Coca-Cola (which would get you a fraction of a share), Coke's DRIP programs allows commission-free additional purchases of as little as $10.

No-load stocks, a term coined by DRIP expert Charles Carlson, refer to a particular form of DRIP, in which the main hassle of most DRIP plans—getting your paws on that first share—is removed. Companies that offer no-load stock plans for their shares act both as DRIPs and brokers. For a small fee—usually way less than you'd pay at even a deep discount broker-age—they'll actually sell you the shares you need to get started. Some programs even offer a discount on shares bought through a DRIP, an edge that can really add up.

Confined to big industrials and utilities just a few years ago, DRIPs and no-load stock plans are increasingly available from a wide range of brand-name companies. At last count there were over one thousand companies administering DRIPs, including some two hundred that offer no-load stock plans. There are now enough available to build a fairly diversified portfolio, including giants such as Gillette, Mobil, Norwest, Merck, McDonald's and Ameritech, although technology and transportation companies have been reluctant to get into the act.

DRAWBACKS:
- Shares owned in DRIPs are slightly harder to sell, or less liquid, than those held in street name (in a brokerage account). Selling shares in DRIPs can also result in a paperwork headache. When an investor sells stock at a profit, he faces taxes on the gain, called a capital gains tax. Assume an investor has two different DRIPs—GM and Ford. He buys ten shares of each to start, then another five each month. Of course, he also reinvests the dividends (that's the whole point). After five years, he's made 160 total purchases, each at a different price—sixty monthly purchases plus twenty quarterly reinvestments times two stocks. The guy's made a different gain (or loss) on each of those purchases, and figuring all that out is a pain that's avoided with a regular broker, who sends summary statements every year.
- To join most DRIPs, investors have to register with the company administering it. So if you create a portfolio of ten different DRIPs, you've got the equivalent of ten different accounts—a lot of paperwork.

These drawbacks can be alleviated by choosing just a couple solid stocks and sticking with them for the very long-term. Most young investors are too quick to sell anyway, so making it a little tougher can act as a hedge against an itchy trigger finger. DRIP investing is not where you park your investment dollars while you save for a car or where you speculate on the next hot Internet play.

Here's where to go for more information:

• "DRIP Investor," a monthly newsletter by the dean of DRIPs, Charles B. Carlson, 7412 Calumet Ave., Hammond, IN 46324; 219-931-6480

• First Share, 800-683-0743

• *Buying Stocks Without a Broker and No-Load Stocks,* DIY books by Charles B. Carlson ($16.95 each, McGraw-Hill)

• "The Individual Investor's Guide to Dividend Reinvestment Plans," The American Association of Individual Investors (updated annually), 625 N. Michigan Ave., Chicago, IL 60611; 312-280-0170

• *The Directory of Companies Offering Dividend Re-investment Plans,* Evergreen Enterprises, PO Box 763, Laurel, MD 20725; 301-953-1861

• The Moneypaper (914-381-5400), creator of those annoying fake-radio broadcast ads that are ubiquitous on financial television. Lists companies that offer DRIPs and also runs its own quasi-brokerage to ease the purchase of the initial share

• A complete list of no-load stocks is available by writing to the DRIP Investor at the above address or on the Internet at *http://netstock-direct.com,* a site that also features searching capabilities and electronic prospectuses and registration from companies that offer DRIPs.

• About one hundred or so companies that offer direct-purchase plans have made their prospectuses available through the Direct Stock Purchase Plan Clearinghouse. Call 800-774-4117 to ask for up to five of the documents at a time. The service, which is free, uses an automated phone tree that eerily knows your name and address after you enter your phone number.

Short Selling

You've heard the saying "buy low, sell high." Well, short selling tries to do the same thing but in reverse order—the investor sells high, then buys low.

In a regular stock buy (also called a "long buy") the hope is that the stock in question will rise in price after the buyer purchases it. But what if an investor thinks a stock is going to drop in price? He can borrow shares

What the Hell's a Stock Split?

When I was a little kid, my friend Kevin was given fifty shares of stock in Wendy's. This being the height of the "Where's the beef?" campaign, he soon told me that because "the stock split," he now had one hundred shares. "Wow, you doubled your money," said I, making the first in a career-building series of financial misobservations.

A stock split creates more shares by dividing the value of those shares already in play. Suppose Intel is trading at $100 per share. Intel may decide that people are growing wary of the stock because $100 seems like a psychological boundary. It decides to split the stock. If you own one hundred shares at $100 when Intel decides to split the stock in half, you will suddenly find yourself with two hundred shares of a $50 stock. Either way, your shares are worth $10,000.

Stock splits are not always two-for-one. They can be five-for-two or ten-for-seven or whatever the board of the company decides. Though splits are essentially a bookkeeping maneuver—not much different from getting four quarters for a buck—they generally signal good news for shareholders. Companies rarely split the stock when the price is declining and stock prices often get a little boost right after a split. Additionally, if a company pays a dividend, it may mean more dough for the shareholder. A company that splits its stock often raises its per-share dividend payment (also called its yield). When Mattel split its stock five-for-four in 1996, it maintained the same dividend—an investor who used to have one hundred shares would now receive 25 percent more in dividend payments for his 125 shares.

Companies sometimes decide to split their stock to decrease the volatility of the share price. With more shares out there, it becomes harder for big investors to cash in on steep moves in price by jumping in and out. Companies also know that certain investors buy stock only in "round" lots (amounts divisible by 100) because they face steeper commissions on odd lots. A two-for-one stock split automatically cuts the price of one hundred shares in half.

The opposite of a stock split is called, mystifyingly enough, a reverse split. Shareholders get one share for every five or ten or two or whatever shares they already had. This is done when a company wants to raise its stock price. Lots of institutional investors—pension funds, insurance companies, mutual funds—have rules forbidding investment in stocks trading for $5 a share or less. A reverse split may be a quick fix, but it is often indicative of a troubled company.

Just in case you're not yet convinced that the world of investing is a barrel of monkeys, you should know the story of legendary investor Philip L. Carret. The joke goes that Carret is so full of vim that when he turned one hundred, he split the stock.

of a stock from his broker and sell them right away. Then when the price drops, he repurchases the same number of shares and returns them to the broker. His profit is the difference between the price he sold the shares at and the price he bought them back at—if the company was at 90 when he borrowed one hundred shares then dropped to 75, his profit would be $1,500.

Sounds obvious enough, but in practice, it's easier said than done. There are also some special risks associated with short selling:

- Even riskier than buying long

When an investor's long, the worst that can happen is to lose 100 percent of your investment—a stock you bought at 50 can go to 0 and no lower. But a stock that rises costs a short seller money, so a stock bought at 50 can go to 100, or 200 and so on. This means that a short seller faces unlimited downside risk and has to monitor his holdings even more closely than if he invested long.

Short sellers are also vulnerable to a treacherous maneuver known as a "short squeeze." This happens when a stock that a lot of investors have sold short starts to rise. Short sellers scramble to buy shares, known as "covering" the short position, before the price gets any higher. But all that buying creates demand for the shares, which drives the price even higher. Shorts who are late to cover can get caught with their shorts down.

• No income

Short sellers do not receive the dividend payments that many stocks pay to their regular holders. Dividends take some of the risk out of regular stock buying: if you're long on Philip Morris, the 4 percent dividend takes some of the sting out of a year in which the stock price goes nowhere.

• Shorts get a bad rap

There's something vaguely un-American about short selling. Basically, you're rooting for bad news, and short sellers often find themselves blamed for rumors that send a company's shares south. This is an unfair perception. Longs do their share of rumor-mongering, and shorts serve a valuable function by reining in unscrutinized hype. Still, short selling is not for beginners or the risk-averse.

Two Sides to Every Trade

Finally, there's one last thing you should consider before making any stock trade. One of the hardest concepts for the newish investor to grasp is the idea that every single trade represents a difference in perception between you and whoever's on the other side of the transaction.

If you are willing to fork over $100 for a share of company XYZ, it's because you think that share will be worth more than $100 someday soon. But that means whoever's willing to sell that share of XYZ to you thinks he's getting a pretty good price. The fact that he's willing to sell means that he thinks the share will either soon be worth less than $100 or that it'll take a lot longer to show a profit than some other place he could put that hundred.

It's the same thing when you sell—if you're convinced a company's future looks cloudy enough for you to bail out for $100, whoever buys it disagrees with your prognosis.

So the question an investor has to ask before every trade is "What do I know that the other guy doesn't?" With ever-larger chunks of the market held by institutional money managed by professional investors versus little guys like you, it's a daunting question. If you sell your shares of Intel, there's a good chance you're selling them to a big mutual fund or pension

fund whose manager smells an opportunity. Are you confident that your research and instincts are better than his?

No, this isn't intended to scare you into never buying or selling a stock.
It just means that unless you're in it for the long haul, wherein even poor
timing will usually be overcome by the general uptrend of the market, your
hunch about a company's prospects had better be well founded. It's im-
perative to resist the belief that your intuition is somehow superior to that
of the people who do nothing but cogitate on the direction of the market.

A study of trading records by University of California-Davis professor
Terry Odean tracked the buys and sells of a particular broker's clients.
Over all three periods—long, medium and short—the stocks that the
clients sold outperformed those that they bought. Over the long term, the
gap was more than 3 percent a year! In other words, the investors would
have done better holding the stocks they held in the first place—and that
doesn't even factor in the extra trading costs that the hot-potato investors
faced.

An example will demonstrate the point. Say there's a fellow—we'll call
him Keith Karson—who fancies himself pretty smart about the market. It's
spring 1995 and the wrecking ball of hyperbole that became Windows 95
has just begun. Wow, thinks Keith, with all this talk about Microsoft, I bet
Apple is a pretty good value right about now. Karson bestows upon himself that most overused of investor clichés—contrarian—as he figures one
of two things could happen: (1) Windows 95 will be a fiasco. Delayed or
buggy, it'll so frustrate PC users who have been holding their breath that
they'll all buy Macs. Or (2) Windows 95 will be a sensation, causing Apple
to realize once and for all that it can no longer go it alone, sparking a bid-
ding war that'll send Apple shares skyward. In July, Karson plunks down
$46 a share, convinced he's looking at a win-win.

Cut to early 1996. Windows 95 met most of its lofty expectations while
Apple has just compounded the mistake of being undersupplied through
the end of 1995 by being way oversupplied for what turned out to be a dis-
astrous Christmas. Management is literally on life support as suitors do indeed hint at a takeover attempt that will pay several dollars from where the
stock is trading. Several dollars *under,* that is.

Karson bails in early February, thankful for the twenty-eight bucks someone else thinks each of his shares is worth. A nearly 40 percent loss, but a cheap lesson for a stock that's at $16 soon thereafter.

It's virtually impossible to outguess the market on a consistent basis. Your reasoning is not likely to outsmart the analyst whose day is spent poring over historic p/e ratios and macroeconomic trends. And if your information's so good that it'll make you money, you're likely to end up sharing a cell with another chastened insider.

On the other hand, you do have some advantages over the money pros out there. For one thing, no one's monitoring your quarterly performance. You don't have shareholders screaming for your head when you underperform the S&P 500. That means you can stick with stocks that haven't been stars but that you still believe will be eventually. And unlike most stock fund managers, you're free to bail out of stocks entirely if you foresee trouble on the equity horizons (though, as discussed, that kind of timing rarely pays off).

I don't expect or advise anyone reading this book to run out and start selling short or buying obscure penny stocks or high-yield bonds. But I included these topics to help complete a newcomer's appreciation for the complexities of investing and to instill a sense that Wall Street is a place where any hunch—that a bond will default, that a company will fail—can be backed with a wager. That sense, that for every idea you have there's someone betting that the opposite is true, is the best remedy I know for the overeager investor.

The bottom line is that average Joes and Janes ought to feel good about buying stocks. There's no better way to learn than by doing, and the fact that stocks have generally produced better returns over the long haul than their safer brethren—bonds and cash instruments—is indisputable. But the key phrase here is "long haul." If you've got a kitty saved up, along with several years to let it ride, by all means buy stock in some stable companies whose business interests you. But don't be the sucker every hustler looks for when he comes to the pool hall. Trying too hard to pretend you know what you're doing might be the best way to convince someone you don't.

Bond Investing

As we've already covered, investing in bonds tends to produce smaller returns over time than investing in stocks. But since the bond issuer has an obligation to pay interest and to repay the bondholder when the bond matures, bonds are generally safer than stocks.

There are two factors that determine a bond's interest rate, or coupon—the term and the quality of the bond. In general, the longer the term, the higher the coupon; since you're guaranteeing the company the use of your money for a long time, it's got to pay you more for the privilege. (There are times when longer-term bonds actually pay lower coupons. This is called an inverted yield curve and occurs when investors expect rates to fall.)

As for quality, an issuer in shaky financial condition may default on the bond, which means the bond buyer is taking a risk in loaning his money. So issuers with questionable credit have to pay higher interest rates in order to attract bond buyers. This all means that a big, stable company is not going to pay as much interest on its ten-year bonds as a tiny, troubled company, and two cities with comparable credit are not going to pay drastically different rates on bonds of equal maturities.

The term of the bond is pretty obvious—it's stated when the bond is issued. But the financial health of the issuer is very difficult to determine. Happily for bond investors, there are companies that keep an eye on the bottom lines of the companies trying to borrow money.

The major bond-rating companies are Moody's and Standard & Poor's. Both use a modified school-style grading scale, with AAA being the highest (Moody's calls it Aaa), AA just below that (Moody's: Aa), A just below that, then BBB, BB, B and so on. U.S. government bonds are not rated, since they're considered as safe as bonds get. *Junk bonds,* or *high-yield bonds,* are those rated CCC or lower (Caa by Moody's). These were made infamous as the instrument of choice for financing takeovers and leveraged buyouts in the 1980s. Predictably, they pay higher yields than bonds of better quality because the risk of default is higher.

As creditors rather than part-owners, bondholders are not entitled to opine on the workings of the company as stockholders can. But in the event of corporate bankruptcy, bondholders come before stockholders when the company's property is being liquidated.

In the old days, when people were shorter and lived by the water, investors bought bonds and held them until they matured. They were content to enjoy the fixed monthly payments that gave bonds the sobriquet *fixed-income securities.* Nowadays, investors often try to make money on top of the interest payments by trading bonds. A bond that cost $10,000 and pays 6 percent interest is worth more or less than $10,000 when interest rates change. If rates fall, bond issuers will be able to lower their rates below 6 percent. So the original bond that guarantees 6 percent is suddenly worth more than the $10,000 its holder will get back at the end of the term. The reverse is true when interest rates rise: bonds are worth less than their par value.

Suppose you buy a bond with a par value of $10,000, a term of ten years and a coupon of 7 percent. If you hold it to term, you'll have collected $7,000 in interest payments by the time your $10,000 is returned after ten years. That means your *yield,* or return, will be 7 percent ($7,000 ÷ 10 years = $700 per year; $700 is 7 percent of $10,000).

But suppose you hold your bond for five years and interest rates suddenly fall. Since banks and other investments are paying less interest, bond issuers of similar quality to yours no longer have to pay 7 percent to attract investors. That means that your guaranteed $700 a year is suddenly worth more than $10,000. How much more depends on how far rates have fallen, the term of your bond and the buyer's perception of where rates are headed next. But let's say you sell your bond for $11,000. Your yield will have risen to 9 percent ($3,500 for five years of interest payments plus $1,000 in profit on the sale of the bond = $4,500. Dividing by five years makes $900 per year, or 9 percent on a $10,000 investment). Let's also say whoever buys the bond from you carries it to term, cashing it in when it reaches maturity in five more years. He'll have made $2,500 on the investment ($3,500 for five years of interest payments—the $1,000 premium he paid for the bond). That's a yield of only 5 percent. So unless rates for similar quality bonds have gone below that, you got the better end of the deal.

The reverse happens when you buy a bond and interest rates rise—all of a sudden your guaranteed payments of 7 percent don't look so juicy compared with what investors can get elsewhere.

If these numbers are beginning to cure your insomnia, just keep these two key points in mind:

- Bondholders get hammered when interest rates rise and make out like bandits when they fall.
- Yield, or a bondholder's return, moves in the opposite direction of price; if a bond's price goes higher, it's yield is lower and vice versa.

Savings Bonds

Though you probably have an abandoned one of these in your underwear drawer, savings bonds are not very sexy investments. Usually sold for half par value, they mature after about seventeen years and keep paying interest for usually up to thirty years total. In general, bond certificates are like cash or stock certificates—when they're lost, the owner's out of luck. Like most bonds, savings bonds are bearer bonds, meaning they can be cashed by whomever holds them. Unlike most bonds, savings bonds are registered to whoever's name is on the front, so they can be replaced by the smart bondholder who remembered to write down the serial numbers from the lower right corner of the bond and store those numbers apart from the bond itself. Series EE U.S. savings bonds are available for as little as $50; investors with at least $500 in EE series or E series (which EE replaced) can change them into HH series, which pay semiannual interest payments of 6 percent (series EE tends to pay slightly less than that, based on a formula derived from what the Fed is paying on T-bills). As with all federal bonds, the interest on U.S. savings bonds is free from local and state income tax, and the federal tax can be deferred until the bonds are redeemed. Those are some pretty good features. But that interest rate is pretty painful for all but those who simply can't withstand even moderate risk. If you do have a savings bond moldering and would like to know how much interest you're receiving, you can call 800-4US-BOND for updated interest rate information.

A Word About High-Yield Bonds

While we're talking about the trade-off between risk and return in bond investing, it's time to mention junk

MISCONCEPTION bonds. Junk bonds are an undeniably speculative investment and definitely not for the faint of heart.

But the bad name they've acquired is somewhat unjustified and attributable, in my opinion, to an irrational and sound-bite-driven dislike for the men who made jillions off selling them, including Michael Milken. It's true that plenty of investors lost their shirts on companies that defaulted when they couldn't make the massive debt payments to junk bond buyers. Plenty of other companies, however, wouldn't have survived the eighties without the discipline and leanness necessitated by those massive debt payments.

From an investment point of view, high yield bonds operate like anything else—the greater the potential reward, the greater the risk. Young investors interested in dabbling in junk ought to do so only with a small percentage of their overall portfolio, and only via a good high-yield mutual fund, such as Invesco High Yield (ticker symbol: FHYPX; Morningstar rating: 5 stars; load: none; minimum initial purchase: $1,000; telephone: 800-525-8085).

Bonds are usually denominated in $1,000 increments, but are sometimes packaged together so that an individual investor can get in only if he ponies up $5,000 or even $10,000. That means unless your portfolio is really huge, you run the risk of being overweighted simply by buying one bond. That's one reason why lots of small fry who want to invest in bonds do so via bond mutual funds (other reasons include professional management and commissions savings).

When assembling a portfolio of individual bonds, the big question an investor faces are maturity and grade. As already mentioned, longer maturities and lower ratings generally equal higher interest payments. But along with those higher payments comes greater risk. In the case of low-grade bonds, there's the risk of the company defaulting—falling into such financial trouble that it cannot pay interest or even repay the principal. With a long maturity, the risk is that interest rates will rise, leaving the bondholder stuck with an underperforming investment for a long time.

How comfortable an investor is with default risk boils down to personality and the amount of high-risk stuff in an investor's whole portfolio. One strategy for lessening the interest-rate risk is called laddering. This involves buying bonds that mature at various intervals, so that you never have all your money in bonds that mature at any specific time.

Some bonds, known as *callable* bonds, can be redeemed by the issuer before the maturity date. Issuers would be inclined to exercise this option if interest rates drop and they can borrow money more cheaply elsewhere. For the investor, that means that a noncallable bond with the same term and rating as a callable bond is a better investment.

The actual process of buying bonds is a cinch. You call up your broker and ask what's available in the grade and maturity you like. The broker will likely pitch you bonds that his firm already has in inventory. Don't worry if that sounds like a conflict—unlike stocks, one highly rated bond is much like another, so long as the maturity and other particulars are identical. Most likely, you'll be buying a bond after its original issue date. That means that you probably won't pay face value for the bond. If interest rates have dropped since the issuance of the bond you're buying, you'll likely have to pay a premium for it, since those issuing bonds of similar term and grade don't have to pay as much interest to attract buyers. By the same token, if rates have climbed since your bond was issued, you'll probably get a discount, since you're sacrificing some income.

The broker who sells you the bond doesn't earn a commission per se, but charges you a markup over what his firm paid for the bond. That markup is usually very reasonable—$10 per $1,000 of bond is typical—which is one reason brokers don't tout the fact that they offer bond-buying as a service. The bond certificate itself is then held in your account at the brokerage (that's called holding it in "street name") unless for some reason you want to hang it on your refrigerator. Your twice-yearly payments will be sent to your account and you'll be notified when it's time to redeem the bond.

Investors buying Treasuries can avoid brokerage markups and bond fund fees altogether by buying their bonds direct from Uncle Sam. As long as the maturity is over five years, Treasuries can be bought direct with a minimum purchase of just $1,000. This method has problems of its own—safekeeping of the security is up to you and selling before maturity is not as easy as calling your broker. But if you're determined to avoid commissions and certain you'll hold the Treasury for at least five years, call 202-874-4000 for details on going toe-to-toe with the Fed.

Mutual Fund Investing

Let's say you had $10,000 you wanted to put to work in the stock market. We've already covered the importance of diversification and the need to have your eggs in many different baskets. So it might not be smart to stick the whole chunk in, say, Coca-Cola, because even a well-run blue chip like Coke can have a bad year or bad several years.

Instead, you'd want to invest a little in many companies, maybe fifty or so. Assuming three quarters of these did well, you'd probably make up for the one quarter that do not. But you'd have to be a full-time stock analyst to follow the goings-on of fifty different companies, let alone the prospects for all the eight thousand companies you haven't bought but one day might. Even if you did buy the stock of fifty companies, your $10,000 would allow you to spend an average of $200 on each. Using a discount broker who charged only $25 per trade in commissions, you'd spend $1,250 on brokerage fees—a whopping 12.5 percent right off the top. And even if you did have the time to follow the stock market, and even if you didn't care about the commissions, owning fifty stocks would be a terrible record-keeping chore. And even if all these barriers didn't stop you from buying fifty different stocks, what would you do if you later had another hundred bucks to invest? Obviously, you couldn't buy $2 worth of all fifty companies. But even spending the whole $100 on just one of them means you'll pay $25 in commissions—25 percent!

A mutual fund neatly solves all of these problems. By pooling the capital of thousands of investors, mutual funds provide individual investors:
* Professional management by a full-time money manager
* The buying power of many investors, so the transaction cost of each trade consumes only a tiny percentage of the value of the trade
* Greatly simplified bookkeeping. Even if the fund manager makes a couple hundred trades during the course of the year, the mutual fund investor only has to keep track of the fund, not the stocks within the fund.
* Welcome mat for small investments. Investors can get started in most

funds for between $1,000 and $3,000 (usually less if the fund is to be held in an IRA). Subsequent deposits can usually be made in increments of as little as $50 to $100.

In addition to the reasons detailed above, mutual fund investing usually offers a variety of smaller but still sweet perks:

• *Painless maintenance.* Mutual funds are great about keeping investors up to date on the value of their holdings, detailing performance and tax stuff on easy-to-follow statements.

• *Encourage the small stuff.* Most mutual funds make adding to your investment as convenient as possible. Not only do they usually accept additional investments in increments as small as $50, but they often offer direct deposit programs, which automatically deduct from an investor's checking account every month any amount the investor wants—great for instilling discipline in an investing program.

• *One-stop shopping.* Many brokerages, including Schwab, Fidelity, Jack White, Merrill Lynch and Smith Barney, operate what are known as mutual fund *supermarkets.* These allow investors to buy funds from a variety of fund companies all from their single brokerage account. Rather than having five statements from five companies, the investor gets one statement, which greatly simplifies record keeping. This is extra-convenient for investors who select different types of funds. An investor can buy a foreign stock fund, a technology stock fund and a bond fund from companies that specialize in those types of funds without having to open three separate accounts—or worse, settling for those types of funds from one mutual fund company that may not do all of them well.

• Convenience. It's easy to know how much your mutual funds are worth on any given day. Funds are sold in shares, just like stocks, and the price of one share is called the *net asset value* (NAV). The fund calculates its NAV by dividing the value of all its holdings at the close of a trading day by the number of shares it has outstanding (i.e., if a fund's investments are worth a total of $100 million and it has 2 million shares out there, each is worth $50). They report that number to the newspapers every day after the market closes, so it's easy for fund investors to tell how their funds are doing. And just about all funds have toll-free numbers investors can call to check out the value of their holdings, and many funds also offer that info online.

But wait, there's more! Mutual funds can access more than just the domestic stock market. A whole world of foreign stocks, bonds (domestic and foreign, government or corporate) and other investments not easily understandable or even available to the average investor, such as precious metals or hot IPOs.

With all these advantages, it's little wonder mutual funds have exploded in popularity over the past several years. Americans have over $4 trillion invested in mutual funds. Funds are also the investment vehicle of choice for the majority of company-sponsored retirement plans, with big fund companies like Fidelity, T. Rowe Price, Putnam and Vanguard administering the 401(k) plans of American corporations big and small.

Mutual funds come in a dizzying array of flavors. In fact, there are more than ten times more funds to choose from than there were in 1980. That means an investor can usually find a fund to suit just about any investment style, ranging from an ultraconservative government bond fund to a wildly aggressive overseas stock fund. But wide variety also means it's tougher than ever to choose the funds that best suit your investment goals.

In general, investors should stick to funds they understand. That doesn't mean you should know the rationale behind every move a fund manager makes—the reason you're in the fund in the first place is because you don't want to concern yourself with the minutiae of investing. But if you have no clue why low inflation tends to hammer funds that invest in gold, then you're probably better off staying out of gold funds.

It's important to have some idea of the kinds of stocks your fund is holding. Even though one of the main reasons you got into funds is to achieve instant diversity, you can still find yourself underdiversified if you invest in only one fund that has a bad year. There's also a similar risk in investing in only one type of fund. That is, one domestic-growth-stock fund often performs a lot like the next. That's why it's a good idea to spread your mutual fund dollars between a few solid funds of different types. An investor who favors domestic stock funds may decide to supplement his holdings with an international stock fund, for example. Someone who's invested entirely in stocks may decide to add a bond fund.

Spread Too Thin?

Mutual funds don't come with the warnings they put on cigarette packs but they can be just as addictive.

Many mutual fund investors get carried away, throwing money at every hot fund they hear mentioned on TV. But studies have shown that chasing hot performers usually doesn't pay off in the long run. Plus, one of the reasons investors like mutual funds in the first place is the ease of record keeping. Owning fifteen different funds can be as big a paperwork problem as owning fifteen stocks, and the performance of them can be just as hard to track. Most investors, especially those with less than $100,000 to work with, will do well to have no more than seven mutual funds.

TIP

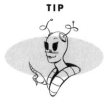

Rating the Funds

The single best source for information on mutual funds is available from Morningstar, a Chicago-based group that lives and breathes funds. Their booklets are packed with vital statistics: performance figures for a variety of time periods, risk assessment, loads and fees, the skinny on the fund's manager, info on reaching the fund and a couple of paragraphs about how the fund operates.

Beyond all that excellent info, there's the star-rating system, where Morningstar awards from one to five stars to a fund based on the success the fund has had in delivering returns, sticking to its stated objectives and minimizing risk. Anytime you see a fund advertising its performance with stars, they're talking about the Morningstar stars. The company makes a big production out of saying that the stars are no big deal, and it's true that a five-star fund isn't all that likely to outperform a four-star fund in the future. But with so many funds around, there's seldom a good reason to invest in any fund that gets less than three stars.

A subscription to Morningstar is way too expensive and extensive for the needs of the average fund investor. But many libraries subscribe to it, and condensed reports are available at Morningstar's website *(www.morningstar.net)* and on their AOL site (keyword: *Morningstar*).

Numbers Do Lie

Ever notice how every mutual fund advertisement you see brags about its four- and five-star funds, while there's a suspicious lack of one- and two-star funds?

Mutual fund companies have devised a few ways to sweep their lame funds under the rug. The first is that these funds simply cease to exist. Let's say a fund company has a family of ten funds that have been around for ten years or more. Five of them are rated four or more stars, and five rated two or worse. If the company simply disbands the dogs, it can say, almost with a straight face, that all of its funds have been around for more than ten years and all are rated four stars or better. This phenomenon, known as *survivorship bias,* allows fund companies to stack the deck.

Another way funds disguise the performance of their laggards is by merging them with more successful funds, then reporting only the results of the better fund. Sometimes entire fund companies are bought for this purpose—to mask the poor results of the buyer's own funds.

You can correct for these maneuvers by ignoring a company's claims about how great all its funds are and concentrating on how the specific fund you're interested in has done over the long term, and whether that performance owes its origins to factors still in place, such as a manager who's had success for a while and a style that hasn't swung wildly or diverged from the fund's stated goals.

Loads, Fees, Rosemary and Time

Often, all that separates the performance of one fund from another is the fees each charges. We've already seen how even a percent here or there can make a huge difference over time, so finding a good fund with low fees can greatly improve your returns.

Unfortunately, mutual fund companies are aware of how averse investors are to paying for access to their funds. So they've developed myriad ways to disguise the different charges and fees. Here's the skinny on what a mutual fund investor is up against, and some advice on how to make the comparisons that will separate the rip-offs from the bargains.

• *Load.* Many mutual funds charge loads, which are used to pay commissions to the brokers, planners and institutions who sell the funds. A load is expressed as a percentage of the investment. A 2 percent load subtracts $2 from every $100 an investor deposits, so only $98 is used to buy shares.[1] If the charge occurs when the shareholder redeems, the load is called a *back-end* load. A 2 percent back-end load takes $2 from every $100 it sends an investor who sells shares. *No-load funds* charge no sales commissions (though they do charge management fees and may charge what are called "12b-1 fees").

• *Management fee.* Mutual fund managers make a lot of money. That money comes from a yearly fee the fund company deducts from accounts. It's expressed as a percentage of the fund's assets, so a fund with a .7 percent management fee will deduct $70 a year for every $10,000 from an investor's account. Larger funds can often afford to lower the percentage they charge, since 1 percent of a billion-dollar fund is a lot more than 2 percent of a $100 million fund. (Um, five times more, in case you're checking my math.)

• *Redemption fee.* This is the fee many funds charge investors when they sell shares; they're designed to penalize investors who sell funds soon after buying them. They function like back-end loads but are paid to the fund company rather than to whomever sold the fund.

• *12b-1 fee.* Some funds charge investors a percentage every year to cover advertising and other marketing expenses.

These fees vary widely, ranging from almost nil to the 8.5 percent—the maximum funds can legally charge. Many funds charge 5 percent or so just to get in, while some of America's biggest and best-performing funds charge no load and minuscule fees. High loads can crush a fund's performance. A 3 percent front-end load means that every time you invest $1,000, only $970 is put to work in your account. And a fund's high management fee can eat into returns even if it's a no-load. Since they're deducted every

---

[1] Andrew Tobias makes a neat point about loads in *The Only Investment Guide You'll Ever Need.* Send $1,000 to a fund with a 5 percent load and you'll actually get only $950 worth of shares. So you're actually paying a commission of $50 on a purchase of $950, not $1,000; that's about 5.26 percent, not 5 percent.

year even if you don't add or withdraw any funds, fees can wreak havoc on mutual fund returns, especially a long-term account.

It's often difficult to judge the effects of various fees. A fund with a 3 percent load and 1 percent yearly management fee may or may not be a better deal than a no-load fund with a 1.5 percent yearly management fee, depending on how long you stay in the fund. The way to think about it in general is that the longer you'll be staying in a fund, the less important the load is and the more important the yearly fees become. That's just a general rule, though—a big load is a drag even for long-term investors, since subsequent deposits will also get hit with the load. It's also not so easy to predict just how long you might stay in a fund. If you've invested in a heavily loaded fund because of its small yearly fees and then have to take a redemption in a year or so, you'll have paid a high price. That's why the best option is often a no-load fund with very small annual fees.

With all this mishegas about fees and loads, one would hope that someone's established a simple way to compare exactly how much funds charge for access to their services. Well, someone has—almost.

Morningstar publishes a statistic called the Annual Expense Ratio (AER) for every fund it covers. This number, expressed as a percentage and usually between .5 percent and 1.75 percent, is the yearly charge the fund deducts for all fund operating expenses, including 12b-1 fees, operating costs, management fees, administrative fees and all other asset-based costs. Thus, a fund with an AER of 1.2 percent takes a total of $12 a year for every $1,000 an investor's got. One problem with AER is that it doesn't include loads, which are often the most significant charge an investor faces. Thus, comparisons between loaded funds with low AERs and no-loads with higher AERs once again boil down to amorphous questions about how long an investor intends to stay in the fund and how frequent and substantial subsequent deposits will be.

 **WARNING!** All this talk about fees and loads brings to mind a penny-wise pound-foolish trap that ensnares many mutual fund addicts, who are so busy avoiding loads and fees that they forget that the main objective is to find a profitable fund. Loads and fees are simply one part of the total return picture. A fund

Wide Load Ahead: One Man's Chilling Tale

Ever hear the saying, "The shoemaker's kids go barefoot"? Well, in this case, the financial writer's mother pays big loads.

A couple of years ago, my mom and I took a good look at her financial picture. To my horror, most of her nest egg resided in her checking account. The few bond funds she had were the notorious variety sold by financial advisors whose clients don't know better. In other words, they were crummy performers with high redemption fees.

A redemption fee is another word for a back-end load. Let's say you've accumulated $5,000 in a fund with a redemption fee of 3 percent. If you cash out the entire fund, you'll get a check for $4,850— $5,000 minus $150 (3 percent).

Typically, back-end fees operate on a sliding scale. That means that they'll be higher (often 5 percent) if you redeem within one year, then get lower the longer you keep your dough in the fund. You might pay 3 percent if you redeem in one to three years, 2 percent in three to five years, and the fees usually disappear altogether after seven or so years.

that consistently outperforms its peers by 5 percent is worth 3 percent in load and expenses. But a loaded fund that matches its no-load peers, or only beats them by a percentage that's smaller than its fees, isn't worth the cover charge.

Index Funds

Index funds have been around for a while, but their popularity surged in the 1990s as the market at large enjoyed an unprecedented positive streak.

Operating on a "if you can't beat 'em, join 'em" philosophy, index funds try to replicate, rather than beat, the performance of a well-known index, such as the S&P 500, the Lehman Brothers Aggregate Bond Index (U.S. and corporate bonds) or any number of foreign indexes. Index funds have

What the Hell's an Index?

An index seeks to provide a thumbnail sketch of the market on which it's based. But before we descend into the murky world of the hypothetical, let's look to the best-known index for a concrete example.

The Dow Jones Industrial Average—universally referred to as the Dow—is the most famous and most widely followed index. When people say, "The market was up sixty points today," they mean the Dow was up sixty points. Comprised of thirty giant American companies, all of which trade on the New York Stock Exchange, the Dow contains only chips of the bluest hue, including DuPont, GM, Exxon, Disney and Coca-Cola. It is periodically updated, as it last was in 1997, when Hewlett Packard and Wal-Mart were among those added, while Westinghouse and Woolworth departed.

The Dow gives a familiar and easily digestible snapshot of what happened during any given day. The Dow is an "unweighted" average. It is computed simply by adding the stock price of each of its component companies, then adjusting by a factor to account for distortions that have been caused by stock splits. That means that the price moves of relatively itsy-bitsy Dow component Alcoa affect the Dow as much as those of behemoth General Electric.

Because the companies included in it total about a quarter of the value of the New York Stock Exchange, the Dow provides a quick gauge of what stocks in general are doing. Quick comparisons are just one use for indexes, however. Providing a benchmark by which to compare the performance of portfolios is another critical function. For this, investors are better served by selecting an index that closely matches the types of investments in one's portfolio. For most equity mutual fund investors, that means the Standard & Poor's 500. Like the Dow, the S&P 500 is a collection of stocks. But it includes four hundred industrial companies, forty utilities, forty financial companies and twenty transportation companies, which gives a far more

representative look at "what the market is doing." The S&P 500 is often used to compare mutual fund performance, both by mutual fund
companies that seek to perform better than the S&P 500, and by mutual fund raters, like Morningstar, which uses the index to judge fund
performance. The S&P 500 is a "weighted index," meaning a company whose total outstanding stock is twice as valuable as another's
would also see its price moves affect the index twice as much as those
of the smaller company.

It wouldn't be the world of investing if there weren't a product for
every perversion. Some indexes are designed to track the fate of small
companies (Russell 2000) and there's one that includes nearly every
stock (Wilshire 5000). There are bond indexes (Lehman Brothers Aggregate Bond Index), utility indexes and lifestyle indexes, such as the
Consumer Price Index. But the aim of all of them remains the same:
to summarize and encapsulate broad, complicated trends in neat little packages.

fund managers, but their main job is to mirror the index they track. The
S&P 500, for example, seldom adds or subtracts a company, so the manager seldom dumps a stock or adds a new one, though the manager does
have to try to maintain a weighting that matches that of the index. When
an index fund is functioning like it's supposed to, its performance will be
the same as the index it follows; in a year when the S&P 500 returns 15 percent, a good S&P 500 index fund will also return just about 15 percent.

Active Management vs. Indexing
The majority of mutual funds one hears about are actively managed. That
means a guy with a Range Rover is paid a lot of money to decide which
stocks (or bonds or whatever) to trade and in what amounts and when.
And then there are index funds. These funds simply track a well-known index, such as the S&P 500, the Lehman Brothers Aggregate Bond Index
(U.S. and corporate bonds) or any number of foreign indexes.

With the S&P on a tear for the last three years, indexing has become increasingly popular. Vanguard, the fund company most closely associated with index funds (though they run a couple of dynamite managed funds, too) has watched its Vanguard Index 500, the flagship fund that apes the S&P 500, become America's second-largest fund. It's currently taking in money even faster than Fidelity's Magellan behemoth, an archetypal actively managed fund that's underperformed the index of late.

Indexing has a lot to recommend it. In fact, I believe a portion of everyone's mutual fund investment dough should be in a good large-stock index fund, such as the Vanguard one mentioned above. But indexing is not the panacea that a runaway bull market can make it appear. Here are some of the pros and cons of both forms of mutual-fund investing.

PERFORMANCE

More than 80 percent of the actively managed stock funds that have been around for ten years failed to match the 14 percent annual return that the S&P 500 posted. So the chances of picking a stock fund that will outperform the market are only about one in five. The success of indexing is frustrating for investors in actively managed funds. After all, goes the reasoning, a fund manager is being paid a fortune to pick stocks and time the market. Shouldn't he be able to beat the guy who simply buys the five hundred biggest companies and sits on them? Fans of indexing, however, including such eminent market thinkers as John Bogle and Burton Malkeil, contend that no fund manager is more efficient than the market over the long term—if you can't beat the market, you might as well join it.

CAVEATS

Because the S&P 500 is comprised of America's largest five hundred publicly traded companies, funds that track that index tend to trail actively managed funds during years in which smaller companies post higher returns than large ones. Of course, there are index funds that track smaller companies. There are also international index funds. But for some reason, those indexes tend not to outperform their active counterparts. And in riskier segments of the market, you're often better off with a manager who's got the freedom to sell his stocks rather than an index fund, which has to replicate its benchmark even if it's spiraling down the toilet.

Individual Stocks vs. Mutual Funds

Why should a novice investor even buy an individual stock when there are so many great mutual funds available?

One of the best reasons to buy a stock is the education gleaned from following its daily machinations. Mutual fund fans, particularly those who favor index funds, are quick to make the case that investing is too important to be used as a learning experience. With a mutual fund, the decision making is left to a pro, so you don't have to worry about how the day's news affects your investments. In fact, that's one of the chief selling points of mutual funds: the fund manager has access to more data than you could ever have, not to mention the knowledge and time to comprehend that information better than an amateur.

It's a point well taken. The lion's share of an investor's portfolio should be under the care of highly rated mutual funds, at least until the investor is proven adept at stock picking and perhaps even then. And, of course, mutual funds provide greater diversity than the average small-time investor could assemble on her own.

But owning stocks is a better way to learn not just how the market works, but the habits of good investing. Stock investors learn to check the stock's price regularly and develop a sense of how news events affect a company and its industry.

Finally, there's that fun factor again. Remember that AIM toothpaste commercial where the towhead brushed longer because it tasted swell? Same thing here: my bet is that those who find stock picking fun plant more of their dough in the market than those who buy a fund and ignore it.

TIP There's also a subtle tax reason to invest in stocks. Mutual funds take capital gains when they like, sticking you with the tax bill. But with individual stocks, you control when the stock is sold, which means you control the tax event. That way you can choose not to take a capital gain until you're in a better position to pay for it. Buying and holding a stock for a long time is almost like having a tax-deferred account—you still have to pay taxes on the dividends, of course, but that's small potatoes.

FEES

Remember that highly paid guy who oversees actively managed funds? Well, it's your money financing those suspender-shopping sprees. Index funds have managers too, of course. But because they're not making heavy-duty buy/sell decisions or allocation weightings, they don't command the superstar wages of their active manager counterparts. And since index funds don't need to hype their performance (one is essentially the same as the next, and the whole idea of "beating the market" is by definition not possible), they also save on marketing. These savings are passed on to index fund customers in the form of lower expenses, which in turn aid the performance.

TURNOVER

The S&P 500 and other indexes seldom add or subtract companies, so index funds seldom buy or sell stock. That means that they incur less capital gains than more actively managed funds, which means investors who stay put in index funds face less capital gains taxes.

FUN

Just as picking individual stocks can be gratifying and educational, picking actively managed mutual funds can be more gratifying and educational than indexing. No, you're not here to have fun. But if the thrill of picking

What the Hell's a Closed-End Fund?

Most mutual funds that you hear about—including all the famous ones like Fidelity's Magellan, Vanguard 500 and the Janus Fund—are "open-end" funds. That means that when you put your money in, you essentially own a fraction of all the securities that the fund owns. When investors add more money, the fund simply issues more shares and buys more bonds or stocks—whatever it is in which the fund invests.

Other funds—including a lot of specialty funds, such as those that specialize in the stocks of specific countries or industries—are "closed-end" mutual funds. Closed-end funds, like their more famous brethren, are also collections of assets that are professionally managed by an investment company. But they resemble stocks in that there's a fixed number of shares. To own a piece of the fund, you buy shares of it from a broker, just as you would if you wanted shares of General Motors. Like an open-end fund, its value is affected by the share price of the companies it holds. But unlike an open-end fund, it also becomes more or less valuable based on the perception of other investors. That is, your shares might raise in value if the public finds them desirable (say if the manager gets "hot," or the fund is the only way to invest in an emerging country like Russia). Since you're buying shares not from the company but from other investors, closed-end funds don't always have 800-numbers and fat marketing programs. But because they tend to be smaller than open-enders, closed-end funds tend to have higher operating expenses. Unless there's no open-end fund around that's doing a good job at whatever it is that interests you about a closed-end fund, stick to open-enders.

a fund managed by the next Peter Lynch makes you more willing to follow the market, you might just invest a bigger chunk of your money.

Building a Mutual Fund Portfolio

One of the best features of mutual funds is their variety. Investors who prefer to stick exclusively to mutual funds can easily find combinations that reflect their personal tastes and comfort with risk. In fact, the same set of funds may be right for very different investors, if used in different proportions.

Let's look at a list of funds that reflect a variety of investment goals. These specific funds are highly rated personal favorites, but by no means the only ones suitable for these purposes.

Stocks

- Domestic Growth

(Dodge & Cox Stock; ticker symbol: DODGX; Morningstar rating: 5 stars; load: none; minimum initial purchase: $2,500; telephone: 800-621-3979)

Index

Large Companies

(Vanguard Index 500; ticker symbol: VFINX; Morningstar rating: 5 stars; load: none; minimum initial purchase: $3,000; telephone: 800-851-4999)

Small and Medium Companies

(Vanguard Index Trust-Extended Market; ticker symbol: VEXMX; Morningstar rating: 3 stars; load: none [but there is a .5 percent "transaction charge"]; minimum initial purchase: $3,000; telephone: 800-851-4999)

Growth and Income (invests in stocks, including many that pay quarterly dividends)

(Fidelity Growth & Income; ticker symbol: FGRIX; Morningstar rating: 5 stars; load: none; minimum initial purchase: $2,500; telephone: 800-544-8888)

- Foreign

(Janus Worldwide; ticker symbol: JAWWX; Morningstar rating: 5 stars; load: none; minimum initial purchase: $2,500; telephone: 800-525-8983)

AGGRESSIVE

Almost entirely invested in stocks, including substantial exposure to overseas stocks and small-cap stocks.

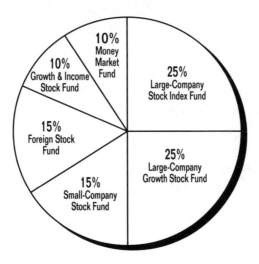

MODERATE

Primarily invested in stocks, including a taste of overseas stocks; supplemented by a small chunk of bonds.

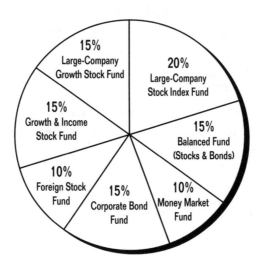

TIMID

About half invested in stocks, including a sliver of overseas stocks; a substantial cash portion and chunks of both corporate and government bonds comprise the rest of the portfolio.

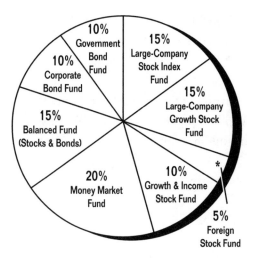

INDEXER
(Aggressive)

Invested entirely in index funds (except for the money market portion), including foreign and small-company exposure, with an emphasis on stocks and a small chunk of bonds.

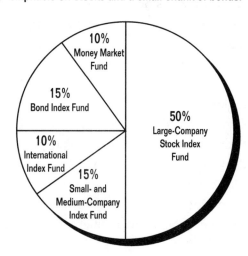

Index

(Schwab International Index; ticker symbol: SWINX; Morningstar rating: 4 stars; load: none; minimum initial purchase: $1,000; telephone: 800-435-4000)

- Aggressive/Small-Cap

(Kaufmann Fund; ticker symbol: KAUFX; Morningstar rating: 4 stars; load: none/12b-1 fees; minimum initial purchase: $1,500; telephone: 800-237-0132)

- Balanced (invests both in stocks and bonds)

(Vanguard Wellington; ticker symbol: VWELX; Morningstar rating: 4 stars; load: none; minimum initial purchase: $3,000; telephone: 800-851-4999)

Cash

MONEY MARKET

As discussed in the "Counting It" chapter, the portion of your assets that are in cash should be considered part of your portfolio. Since the best place to combine the needs for safety, easy access (liquidity) and returns for the cash portion of your portfolio is in a money market mutual fund, we'll include this as a component of your mutual fund portfolio.

(Brokerage-based "sweep" account such as Merrill Lynch's CMA Money Fund, Fidelity's Cash Reserves or Schwab's Money Market Fund or dedicated cash fund such as Citizen's Trust E-Fund or the Reserve Fund's Cash Performance Account)

Bonds

- Corporate Bonds

(Invesco Select Income; ticker symbol: FBDSX; Morningstar rating: 5 stars; load: none/12b-1 fees; minimum initial purchase: $1,000; telephone: 800-525-8085)

- Government Bonds

(Strong Government Securities; ticker symbol: STVSX; Morningstar rating: 5 stars; load: none; minimum initial purchase: $2,500; telephone: 800-368-1030)

Index

(Vanguard Bond Index-Total Market; ticker symbol: VBMFX; Morningstar rating: 4 stars; load: none; minimum initial purchase: $3,000; telephone: 800-851-4999)

Using the "sleep well/earn well" parameters established in the section above on asset allocation, let's see how investors of different risk tolerance can all use these funds to suit their needs. Suppose three investors of different levels of risk comfort each has a chunk of money they're planning to invest for at least ten years.

Sample Mutual Fund Portfolios

Remember, an investor isn't forever sworn to one style or another. The same person can belong to different classes at different times, such as when an investor who normally takes lots of risk is saving for a specific short-term goal.

Retirement Investing

I know, I know. Retirement is a million years away. Who's got an extra two grand for the distant future when there are so many cool things to buy now?

Too many young people shy away from retirement investing because of the long-term commitment required. It's scary for a twenty-five-year-old to kiss hard-earned cash good-bye for thirty-five years or so.

It's also critical. With pension plans going the way of the Betamax and Social Security scheduled for a meltdown when the boomers retire, self-directed retirement plans may be the only line of defense between a young person and a retirement spent in some kindly relative's attic.

Look, I want everyone to have cool clothes and vacations and a home and enough cash on hand to tell their boss to sit and spin. But even when saving for a specific short-term goal, retirement investing should be among the top financial priorities for most young people.

Tax-Deferred Investing: The Holy Grail

You know how you get your first paycheck from a new job and you just stare at how small it is after all the taxes have been removed? Well, investment gains are also taxed, and that eats into their total return.

Tax-deferred investments, on the other hand, grow tax free as long as they stay in tax-deferred accounts, such as IRAs, 401(k)s and 403(b)s. So the gains from investments are larger, plus the power of compound interest has more raw material on which to work its magic.

It adds up. Say you put $2,000 into a brokerage account and gained 10 percent over a year. If you're in the 15 percent tax bracket, your $2,200 ($2,000 + $200) would end up being worth only $2,170. So your actual gains would be 8.5 percent. At the risk of sounding like a broken record like a broken record, these small differences are huge over time. And they get huger as your income propels you upward through the tax brackets.

Who's dying for another example? You? Good! Suppose you're in the 31 percent tax bracket. You buy $20,000 worth of a mutual fund in a regular account and let it sit for ten years. The fund earns 8 percent a year. After paying taxes every year, your account would finish the decade at $34,229—an after-tax gain of $14,228. If you had purchased that same mutual fund with money from your IRA, it'd have grown to $43,178 in ten years—a gain of $23,178. In other words, the sheltering of the IRA upped your ten-year total return from about 70 percent to 110 percent. Not bad.

Before you get completely infatuated, you should know that you will have to pay the piper eventually. When you begin to take money out—as early as fifty-nine and a half or as late as seventy and a half—you'll have to pay taxes on the withdrawals. But by then, your money will have enjoyed the benefits of tax-deferred compounding for long enough to offset those taxes and then some. Plus, there's a good chance you'll be in a lower tax bracket by then, so you'll surrender less.

The reason the government provides this tax break is to encourage Americans to save for retirement. While you're permitted to withdraw from retirement accounts—hey, it's your money—the penalty is steep for withdrawing before age fifty-nine and a half. Not only will you owe the taxes on whatever part of the withdrawal you haven't yet paid taxes on, but the IRS adds an extra 10 percent spanking on top.

Let's take a closer look at the most common methods of tax-deferred investing.

Individual Retirement Account

Anyone with earned income—working for someone else, self-employed or alimony—can invest up to $2,000 a year in an IRA ($4,000 for married couples with one working spouse). Bear with me for an example.

Two investors, Harvey and Joyce, each begin investing $2,000 a year at age thirty. They buy the exact same mutual fund, which returns 10 percent a year, and both are in the 28 percent tax bracket. Harvey invests in the fund through a regular brokerage account, while Joyce sticks it in her IRA. By the time they retire at age sixty, Harvey's account has grown to $211,000—not bad for an investment of $60,000. But Joyce's sixty grand is now worth a whopping $376,000. That extra $165,000 will be more than enough to pay her taxes when she starts withdrawing.

As if you're not already convinced, there's another benefit to an IRA: certain investors are eligible to deduct their contribution from their gross income. If you (and your spouse, if you got one) are not eligible for a retirement plan through your job, you can deduct the whole IRA contribution. So if you make $20,000 and put $2,000 into an IRA, you'll be taxed as though you earned $18,000. That saves you $300, since you'd be in the 15 percent tax bracket.

If you do have access to a retirement plan, you can still deduct your full IRA contribution, so long as your income is under $30,000 ($50,000 for a joint return), with the limit rising every year until it hits $50,000 ($80,000 for marrieds), thanks to 1997's budget agreement. If you earn more than $30,000, you may still get a partial deduction. But even without any deductibility, IRAs are a smart move because you still get the benefits of tax-deferred compounding.

If you're really strapped, you can take a withdrawal from your IRA—you've got sixty days to repay it without penalties. Under certain circumstances—to pay medical expenses that total more than 7.5 percent of your adjusted gross income or health insurance if you've been unemployed—you can use IRA money without penalty.

An IRA is an account, not an investment. You can put just about whatever you want into your IRA—stocks, CDs, mutual funds, cash, bonds, whatever (except **MISCONCEPTION** options and other complicated derivatives that you wouldn't want to be in anyway if you're reading this book).

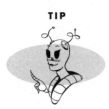

TIP

Keep your IRA wherever you have your regular brokerage account. (It's easy to transfer an IRA, so don't worry if you've already got your brokerage and IRA in two different places.) Having both accounts under one roof will simplify record keeping, and also makes it easier to contribute to the IRA. Suppose you need to sell a stock or bond to fund the IRA contribution. If both accounts are in the same place, you can do the transfer with one phone call. If they're separated, you'd have to get the check from one broker, deposit it in your checking account, then write a check to whoever's got your IRA.

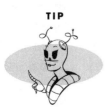

TIP

I recommend keeping your IRA at a discount brokerage, such as Schwab, Fidelity, Jack White or Quick & Reilly, rather than at a specific mutual fund company or, heaven forbid, a bank. A brokerage combines the ability to purchase stocks, bonds and other securities with the ability to purchase the mutual funds of a variety of companies through their fund supermarkets.

WARNING! Early withdrawal from IRAs generates big tax headaches, especially if some contributions were deductible and some were not. All the more reason not to touch that money until retirement.

 **WARNING!** Don't you dare pay an annual fee to whatever company warehouses your IRA. Some companies still try to collect $20 to $50 a year for this service—on top of whatever commissions you generate from buying securities in the account. A pox on them.

401(k) Plans (or 403(b) Plans, for Nonprofit Employees)

These are simply the best retirement savings option around. Invented only about thirty years ago, 401(k)s have quickly become the vehicle of choice for millions of Americans, as more and more employers offer them.

401(k)s enable employees to take a chunk of their paycheck and invest it directly into accounts that they control. Like IRAs, gains in 401(k)s grow tax-deferred. 401(k) contributions are deducted from your income, so tax bills are lowered right off the bat. Best of all, 401(k)s are often matched to some degree by employers. A typical plan will allow contributions of up to 10 percent of pay, with the first 6 percent being matched by the employer. For a fully participating employee making $50,000, that would mean a contribution of $5,000, which would grow tax-deferred and take five grand off taxable income—plus a free $1,500 from the employer. Can't beat dat.

Usually the employer hires a mutual fund company to administer the plan. Then the employee has a choice of several investment options offered by that mutual fund company, typically ranging from conservative (money market funds) to moderate (corporate and government bonds) to aggressive (growth funds and even small-company funds). The better plans allow the employee lots of control over the account, including the ability to blend the offered mutual funds any way he likes as often as once a month. Many plans also allow employees to borrow against the value of their 401(k), deducting money right from the employee's paycheck to repay it. You have to pay interest, but since you're paying it to your own account, that's not so bad.

Invest as much as you possibly can afford in your 401(k), and at least the amount that's eligible for matching funds.

Save Social Security

Most young people think Social Security is doomed. An oft-quoted survey by the whippersnapper activist group Third Millennium found that more Americans under thirty-five believe in UFOs than believe they will ever receive a Social Security check.

The problem boils down to demographics. Americans are living longer and having fewer children. That means more people are staying around to collect Social Security payments from fewer earners. (Remember, Social Security is a "pay-as-you-go" system. That means the money deducted from your check goes to a Social Security recipient today, rather than being stored somewhere for your use later on. Then, when you retire, your Social Security check is supposed to be funded by deductions from the paychecks of those still working.) In 1960, there were about five working Americans for every SS recipient. By 2020, about when the first wave of baby boomers becomes eligible for payments, there will be only about two working Americans to fund each check.

Despite the relatively obvious roots of Social Security's fiscal precariousness, many Americans attribute its troubles to that catch-all bogeyman "government mismanagement." In fact, Social Security is one of the most popular—and successful—government programs in United States history. Whatever your politics, it's hard to deny that the intent of Social Security—a safety net for those who are disabled or have spent their lives working and paying taxes—is noble. Unfortunately, the current perception has a brutal effect on efforts to alter the system for the better. "Why shouldn't I get every penny coming to me or pay lower taxes when it's some government bureaucrat who fouled up the system?" seems to be the current thinking of an electorate that won't even allow a politician to raise the issue of Social Security.

Social Security is the single largest government expense by a wide margin, far surpassing even national defense. Currently, about one of every six Americans receives a monthly check, totaling some $350 billion a year. And many people who currently receive Social Security have no other income. So it's not feasible, or even imaginable, for the program simply to disappear. But America ain't gettin' any younger. By the turn of the millennium, there will be more than 100,000 Americans over the age of one hundred. In 1980, there were 25 million Americans over the age of sixty-five. By 2003 there will be more than 35 million and by 2030, there will be 65 million.

So it's clear that Social Security is facing some challenges. But there are some stop-gap measures that can be taken. Already, the age at which Americans can begin receiving full benefits has been inched up to sixty-seven and there's talk of it rising more. Others advocate allowing Americans to save for their own retirement with a portion of what they currently pass along to current Social Security recipients. Those who invest in U.S. stocks, the theory goes, will do better at working the money than the current fund, which invests surplus funds in ultrasafe low-yielding U.S. Treasuries. Others advocate aggressively taxing the Social Security benefits of wealthy recipients.

There are shortcomings to all the proposed methods, and groups advocating rival reforms have done a good job maintaining the status quo simply by shouting each other down. But if you believe, as I do, that Social Security is worth saving, there are some things you can do to make your voice heard. In addition to contacting your representatives, look to any of these places for more information:

• Third Millennium *(http://thirdmil.org),* a self-appointed generational watchdog group that does good work on lots of stuff that many people find too boring to examine

• Economic Security 2000 (202-408-5557), a grassroots advocacy group working to reform Social Security

• Junior Chamber of Commerce (800-Jay-Cees), the venerable do-gooder group that has now made Social Security's salvation a priority

MISCONCEPTION Younger employees sometimes say they can't afford to contribute to their company's matching 401(k) plan. While I sympathize, this is one of those "can't afford not to" situations. Saying no to your company's matching funds is the exact same thing as saying no to a raise.

WARNING! Some employers offer company stock as an option for the 401(k) plan. I'm a fan of owning stock in one's company, but be careful not to allow its weighting to throw a 401(k) out of whack. If the company goes out of business, overindulgers could face a double whammy—no job and a worthless 401(k).

Keough and Simplified Employee Pension (SEP)

These plans are for self-employed people. Both function as hybrids of pension plans and IRAs with the main benefit being a much higher ceiling on contributions than the latter. Self-employed individuals with no employees should opt for the SEP because it's easier to administer, but both require an accountant to calculate the precise amount of allowable contribution.

WARNING! Don't put tax-advantaged investments inside retirement accounts (i.e. Treasury bonds or a variable annuity in an IRA). Tax-advantaged investments always yield less than equivalent non-tax-advantaged investments—investors are willing to sacrifice some yield in order to escape the taxes. But keeping tax-advantaged investments inside retirement accounts is like carrying two umbrellas at the same time.

More Investment Strategies and Concepts: The Not-So-Basics

Timing the Market

Of all investing clichés, perhaps the most overused is "buy low, sell high." While that is, of course, the key to successful equities investing, it's also too often misinterpreted as an invitation to jump in and out of the market.

No one can reliably call the day-to-day direction of the market. By sheer chance, there will always be a few market timers who successfully predict the crashes that occur from time to time. These people—and their firms and newsletters—then become the next big thing, with investors following them around like Hamelin rats.

Don't believe it. Expert after expert has proven incapable of consistently predicting the highs and lows of the market. Investors chronically pile on whatever was hot last year. Technology mutual funds, for example, repeatedly reap high inflows just as they've hit their peak, and pay high withdrawals after returns start to sink. That means that those investors stayed in just long enough to lose money.

Another form of market timing is less obvious but equally toxic, and it's a mistake that market newcomers make all the time (yep, I'm guilty, too). Ever thought to yourself: I want to invest, but the market's been rising so much lately? The corollary thought is: The market's really been tanking lately, maybe I should get out.

These thoughts are understandable. But they're also the exact kind of sentiments that get young investors into trouble. It's tough to take the plunge when the water suddenly turns chilly and it's tough to stay in the action when the market's overheating. But the notion that the market's too high or too low is just another form of timing that young people ought to avoid.

Think of it this way. Being afraid to buy after a market drop is equivalent to going to a store and being excited about a pair of shoes. Suddenly, the clerk notices that the shoes had been mismarked and lowers the price. But the new, lower price makes you not want them anymore. While a big drop in an individual stock often warrants a closer look (though there, too, panic selling isn't going to help), a dip in the market as a whole should be viewed with a cool head.

Another classic timing mistake is overreacting to news that's already widely available. You'll hear people say stuff like "I just heard on CNBC that Merck is going to release a new drug that's going to make a pile of money so I'm going to buy some shares of Merck." By the time news that will affect a stock price is in the paper or on TV, you can bet that it's already built into the price you'll end up paying. Unless you have some sort of information so inside that it's illegal to act upon, count on being beaten to the punch by people who do nothing but follow the health care industry. They've already acted on the news, which drives the price up, and thousands of other viewers or readers are already on the phone to their brokers, driving the price up further. By the time you get there, the price will have likely gone even higher than is justifiable by the good news—and you'll be left holding the bag when those who bought for the quick lift start selling and the price settles back to where it "should be."

Investors' tendency toward bad timing was recently proven by an exhaustive look at trading records by market analyst and finance professor Terry Odean. Using data from a discount brokerage, Odean found that 10 percent of the traders made more than 50 percent of the trades. But he noticed a disturbing trend: most investors bought at the tail end of a stock's run-up and sold at the bottom of a crater.

More often than not, individuals who buy on good news and sell on bad news shoot themselves in the wallet, getting in at tops and selling at bottoms. Reactive, short-term investing decisions are almost always regretted. Investors will do better to come up with a sensible long-term strategy and stick to it. If you're in a stock for the long haul, you'll enjoy the benefits from those who pile in every time there's good news. So do your best to analyze companies based on your expectations of their long-term performance. By all means, be prepared to make a change if whatever attracted you to the stock is no longer valid. But take the daily news events with a big dose of salt—over the long term, those zigs and zags will likely be smoothed.

MISCONCEPTION One example from recent stock market history demonstrates how timing the market can be more dangerous than buying and holding. The strong market of 1982–87 lasted 1,276 trading days and returned an average of 26 percent a year. An investor in the S&P 500 who missed just the top ten days during those five years would have had an annual return of just 18 percent. Missing the top twenty days would have meant a 13 percent annual return, while missing the best forty days would have produced a 4 percent return.

Dollar-Cost Averaging

Dollar-cost averaging means investing an equal chunk of money at regular intervals, usually monthly. The point is that when the price of whatever you're buying is low, your fixed amount automatically buys more shares up, and when it's high, you get fewer shares—all without having to follow the ups and downs or trying to time your investment decisions.

Here's how it works. Say you've got $20,000 that you want to invest in the stock market. You've picked a stock mutual fund and on January 1 you put your first $5,000 in. If the fund is selling at a net asset value (NAV) of $50 per share, you end up getting one hundred shares. On February 1, the NAV has fallen to 40 so your next five grand buys 125 shares. On March 1, the NAV of 64 equals $78\frac{1}{8}$ shares and on April 1, the NAV has returned to 50, meaning another one hundred shares.

All told, your $20,000 has bought 403.125 shares. So even though the average price of the fund during your four months of investing was $51 ($50 + 40 + 64 + 50 = 204; 204 ÷ 4 = 51$), you only paid an average of $49.61 ($20,000 ÷ 403.125 = 49.61$). I call that a bargain.

Beyond the nifty little price break produced by dollar-cost averaging, there's the moderating effect it has on your portfolio. Even though the fund began and ended at the same place, there was a lot of volatility in between. The investor in this example, however, didn't have to worry about tracking the fund in the paper or worrying about when to dive in: she was guaranteed not to overbuy at the high price and to pile on at the low.

The strategy works the same way with other types of mutual funds and with individual stocks (perhaps even more effectively as an evening force because of the greater volatility of a single stock compared with mutual funds). This example presumes a large chunk of uninvested cash, say from an inheritance or lottery windfall. A more common form of dollar-cost averaging occurs when people have automatic payroll deduction into retirement plans.

 **WARNING!** Dollar-cost averaging is easy and effective. But it's not always the magic bullet it's hyped to be and there're some things you should think about before embracing it.

Even though it's touted as a way to avoid "timing the market," dollar-cost averaging is itself a form of market timing. Nobody knows where the market's going from one day to the next. But because the market does have an upward bias, doling out your money in smallish increments is a way of trying to protect yourself from a collapse the day after you plunge head-long. Young investors, who have time and earning power on their side, may be better off diving in all at once. Some studies have indicated that long-term investors face greater risk missing bull markets than they do getting clipped by sudden dips.

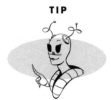

TIP

If you decide to employ dollar-cost averaging, whether through lump-sum intervals or payroll deduction, there's an easy and little-known way to tweak the process. Over the past sixty years, stocks have tended to perform significantly better during the first half of the month than the second. Try to arrange your monthly deposits so that your purchases are made about two to three days before the first of the month. The difference won't be jaw-dropping, but every bit helps.

All Around the World: Investing Overseas

Dying to travel but don't have the bread? Well, here's a way to participate in the best part of globe-trotting—spending money—without leaving your couch. Now that you're convinced that you need to put your investing eggs in as many baskets as possible, it's time for a primer on the ways to send some dollars abroad.

Dozens of strategies exist for Americans to take advantage of international investing. But there are three methods particularly well suited to novice investors, or those not eager to pay for translators and subscriptions to overseas business papers. Here they are, listed from simple to slightly more difficult.

1. *U.S.-based multinational corporations.* Many well-known American companies derive a substantial portion of their revenue from overseas operations, and those are often the fastest-growing parts of their companies. So your investment dollar stays safe and visible in the U.S. while reaping exposure to foreign markets and overseas opportunities. For example, Mc-

Donald's (MCD-NYSE) derives half its profits from the one third of its restaurants outside the U.S.

Other domestic companies, such as Philip Morris (MO-NYSE) or Coca-Cola (KO-NYSE), seek to cash in on emerging markets playing catch-up. The thinking goes that strong American brand names are inevitably desired by those newly able to afford the vices the West advertises so effectively. A billion Chinese mean a lot of 'boros and Sprite. Toilet maker American Standard (ASD-NYSE) is betting that people in the Third World are as eager to pee in porcelain as Yankees—the company currently gets almost half its sales overseas.

Investing in companies with substantial overseas business gives an investor some diversity through exposure to international economic events while also providing the peace of mind from investing in a big American blue chip.

2. *Overseas mutual funds.* These are exactly what they sound like: mutual funds that invest in companies headquartered in foreign countries. (There are overseas bond funds, of course, but American investors interested in the safety of bonds can find plenty to choose from at home and needn't look abroad.)

Foreign funds are a terrific way to achieve a double dose of diversity: you get the multiple stocks of a mutual fund and the overseas exposure of foreign markets. And the whole thing's in the hands of a manager such as Helen Young Hayes (Janus fund, 800-525-8983, no load), who has a handle on the companies and economies of wherever she invests.

Because they are investment products, the names of these funds are confusing. *International funds* invest exclusively in foreign stocks. *Global funds* typically keep 75 percent of their assets in stocks from the U.S., leaving only a quarter for overseas stocks. There are also regional funds, which specialize in investing in Europe, Latin America or the Pacific Rim. Specific countries also have funds, but these are usually closed-end funds that trade on exchanges like stocks and can be quite volatile. Then there are WEBS, which function like index funds of specific countries and trade on the American Stock Exchange much like closed-end funds.

3. *American Depository Receipts.* Created to make investing in foreign companies convenient, ADRs are negotiable dollar-denominated shares

that trade just like domestic stocks. Investors can hold them in regular brokerage accounts and the dividends are paid in dollars.

Stick with ADRs that are "sponsored." That means companies like
Honda Motor Co. (HMC-NYSE) or British Airways (BAB-NYSE) that
trade here on a major exchange (New York Stock Exchange, American
Stock Exchange or NASDAQ) and comply with American accounting and
reporting standards. Plenty of solid foreign companies are unsponsored
(Swiss food giant and baby formula pusher Nestlé, for example), so that
doesn't imply that sponsored ADRs are more reliable investments. But
with about 450 sponsored ADRs listed on the three major exchanges, investors have a pretty good selection and should stick with those until they
have a surer handle on the whole concept.

Depository receipts are a great way to dip your toe in foreign waters with
the convenience of domestic investing. But because information on foreign
companies is harder to come by, view ADRs as long-term investments to be
made only with a small portion of a portfolio.

TIP

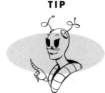

For a free directory of all available ADRs, contact
The Bank of New York, ADR Division, 101 Barclay St.,
22nd Floor, West Bldg., New York, NY 10286; 212-815-
2175.

WARNING! Overseas investing carries with it risks beyond the ups and downs of the security's value. Currency fluctuations can cut into returns (or enhance
them); a strengthening dollar (i.e., a dollar buys more yen or marks than it
did before) can cripple an otherwise good investment. Furthermore, the
more volatile the economy of the country, the more volatile you can expect
investments there to be. That means that emerging market funds are likely
to produce higher highs and lower lows than a fund that invests in established European companies. During a bull market like the one the U.S. has
enjoyed for the last seven years, investors might be tempted not to bother
sending money overseas. But because foreign economies often provide a
counterweight to the cycles of the American economy, the peak of a domestic bull market at home is often the best time to begin investing abroad.

Socially Responsible Investing

If you disapprove of a company's business practices, chances are you avoid their products, right? Well, many investors are not willing to buy stock in those companies whose success comes from activities of which the investor disapproves.

The solution is pretty obvious for those who buy stock in individual companies: don't buy companies whose business or practices you don't like. But with more Americans doing the majority of their investing through mutual funds, it's not so easy to invest with a clear conscience. When you invest in a mutual fund, you're handing control of your money to the fund manager. Not only can't you tell her what companies to buy, you don't even know what all of the fund's holdings are. So there's a whole mess of investors who want the benefits of mutual funds but not the onus of owning shares in companies they dislike.

Enter socially responsible mutual funds. These are mutual funds that avoid the stocks of certain industries. Using "screens" to filter out companies that pollute or make weapons or tobacco or whatever, these funds believe it's possible to do well and do good at the same time.

The big knock against SRI is its allegedly inferior performance. It's true that SRI funds as a class have not kept up with many of their vice-loving peers. But the tide may be turning. In 1996, several SRI funds beat the 22.98 percent turned in by the S&P 500, including the Green Century Balanced fund (24.9 percent) and the Dreyfus Third Century (24.3 percent).

Any fund can have a lucky year, but there's reason to believe SRI is about to benefit from changing public perceptions. The thinking is that the costs faced by companies screened out of SRI funds—environmental clean-ups, tobacco lawsuits, etc.—are going to drag down the returns of these companies. Funds that don't buy those companies will sidestep those costs and enjoy relatively better returns. Or so the argument for SRI goes, and has gone for years. There is some hard evidence. A study by Lloyd Kurtz and Dan DiBartolomeo in the *Journal of Investing* compared the returns of the S&P 500 with the Domini social index, an index of four hundred companies that have passed the usual SRI tests. From 1991–96, the Domini index racked up 169.9 percent in cumulative gains against 150.4 percent for the S&P 500.

Screens exist for nearly every imaginable social value. If you support gay rights, there's the Meyers Pride fund (800-410-3337), which purchases stock only from companies that are "gay-friendly." If dwindling natural resources is keeping you up nights, there's the New Alternatives Fund, emphasizing solar- and alternative-energy investing and the environment. It shuns weapons makers and nuclear power companies. Concerned about the lack of hope in the Third World and want to put your money to work there? Call the Development Capital Fund (800-371-2655), which provides small business advice and start-up money to the world's working poor. There's even an animal-rights fund, Beacon Global Advisors' Cruelty-Free Value Fund (800-892-9626), which avoids circuses, trappers and companies that test products on animals.

Although SRI is usually associated with those left of the dial, conservatives have parking places for their conscience dollars, too.

The Timothy Plan (800-846-7526) avoids companies involved in pornography, gambling, tobacco, alcohol and abortion. Blacklisted companies include American Express, which contributes to Planned Parenthood, and Disney, which according to the Timothy people, "advertises in pornographic magazines." Amana Mutual Funds Trust invests according to Islamic principles—meaning no *riba* (interest), and no businesses involved in alcohol, wine, casinos, pornography, gambling and non-Islamic banks (800-SATURNA/206-734-9900). Then there's a no-loader with a Catholic bent, aptly named the Aquinas Fund (800-423-6369).

Finally, there's Morgan Funshares, a closed-end fund (which means it trades on an exchange, much like a stock—it's ticker is MFUN). It invests *only* in "sin" companies—tobacco, gambling, condom makers, alcohol. Recession proof!

The reason many SRI investors give for avoiding the stock of companies they don't approve of is that they "don't want to give those guys my money." That may be

MISCONCEPTION a noble aim, but it's not exactly correct. When an in-

vestor buys a stock, the money he pays for it goes not to the company that
issued the stock but to the investor selling the stock (unless buying during
the company's initial public offering). In other words, buying the stock
doesn't fund the evil-doings of the company.

There's a lot to be said for not wanting to profit from activities one
doesn't condone, and as mentioned above there's a case to be made for socially responsible companies strictly from an investment point of view. It's
also conceivable that if enough investors share one's point of view, demand
for the stock might suffer, its price would drop and its shareholders might
pressure management to alter whatever policies are causing conscientious
investors to avoid owning the stock. Some investors think the better way to
effect change in a company's policies is to buy the stock, which provides a
vote and the right to attend shareholder meetings. It's hard to say for sure
why companies do what they do, but there's little doubt that shareholder
activism has forced some companies to alter their practices. Shareholder
pressure on Pepsi, for example, is often cited as a factor in the soda conglomerate's decision to stop doing business in Myanmar, a country with a
notorious human rights record.

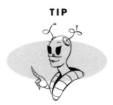

TIP Shareholders trying to enact change can try to get resolutions included on the proxy statements that all investors are mailed. Big companies such as Merck and
American Express have responded to shareholder resolutions demanding that outside directors stop receiving
fat pensions for performing little work. The Investor Rights Association of
America helps small investors craft resolutions. Reach them at 516-864-
1758 or by e-mail at *aquilla@worldnet.att.net*.

Investment Clubs

Simply put, a bunch of friends share in investing decisions, returns and
heartbreaks. For the most part, an investment club is an excellent way to
learn how the market works and share advice. Of course, the usual rules to
social gatherings apply: don't join one with people who irritate you, and be
sure your comrades are trustworthy.

Usually, each member puts up a certain stake, say $1,000, and is expected to add to that at regular intervals. If there are ten members, the group starts a portfolio with the initial $10,000. The buying power of the group lowers the percentage spent on trading costs, in much the same way a mutual fund does. But the fun part is that, unlike a mutual fund, you have some say over what the group buys and sells and when.

As small-fry investors have fallen in love with the market, investment clubs have multiplied. The nation's best-known club, The Beardstown Ladies, are pretty typical of the fun and camaraderie that mark the best groups, even if their supposedly market-beating returns are not so typical (and not so easy to verify, since they're reluctant to disclose them).

One problem with investment clubs arises when a member withdraws, either because he needs the dough or is unhappy with the investing style of the club. Unlike mutual funds, which keep a small percentage of their assets on hand to cover redemptions, clubs are typically fully invested. So when someone bails, the club has to buy the party-pooper out. That means selling shares, which triggers commissions and perhaps occurs when market conditions don't favor the move. Some clubs pass these costs on to the departing member as a sort of back-end load—"leave the club and we'll dock you 2 percent"—while others have a waiting list of investors willing to buy out the departing member's share of the holdings.

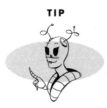

TIP

If you and some buddies form a club, I strongly recommend contacting the National Association of Investors Corporation (711 W. 13 Mile Rd., Madison Height, MI, 48071; 810-583-6242). For $35, plus $14 per member (not all members of your club have to join), your club receives a kit for getting started, tracking your group's portfolio (harder than it sounds when you factor in reinvested dividends), special prices on NAIC software, free reports on the 115 companies that NAIC tracks, access to DRIPs of certain companies and the NAIC's pretty useless magazine, *Better Investing*.

How REIT[2] It Is: Buying Real Estate Without a Real Lot of Money

You already know that mutual funds are a good way to diversify into stocks or bonds—buying a stock fund, for example, puts fifty or so different stocks in your pocket, which would be costly and cumbersome to accumulate and manage on your own.

But what if you want to invest in real estate? Since you know better than to put all your investing eggs in one basket, and since you wouldn't be reading this book if you had the means to buy several pieces of real estate, you might think you're out of luck.

Fear not, gentle soul. Real estate investment trusts (REITs) function essentially as mutual funds for real estate. You put dough into a fund that buys and manages properties and mortgages, producing income by renting or selling them.

The three basic benefits of REITs are just about the same as those of a mutual fund:

- Professional management

Feel like the rental market's about to take off but don't want to wake up at 3 A.M. to fix a tenant's leaky sink? REITs allow you to participate in gains (and, uh, losses too) of the real estate market without the hassles of managing the properties yourself.

- Liquidity

Buying and selling shares of REITs—which trade on exchanges with their own ticker symbols, much like stocks—is a heck of a lot easier than buying and selling apartment buildings or shopping malls.

- Diversification (times two)

In itself, a REIT gives you the diversity of several different real properties, so if one fails, other properties will hopefully offset the loss. Additionally, REITs provide diversity to an entire portfolio. In other words, if your portfolio consists mostly of stocks and bonds, a REIT can cushion the blow if those two asset classes, which often travel in lockstep, take a nosedive. Real estate is also a classic hedge against inflation—while stocks and bonds get creamed by it, "real assets" such as gold or land tend to weather it better.

---

[2] REIT is pronounced "reet."

As an investment class, REITs have earned their investors even more than stocks over the past five years, averaging about 13.8 percent per year, compared with the 13.6 percent the stocks of the S&P 500 have returned. Also, for tax reasons you don't want to know about, REITs typically pay a bigger dividend then stock funds, but you're probably better off reinvesting those dividend payments in more shares of the REIT.

Most REITs stick to a particular type of real estate, so a better idea for someone who doesn't want to own four or five REITs would be one of the many mutual funds that invest in REITs.

Some good mutual fund REITs include Cohen & Steers Realty Shares (ticker: CSRSX -RFI), Vanguard's REIT Index (VGSIX) and Fidelity Real Estate Investment (FRESX). Investigate on your own, too, but that's tough in the world of REITs, which don't get much attention from the personal finance press.

• Get a free list of REITs by sending a SASE to NAREIT, 1129 20th St. NW, Suite 305, Washington, DC 20036-3483.

Throwing Good Money After Bad

Let's say a bunch of your friends want to go to the Billy Squier fiftieth birthday concert at Poplar Creek. Tickets are $25 each for general admission seats. It's a little more than you wanted to spend, but not too steep to keep you from reliving "The Stroke" and "Everybody Wants You." Then, a week before the show, your cat eats the tickets. You hear there are seats still available. Do you spring for another ticket or stay home while your friends flick lighters and yell for an encore?

As it turns out, a lot of people who would never have bought the ticket had it cost $50 to begin with would buy another ticket after having lost the first. Either way they've spent $50 on a ticket. But something about having already spent $25 and not seeing the concert seems even worse than overpaying for the show.

There's a whole mess of clichés that could apply here: "Cut your losses," "Don't throw good money after bad," "Don't give Ticketmaster your money."

Investors buy a stock expecting it to rise. When that expectation doesn't work out, people often pour more money into the idea. If what got you into the position originally is still valid, adding some more after a dip can be a good idea. (That strategy is known as averaging down, since it lowers the buyer's average cost per share.) If a stock looked good at $20, it tends to look great at $15, especially when an investor's smarting from the rough luck that knocked the stock down $5. It's also hard to walk away from a stock after you've put a lot of time and research into it. But there's a good chance that what's driving the share price down is something the investor overlooked in the initial analysis. Before adding more dough, you're better off reassessing the reasons for getting into the stock in the first place. If something's dragging the stock down, it's probably not a bargain even at the lower price.

Economics and Investing: A Ghastly Oversimplification

The Ravages of Inflation

When I was in grade school, nothing beat skipping a day of school with a fake illness. I relished the extra pampering at home and the relief from the tedium of Hickory Point Elementary School. But the real thrill was the chance to catch my favorite daytime program, "The Price Is Right."

One game's premise was simple: the contestant was shown a sparkling new car and given several guesses to determine which numeral went in each of the four digits of the price of the car. This was a long time ago, back when Bob Barker and I were still eating meat. Smart players would invariably start with "4" because all of the cars in the show were always in the $4,000 range. Today, the average price of a new car is about $20,000; you'd be lucky to get a ten-year-old beater for four grand.

Inflation is a fact of life. The dollar that used to net you four Snickers bars now buys only one and a half. That dip in buying power is no big deal when you're talking about candy bars, but it can wreak havoc on an investing program.

Over the last seventy years, inflation has averaged about 3.1 percent a year. Assuming that rate continues, you have to subtract 3.1 percent from whatever return you plan to enjoy. This factor dramatically affects the real rates of return for the various investment classes. Let's look again at the rate of return of some major investment classes from 1925 to 1995.

Annual Returns by Asset Class 1925–95

Small-company stocks	12.5 percent
Large-company stocks	10.5 percent
Corporate bonds	5.6 percent
Government bonds	5.2 percent
Treasury bills (short-term)	3.7 percent

(Source: Ibbotson Associates, Chicago)

A risk-averse youngster might think, "The historical return from corporate bonds is more than half that of large-company stocks, so I might as well avoid the ulcers of the stock market." But what about the effects of inflation?

Inflation-adjusted Annual Returns by Asset Class 1925–95

Small-company stocks	9.4 percent
Large-company stocks	7.4 percent
Corporate bonds	2.5 percent
Government bonds	2.1 percent
Treasury bills (short-term)	0.6 percent

(Source: Ibbotson Associates, Chicago)

Subtract that 3.1 percent from those historical returns of large stocks and you get investing coming in at 7.4 percent and corporate bonds at 2.5 percent. So the buying power of the bond investor's retirement nest egg in today's dollars is only about one third that of the stock investor.

Let's take a quick look at how this impacts the real-world plans of these two investment strategies. Hopey and Maggie are both twenty-five years old and plan to retire at age sixty-five. Each invests $100 a month over those forty years. Hopey sticks with corporate bonds, her $48,000 turning into $178,811. Maggie, more risk tolerant, invests her hundred a month in large-company stocks, ending up with $736,904. (We'll assume that historical rates of return repeat themselves exactly, which they can be counted on *not* to do, outside of examples in personal finance books.)

More remarkable than the gap between those two totals is what Hopey and Maggie will be able to buy with their nest eggs. Both will have their returns eroded by inflation, but that 3.1 percent will hurt Hopey a lot more than Maggie. In today's dollars, Hopey's nest egg will be worth just $82,342, while Maggie's will be worth $293,892. And the investor who thinks he's being smart by burying his $50,000 in the backyard for forty years of safekeeping shouldn't be surprised to find that he can buy only about $7,500 worth of stuff, adjusted for inflation.

As noted throughout this book, an individual's comfort with risk is a personal decision. It's not my goal to establish any sort of "right" amount of risk an investor should take, and what's good for one person might be totally wrong for someone with identical circumstances but a different risk tolerance. But as you can see from the inflation-adjusted returns of the different investment classes, sometimes the riskiest thing to do is to assume too little risk.

Economic Indicators: Predicting Inflation and Recession

What causes inflation is a subject that sparks intense political debate. But there's little disagreement about the fact that certain signs often clearly point to coming changes in the economy.

We've already seen how rising inflation can ravage an investing program. I'm not an advocate of the defensive moves some people advise when inflation appears to be climbing, such as buying gold and gold-mining stocks. The novice investor is probably better off waiting out inflationary periods than trying to time a phenomenon that's vexed even the sharpest economists. But that doesn't mean one shouldn't try to see what's around the corner.

Watch these indicators for signs of inflation:

- Rising Employment Cost Index
- Rising Gross National Product (higher than 3 percent or so)
- Falling dollar

Watch these indicators for signs of a recession:

- Rising rates on short-term government bonds
- Rising inventories (the Commerce Department publishes a monthly figure that compares the dollar value of waiting-to-be-sold stuff with the value of stuff sold. A number higher than 1.5 may point to a slowdown)

- Falling Gross National Product (lower than 3 percent)
- Falling stock market

MISCONCEPTION Inflation isn't always a bad thing for everyone. While I'm reducing economics to a level so skeletal it actually pains my friends back at the University of Chicago, let me generalize a little further. Creditors—those to whom lots of money is owed, including rich guys with bonds, and banks that have written lots of fixed-rate loans—hate inflation because it lessens the buying power of the payments they collect. Debtors—such as a working-class guy with a fixed-rate mortgage or a kid with a student loan balance—look much more kindly upon inflation. Young people with low-interest debt may benefit from inflation because the twenty grand they use to repay their student loans won't be worth as much as when they borrowed it.

People with fewer assets tend to concern themselves more with the unemployment rate. With high unemployment, supply of labor is high so demand is low, which keeps wages low. To a degree, this condition favors employers, who are purchasers of labor. (Taken too far, however, high unemployment favors no one—out-of-work people don't have money to buy what factory owners produce.) The fact that the term "full employment" is used to describe a situation where 5 percent of people are out of work says a lot about whether it's the rich people or poor people who make the terminology.

Good News = Bad News?

Even under the best of circumstances, the stock market is a scary place for new investors. But when good news sends the market reeling and bad news sends it climbing, newcomers can feel like they've gone through the looking glass.

The government and other organizations release flurries of economic data on a regular basis—employment rates, consumer confidence measures, figures on home building. It's pretty obvious why these numbers affect the stock market. What's not so obvious is the direction they'll move stocks.

I got a "Dear Kenny" letter in 1996 that raises some good questions about the apparent disparity between "good news" and the stock market.

DEAR KENNY: When the Dow goes up 40 points the day AT&T lays off 40,000 people, then takes its biggest plunge in four years when the unemployment rate drops, why is a neo-anarchist Clinton-Dole-Greenspan-hater like myself not supposed to wish devoutly that everyone on Wall Street would be lowered naked into a bubbling cauldron like so many restaurant lobsters?
—Bill W., Brooklyn

DEAR BILL: Because your letter's tone so recalls my own restrained prose, I simply must reply. And it's a damn good question. Wall Street's appearance of glee at Main Street's bad news and gloom at good news can make an average Joe or Joann feel like the denizens of Wall Street are of an entirely different species from those of Main Street. While that may have once been true, those days are gone forever. Let's take a look at how the two have collided in the years since I was paroled from high school.

In 1986, 94,000 companies offered 401(k) plans, holding assets of $155 billion. Today there are well over 300,000 plans, with assets of about a trillion dollars. The number of Americans who participate has more than doubled, from 8.6 million to 20.8 million and will hit 25 million by the year 2000.

So who are these 25 million people? In 1994, stocks comprised more than half of all assets held in 401(k) plans for the first time. So when AT&T's stock price bolts skyward on news that it has laid off 40,000, it may seem heartless. But companies are owned by shareholders. More and more, shareholders include regular Joes. And if you were an AT&T shareholder, you'd expect the management—your management—to do whatever it thought was best for the company's competitiveness. This, of course, begs the question of whether slashing employee numbers actually does help long-term competitiveness, or simply provides a quick mask to disguise management's foibles.

For AT&T, a strong case can be made for the latter. Not only did the company have to drastically curtail the number of people it had planned to lay off, but the company's management continued to be outmaneuvered by its competitors. Its stock price hit a high on January 3, 1996, the day after the layoff announcement. Then it spent the next year floating back to earth, a result that's particularly disappointing in light of the terrific performance of the market at large during that period. Adding insult to injury, AT&T paid CEO Robert Allen $16 million for his performance in 1995, a move that was protested (to no avail) at AT&T's annual meeting in 1996 by some large shareholders, including representatives of union pension funds.

That's not an anomaly. The Institute for Policy Studies looked at 22 U.S. firms that announced layoffs of at least 3,000 workers in 1995. They found that at least 14 of those companies' CEOs received raises that were higher than the average CEO got. What's more, the 22 CEOs held more than 22 million stock options (this kind of option allows its holder to buy 100 shares at a certain price), which meant that they directly benefited from the boost in share price that resulted from the layoffs they ordered. Funny how big layoffs seldom seem to include the jobs of those at the top.

But let's say you owned stock in widget company XYZ, which has four employees for every 1,000 widgets it produces. If company ABC is turning out widgets of comparable quality with only three employees per 1,000 widgets, they'll be able to charge less per widget, and presumably still have money left over to pay the three widget makers better, thus landing the top widget makers around (which isn't to say company good fortune always filters down to the employees). XYZ will sell fewer widgets, meaning less profits (earnings). You'll then receive a smaller dividend and the stock price will fall. Unless XYZ finds a way either to cut its labor costs or use that additional labor to create a widget that people will pay more for, XYZ will go out of business, which hurts its workforce even more than layoffs. Hey, it's not always pretty to live in a world that resembles a PBS documentary on the food chain.

Whether firing en masse turns out to be a smart business move is often difficult to gauge. It's incumbent upon shareholders to examine the reasons behind big job cuts at companies where profits are fat. A shrewd investor wonders whether it's a quick fix to prop the stock price temporarily, rather than a necessary bullet bite to streamline operations over the long haul. If a company succumbs to the temptation of short-term results at the expense of R&D money, facility upgrades and salaries that workers are going to view as enough to keep them not just placated but productive and enthusiastic, then a long-term investor ought to avoid the company's shares for reasons of both principle and principal.

Then there's the swoon that the stock markets tend to take upon positive unemployment news. Investors buy stocks taking a variety of probabilities into account. When economic indicators look positive, the Fed is less likely to lower rates to stimulate the economy. That means borrowing stays relatively expensive. If you bought an interest-rate sensitive stock, a bank, for example, you may have paid a higher price than you otherwise would have, in anticipation of the rate cut. When the positive unemployment number was released, your premise became less valid— dumping the stock would be the expected reaction. In no way does that imply that investors are somehow bummed that Americans found a lot of jobs or that they're gleeful when others are hurting.

So what's an investor to do when confronted with economic news? Much of the mystery can be removed if you figure what affect a particular piece of data will have on interest rates. News that will drive up interest rates can be counted on to hammer stocks; expected interest rate dips will usually be a friend to the market.

Why do higher interest rates hurt stocks?

• Remember, a stock is a gamble on the future ability of a company to grow and become more profitable. If the Fed raises interest rates, it is sending a signal that it wants the economy to cool down. It'll be harder for companies to become more profitable if the economy is cooling. Thus when interest rates rise, it's reasonable for investors to assume stocks will have a harder time being as profitable as had been hoped.

• In order to grow, companies borrow money, either from investors in the form of bonds or from banks as plain old loans. Higher interest payments will cut into the company's profitability.

• Higher interest rates mean bonds pay more, which makes them relatively more attractive than stocks. As investors divert their money from stocks to bonds, demand for stocks shrinks, taking prices down.

If the market is expecting an unemployment number of 5 percent and it turns out to be only 4 percent, a whole chain of thinking is instantaneously unleashed that can be expected to send the market down. If more people have a job than was expected, fewer people are looking for a job. Employees, knowing there are fewer people who can step in to replace them, may be able to exert pressure for higher wages. If employees are paid more, they can buy more stuff. Since no one's necessarily producing more stuff, prices rise—inflation. Thus, the Fed may raise interest rates to nip inflation before it begins. All this happens in the blink of an eye—the lower-than-expected unemployment number comes out and stocks tumble.

Unfortunately, it's not enough to guess which way a particular piece of data is going to come out. You'd also have to guess which way the market thinks it's going to come out. Say the last announced unemployment rate was 5 percent. You think that the number to be released tomorrow will be 4 percent so you sell all your stocks in anticipation of a market dip. But what if everyone else in the market thinks the number will be 3 percent? They'd have been paring their stock positions in anticipation. So when the 4 percent number comes out, even though you were "right" in your prediction, the market will react positively, since unemployment is higher than expected. So even though you were right about the number, you were wrong about its effect on the market.

So how should a small-fry investor respond? By doing nothing. That's the beauty of a long-time horizon: there's no need to try to guess exactly when the market will zig and zag. Don't feel like you're missing out by ignoring the analysis of this stuff. And even the pros who seek to stay a step ahead of the market by anticipating these events often get burned.

Some things that can be expected to hamper the stock market:

- Rising interest rates
- Rising inflation
- Declining or flat corporate earnings (actual earnings that are less than expected)
- Political uncertainty, like before a hotly contested election or when a budget agreement is in doubt
- International conflict

4. Protecting It

TAXES

LOVE AND MONEY

INSURANCE

AND SOME MISCELLANEOUS PROTECTIONS . . .

Okay, you've counted your money, invested wisely and dutifully repaid your creditors. You smile to yourself, rightfully pleased at having aced some pretty serious tests of your financial endurance. Just when you're ready to let your guard down and enjoy the ride, you spot some financial villains that make the Legion of Doom look like The Osmonds.

Taxes, disasters, relationships, oh my. Isn't it just like this mean old world to produce a million little dangers trying to tear down all the nice work you've done?

It doesn't have to be that way. While taxes and insurance are certainly among the less fun personal finance topics, both produce a pretty big bang for the buck. I don't know about you, but I feel better knowing that a small portion of my tax dollars helps fund school-lunch programs. And I sleep easier at night knowing I'll be reimbursed if my car is stolen by the gang of ruffians I noticed fiddling with something called "The Club Master Key."

So here are some challenges to your newfound financial stability, and a utility belt's worth of devices that'll serve you well as you fight to keep what's yours.

Taxes

Taxes? I got an uncle in Taxes.

Paying taxes sucks. You get your paycheck and the chunk taken out is always bigger than you feared. Taxes are so high that it now takes the average American until May to start earning for himself or herself—in essence the money he or she earns until then only covers the tax bill. But what really makes it sting is the feeling that others are finding loopholes and shirking their fair share while you're paying tons. Looking at a gutted paycheck or a whopping tax bill, it's hard not to feel like one of the little people. As in the suckers New York hotel queen Leona Helmsley was thinking of when she said, "We don't pay taxes. Only the little people pay taxes."

On the other hand, Americans are awfully fond of the services these taxes fund. Don't think much of the $6.20 you pay for Social Security every time you earn a hundred? Tell it to your beloved grandma, who depends on her monthly check and ain't exactly living large from it. You're not thrilled about the $1.45 you pay into Medicare whenever you score a C-note? Tell it to Gramps, whose hilarious stories and old-world aphorisms might not be heard without the medical care you're helping to fund.

Hey, I'm no shill for entitlements. But there's a lot of truth to the motto that hangs outside the IRS headquarters: "Taxes are the price we pay for a civilized society."

MISCONCEPTION   A lot of people think that the Social Security (FICA) money that's deducted from their check goes into some sort of account that'll be available when they reach retirement age. Not so. Our Social Security program is a pay-as-you-go system. The money you pay now funds the check a current Social Security recipient gets. Then when you retire, your check will be funded by the deductions from some whippersnapper who curses when he sees his pay stub—just like you do now.

Regardless of your feelings about the justice of paying taxes, there's little doubt that the tax code as it stands today is a disaster. It is arbitrary, capricious and autocratic, but most of all, overwhelmingly complicated. In 1997, *Money* magazine gave a hypothetical family's records to forty-five tax pros. They got back forty-five different bottom lines, with two thirds of the preparers missing the correct amount by more than $1,300. In a further irony, a *Forbes* story a few years ago found that twelve of the thirteen members of the Senate Finance Committee don't even fill out their own returns.

A system so convoluted that professionals can't make heads or tails of it is clearly broken. Worse than simply causing anxiety is the way our tax system intimidates people and adds to the general sense of distance many Americans feel from government. So it's the method as much as the amount that riles people. Survey after survey reveals that Americans are willing to pay their fair share. But unless that share is collected in a way that doesn't seem arbitrary and stacked against the little guy, taxes will remain a four-letter word.

Various forms of relief are constantly rumored to be in the works. Though there's little chance of a true flat tax or national sales tax replacing the current Byzantine system anytime soon, there have been nods in the direction of customer service and better communication. After the 1988 Taxpayer Bill of Rights eased some of the IRS's audit and collection practices, the sequel was signed last year. The IRS now accepts returns via delivery services other than the U.S. Mail and has better staffed its website and 800-numbers. It has also created the position of tax ombudsman, designed to give taxpayers better redress to the IRS, the only agency in which "guilty until proven innocent" is the actual guiding principle.

How to Reach the IRS

• All tax forms can be ordered by calling the IRS at 800-TAX-FORM.

• Call 800-TAX-1040 to ask the IRS general and specific tax questions. If you're calling in late winter or early spring, prepare for a long wait.

• Head scratchers can call the IRS's automated TeleTax service (800-TAX-GIRS) for recorded answers on about 150 common tax topics and learn the status of their returns.

• The website (*www.irs.ustreas.gov*) has downloadable forms and a ton of information, particularly about recent tax changes.

• Publications of interest

All of these snappy titles are available for free by calling 1-800-TAX-FORM. Here are some which should be ordered if they apply to your situation:

Publication #1	Your Rights as a Taxpayer
Publication #4	Student's Guide to Federal Income Tax
Publication #17	Your Federal Income Tax

Publication #334	Tax Guide for Small Business
Publication #501	Exemption, Standard Deduction, and Filing Information
Publication #502	Medical and Dental Expenses
Publication #503	Child and Dependent Care Expenses
Publication #504	Divorced or Separated Individuals
Publication #505	Tax Withholding and Estimated Tax (good for those with "creative" second jobs)
Publication #508	Educational Expenses
Publication #525	Taxable and Nontaxable Income
Publication #526	Charitable Contributions
Publication #529	Miscellaneous Deductions
Publication #530	Tax Information for First-Time Homeowners
Publication #531	Reporting Tip Income Tax
Publication #533	Self-Employment Tax
Publication #550	Investment Income and Expenses
Publication #553	Recent Tax Changes
Publication #560	Retirement Plans for the Self-Employed
Publication #564	Mutual Fund Distributions
Publication #587	Business Use of Your Home
Publication #590	Individual Retirement Accounts (IRAs)
Publication #596	Earned Income Credit
Publication #908	Bankruptcy
Publication #910	Guide to Free Tax Services (a complete list of all these publications)
Publication #929	Tax Rules for Children and Dependents
Publication #936	Home Mortgage Interest Deduction
Publication #1546	The IRS Problem Resolution Program

TIP

What's the Hurry?

Deciding when to file is actually not that tough. If you expect to get a refund, file as early as possible. If you expect to owe additional taxes, send your return on or just before April 15. Why? Interest. When you are owed money, the government is essentially borrowing that amount from you in-

Tax Brackets: A Common Misconception*

When the phrase "Joe's in the 31 percent tax bracket" is tossed around, it's easy to see why some people would think that Joe's entire taxable income is taxed at 31 percent. In fact, only the amount one earns that exceeds each bracket is taxed at the higher rate.

Example:
For 1997, the tax brackets for single filers are as follows:

$0–24,650	15 percent
24,651–59,750	28 percent
59,751–124,650	31 percent
124,651–271,050	36 percent
271,051 and up	39.6 percent

If Joe has a taxable income of $125,000, he's said to be in the 36 percent bracket. But that's just the *highest* tax rate he'll face. This is also known as the *marginal rate.* But that doesn't mean he pays 31 percent of $125,000 ($45,000) to the IRS. Instead he pays 15 percent on the first $24,650, plus 28 percent of the amount up to $59,750, plus 31 percent of the amount up to $124,650, plus 36 percent of the remaining $350. His total tax bill: $33,770.50 (3,697.50 + 9,828 + 20,119 + 126 = 33,770.50).

Why is it set up that way? Otherwise, it would unevenly penalize those just above the borders. Suppose you simply paid whatever percentage bracket you were in on the full taxable amount. A guy making $124,651 would pay $45,000 while someone making exactly $124,650 would be in the 31 percent bracket and face only $38,641.50 in taxes. That's over $6,000 in penalties for an income of only $1. Not that a Joe making that kind of coin can't cover it. But you can bet he'd do whatever it took to take that last dollar in some

other form of nontaxable compensation, depriving the government of
the revenue it needs to do all the grand things it does.

(*It's great fun to dub something "a common misconception" even
if the only one who misunderstands it is me.)

terest-free. The sooner you get your return, the sooner you can put that
money to work. If you owe money, they don't offer brownie points for filing early—keeping the money in your interest-earning account as long as
possible will produce a few extra dollars to cover that outrageous tax bill.

Taxes on the $250 I Got from CBGB's? Bummer.

Just about every hipster these days has at least two careers—a "real job"
and a "creative job." Because these alter-ego careers don't generally
generate a lot of income (if they did, they wouldn't be second jobs), it's
easy to forget about the tax implications. Whether you're a waiter/actor,
sales rep/novelist or journalist/superhero, any income generated from
these side gigs has to be reported. The worst part is that you have to keep
track of these earnings and pay taxes on them every quarter. And the even
more worst part is that if you earn over $400 from the second job, you
also owe the self-employment tax for Social Security and Medicare on top
of the income tax. (On a regular paycheck, your employer pays half of
your Social Security, while on self-employed income you have to pay all of
it.)

Your quarterly payments must add up to either 100 percent of the
amount you owed last year or 90 percent of the amount you're going to
owe on that income this year. File Form 1040ES, which includes a worksheet to estimate your taxes; it's due on the fifteenth of April, June, September and January, so it's not a true quarterly payment.

Note: Only those employers who pay you more than $600 are required
to file Form 1099, letting the IRS know you got that money. Jobs that pay
less than that may or may not rat you out, so you're taking a risk if you
choose not to report small earnings.

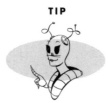

TIP

The tax agreement of 1997 tosses a bone to the self-employed. Beginning in tax year 1997, those who pay for their own health insurance will be able to take deductions on their federal taxes of 40 percent of the premium costs. In 1998, the deduction climbs to 45 percent and keeps rising until 2007, when the amount paid for health insurance is fully deductible.

Earned Income Credit

Of the millions of arcane tax rules, one that deserves special mention for those just getting started is the Earned Income Credit, which can be a huge help to a low-income family. If you have earned income (meaning income from work, not from interest, alimony or government programs), you can collect a credit from the government if your income, or the total of your income and your spouse's, is less than a certain amount. (The amount changes each year; in 1997, it was $25,760 if you had one dependent, $29,290 with two and $9,770 if you have no dependents. If you have no dependents, you must be between the ages of twenty-five and sixty-five to get an EIC; with dependents, age isn't a factor.)

That means that you get a check from the government free and clear; if you expect to receive an EIC, you can even receive payments as part of your paycheck so you don't have to wait until the end of the year (file Form W-5 EIC Advance Payment Certificate with your employer.) The amount to which you're entitled varies with your income and number of dependents, but it's not chump change: In tax year 1997, someone with income of $12,000 and one dependent would get a credit of about $2,200. Call 1-800-TAX-FORM and request IRS Publication 596 for more information about the Earned Income Credit.

Credit vs. Deduction

A tax *deduction* allows a filer to deduct an amount from his or her taxable income. So a filer who owed tax on **MISCONCEPTION** $35,000 of taxable income before figuring in a $500 deduction would end up owing tax on only $34,500.

A tax *credit* allows a filer to deduct an amount from his or her tax bill. So a filer who owed $2,000 in federal taxes before figuring in a $500 tax credit would end up owing only $1,500.

This means that a tax credit of $500 is much more valuable than a tax deduction of $500. With a credit, you save the full $500; with a deduction you save only a percentage of that $500 equal to whatever tax bracket you're in (if you're in the 28 percent bracket, your $500 deduction saves you $140).

Examples of tax credits include the Earned Income Credit, which benefits taxpayers with low income, and the kiddie tax credit, which allows those couples who earn less than $110,000 (or individuals who earn less than $95,000) to deduct $400 per child sixteen and under (goes to $500 in 1999).

To Itemize or Not

The IRS allows you to deduct the cost of some things from the amount of income on which you owe taxes.

MISCONCEPTION These things are called deductions and are many and varied in nature. Here are some examples of legal deductions:

- work-related expenses
- medical expenses
- IRA contributions
- interest on your mortgage
- property taxes
- moving expenses
- charitable contributions
- job search expenses

All carry conditions and are subject to specific terms. A $2,000 IRA contribution, for example, is fully deductible for someone who earns $20,000, but not at all for someone who earns $50,000 and has a retirement plan at work. These rules can be a pain, but don't abandon itemizing just because it'll take a little work. Most conditions are discernible through scrutiny of IRS Publication 529 or simply by asking your tax preparer.

Then there's the standard deduction you get simply for being alive. The standard deduction for 1997 was $4,150 ($6,900 for married couples filing jointly) and rises a little bit each year. This is an either/or situation: you can either claim the standard deduction or add up all the little deductions—known as itemizing—and claim that total as your deduction. Because you can't do both, you want to pick the method—standard deduction or itemizing—that produces the higher deduction. In other words, if the total of your itemized deductions is greater than $4,500, it makes sense to itemize; if it's less, take the standard deduction.

Unfortunately, unless you know you have either very little or a ton of de-

The New Budget

The new budget, universally referred by unimaginative writers as "1997's historic budget agreement," has a lot to offer young people. Included in 1997's historic budget agreement:

• Interest deduction for student loan interest. This sweet plum means that students paying back student loans can deduct the portion of the payment that's applied to interest from their adjusted gross income. There are limits, but they're pretty liberal—up to $1,000 in 1998, $1,500 in 1999, $2,000 in 2000 and $2,500 in 2001 and thereafter. The deduction starts to phase out for individuals making $40,000 and couples making more than $60,000.

• The self-employed can now deduct health insurance premiums.

• The tax rate on long-term capital gains is being cut, to a maximum of 20 percent for stocks held at least eighteen months. A capital gain is a tax on the profit an investor realizes when selling something for more than he paid. The government encourages investors to hold stocks for a long time by rewarding them with a lesser tax rate—one more reason not to jump in and out of stock positions on a whim.

ductions, the only way to know which amount is larger is to fill out the
Schedule A that comes with Form 1040. If it's a close call, you might want
to choose the standard deduction simply to avoid the hassle of itemizing.
But be sure your version of "close call" didn't neglect some juicy deductions that can save you money. If you do think you stand a chance of ben-
efiting from itemizing, be sure to save proof of all the expenses you're
going to claim. A simple folder marked "Deductions '98" will do—just put
your receipts and year-end statements together and sort them out at tax
time.

You Can Go Your Own Way

There is no better way to learn about taxes than by filling out your own return. Understandably, learning about taxes ranks one notch below reread-
ing *Beowulf* on the average person's priority list. But if you're filing a
relatively simple form, and certainly if you're among the third of Americans
who use the 1040EZ or 1040A, you should definitely consider preparing
your own return.

The first thing any file-it-yourselfer should do is call the IRS for two free
booklets. Dial 1-800-TAX-FORM and ask for Publication 17, "Your Federal Income Tax," and Publication 1, "Your Rights as a Taxpayer."

You're eligible for the 1040EZ if you are not itemizing and meet the following conditions:

- Single or married with no dependent
- Under sixty-five and not blind
- Total income under $50,000, all of it from work, scholarships or
grants (no Social Security or unemployment insurance, etc.)
- Interest and dividend income under $400
- No earned income credits

If you've already decided not to itemize and are eligible for the 1040EZ,
that's definitely the way to go. It takes about fifteen minutes and can be
completed by anyone who can add and subtract.

The 1040A is the next step up. This is the way to go if you are not itemizing deductions, and your total income is less than $50,000 from all

sources, including wages, tips and salary, Social Security, IRA withdrawals, unemployment, interest and dividends. The 1040A is slightly tougher than the EZ because more forms of income are allowed. Still, we're talking about only thirty-three lines here—it's a cinch if you have your records at the ready and can deal with simple arithmetic.

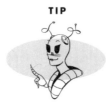

TIP

Save Time, Work, Math, Wails

If you're using either the 1040EZ and the 1040A, you don't even have to do the computations. Simply fill in all your information and let the IRS figure the amount you owe or are owed. Attach your W-2s and get the thing in at least a month before April 15. The IRS will either send you a check or bill you, and that's perfectly legal and acceptable. Be careful, though—they're not errorproof; it pays to have a ballpark idea of your tax liability so you'll recognize a number that's way off base.

TIP

New for 1998! A little-mentioned provision of 1997's landmark budget bill means that tax year 1997 is the first year the government will allow filers to pay their yearly federal tax bills with a credit card. There're simply so many jokes to be made about such a scenario that I'm going to do us all a favor and not make them.

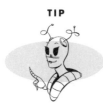

TIP

New Budget = Break on Student Loans

Thanks to the new budget, borrowers will be able to deduct the interest they pay on student loans from their federal tax bill. Beginning in 1998, up to $1,000 of the interest portion of one's student loan payments can be deducted—that's a $150 savings for someone in the 15 percent tax bracket. The eligible amount rises $500 per year until it tops out at $2,500 in 2001. Best of all, unlike most deductions, this one's available to those filers who don't itemize—in other words, it's easy to claim, even if you use the 1040EZ or 1040A.

Then there's the 1040, the form most Americans use. This is what you'll use if you are itemizing deductions, make more than fifty grand or have

any number of complications that will require the attachment of supplementary forms known as schedules. Don't get all freaked out here.
Even the dreaded 1040 is manageable for an ambitious do-it-yourselfer.
However, I recommend hiring a tax pro for at least the first year you itemize. Should you choose to go it alone in subsequent years, you'll at least
have a model to work from, and a memory of some deductions he or she
asked you about that may not have worked one year but might apply the
next.

Tax-preparation software is a true friend to the do-it-yourselfer. It will
walk you through the filing process exactly as a human preparer would do.
After filling in the basics—name, address, Social Security number—the
user is hit with a barrage of questions about income, possible deductions
and all the other vital statistics. After the interview process is complete, the
program uses your printer to spit out a pretty return that you simply mail
to the IRS.

TurboTax (for Macintosh, it's known as MacInTax) and Kiplinger Tax-
Cut are the simplest and most thorough programs (about $20 for TaxCut
and $35 for TurboTax or MacInTax). All three allow your data to be im-
ported directly from your personal finance software (TurboTax is made by
the same company that makes Quicken, so that import is particularly seam-
less), but unless you're the kind of user who religiously enters everything,
don't rely on the import alone. It's a drag to have to buy yearly updated edi-
tions, but they're pretty cheap and it's necessary to have the new rules and
rates factored into your return.

Electronic Filing

Whether by your own computer or a preparer's, electronic filing is a bad deal. It's not all that convenient because the accompanying W-2 forms still must be mailed in, along with
Form 8453-OL. Plus, the filer pays a fee (about fifteen bucks) for the privilege of saving the IRS the cost of hiring people to open envelopes and scan
forms. Even if you get a $1,000 refund thirty days faster, you'd have to in-
vest that grand at about 17 percent to cover your $15.

Hired Help

The term "accountant" is loosely tossed around to describe anyone who gets paid to help prepare tax returns. In fact, there are several types of tax professionals, many of whom are not accountants, with varying levels of expertise. No matter whom you hire, it's a good idea to establish the fee structure in advance. Here are the levels of tax help you're likely to encounter.

TAX PREPARERS

This is who you'd find at H&R Block, Jackson Hewitt, as well as smaller firms that spring up in malls around tax time. Tax preparers are not licensed by anyone and often do tax work only during the tax season. They also charge the least—a basic 1040 return without many deductions or other complications will usually run about $100. The disadvantage is that a preparer may be more likely to miss a sweet deduction or credit than someone who relies on customer referrals and return business. If you have a simple return but are dead-set against doing it yourself, a preparer should be fine. But if you have lots of questions and want a professional who'll be around in six months, you're better off with someone with a higher level of experience.

ENROLLED AGENTS

An enrolled agent is licensed by the IRS, which means he must prove he's attained a certain amount of tax expertise and also continued his education; an EA is also legally qualified to represent you before the IRS if you are audited. This is a good choice for someone with a complicated return— lots of Schedule A deductions or a large number of capital gains and losses (taxable sales of securities at a profit or loss), or if you're self-employed. Expect about double the price of a tax preparer, but more expertise and the ability to contact the EA throughout the year for questions and advice. You're also more likely to use the same EA year after year than you would a regular tax preparer, so you may save time in the interview portion of the return-filing process. You also stand a good chance of getting advice on tax planning: what you should do next year to lower your tax bill.

- The National Association of Enrolled Agents (800-424-4339) will mail you a list of EAs in your area, but as with any professional, testimonials from trusted friends trump recommendations from trade groups. They also have a suitably dreary site on America Online, keyword: *NAEA.*

CERTIFIED PUBLIC ACCOUNTANTS

These are the big guns of tax preparation. Their training is rigorous and ongoing, they can represent you before the IRS and they tend to have the fiercest collection of pens in their pockets. They also charge a real lot—from $125 an hour and up. Unless your return is extraordinarily complex, CPAs are best hired on an as-needed basis, such as if you form a partnership or have a home office that employs others.

No matter whom you hire to prepare your return, you'll need to have the following documents at the ready:

• Last year's return, and the prior year as well, if you still have questions about last year's

• All W-2 and 1099 forms you received from employers, banks and investment firms

• Tax form and address labels sent by IRS and your state

• Summary of your previous year's investment gains and losses (end-of-the-year brokerage account statements include this info)

• Summary of everything that could conceivably be deducted: medical and dental expenses; proof of charitable contributions (canceled checks will do for small gifts; over $250, you should have a receipt from the charity); dependent care expenses (if you're providing more than half of someone's total support); business expenses, including car records if you use your car for work; subscriptions for work-related magazines; home expenses (especially if you've spent any money on improvements or additions); investment expenses (ask before you deduct this book); receipts for tax books, etc. Err on the side of bringing too much and your preparer will let you know if you can claim it.

• If you're a homeowner, Form 1098, which lists mortgage interest and points expenses, and your property tax statement

• A summary of retirement plan contributions

• If you've had a "casualty loss"—your prized Picasso was destroyed by

fire or thieves stole your wedding ring—bring a copy of the police/fire report and any records that verify the value of the item

Charity

When Oscar Wilde said "Charity creates a multitude of sins," he probably
didn't anticipate the tax deduction with which the IRS rewards donors.
Donations to qualifying charities can be deducted by anyone who itemizes
his deductions—remember to keep receipts for any donation over $250
and get the charity's tax-exemption certificate. "Qualified charity" means
the IRS recognizes the group as worthy of your tax-deductible dollar: religious organizations, parks, schools. Big-name charities like the Red Cross,
Planned Parenthood and the Nature Conservancy all qualify. Donations to
labor unions, social clubs, lobbyists, politicians and PACs, and tuition do
not qualify.

Money isn't the only way to help the charity, and yourself. Don't forget
to tally the value of clothes you've given to the Salvation Army and that old
computer you gave to the Boy Scouts. The IRS allows a deduction of fair
market value for clothing and goods—with the way old Levi's are priced at
chichi thrift stores, that could add up. If you're in the 28 percent tax
bracket and your state tacks on another 5 percent, a donation of $500
worth of old clothes will shave your tax bill by $165.

How Many Exemptions Should I List?

Working Americans are required to file a W-4 form, which establishes the
percentage of money to be deducted to pay Uncle Sam. These forms are essentially estimates, and the main variable besides salary is the number of
withholdings (commonly referred to as exemptions, but properly called
"allowances") a worker takes—the more exemptions, the lower the
amount deducted.

Choosing the appropriate number of exemptions can be a vexing question. Those who claim too many exemptions may have too little deducted
from their paychecks and face a big bill at tax time—and can also face
penalties for withholding an unrealistically small amount. Others, who are
chronically broke and don't want to get stuck with a tax bill they can't pay,

purposely claim zero exemptions in order to avoid that fate—or to enjoy a lump-sum refund.

In general, both strategies are awkward. Claiming zero exemptions means giving the government an interest-free loan of money that could be working for you. On the other hand, plenty of people get into a pickle claiming six deductions and then having to scramble come April 15 'cause they blew the cash on Newports and jawbreakers. So meet the IRS halfway. If you're single and childless, claim at least one but no more than two exemptions. Meantime, leave yourself some cash in an interest-earning money market fund to cover unexpected surprises.

Further Research

Taxbooks are as lethally dull as you'd expect them to be. A few that rise above the heap are *Taxes for Dummies,* the *Consumer Reports Guide to Income Tax* and, for step-by-step filing help, *J.K. Lasser's Tax Guide.*

Love and Money

Don't kid yourself about there being any big wall between love and money—they intersect at a surprising number of places. Taxes, banking, home buying, credit, debt—all these areas present financial issues for couples different from those for individuals. Some, such as the decision to commingle finances, boil down to thinking about the different styles of handling money that each person brings to the relationship. Other decisions, like whether to file joint or separate tax returns, are more cut-and-dried financial questions.

Relationships are hard enough without allowing money to get in the way. With a little effort the financial strengths of each partner can be brought to bear—one mate's shopping skill can complement the investing acumen of the other. Remember, though, it's only money. An empty wallet's easier to fill than an empty heart.

Banking

As though choosing toothpaste brands and sharing the remote are not tough enough for most couples, there's also the question of how the household money is treated. Separate versus joint bank accounts is the big question a couple faces when they decide how to commingle their financial lives. Separate accounts are familiar—each partner keeps his or her own money in it and retains sole authority to dip into it, just like single days of yore. Joint accounts are accessible to both partners for both deposits and withdrawals. So even if how they function is self-explanatory, the reasons for choosing one over the other are not always as clear.

Here's a list of the strong points of each method:

SEPARATE

• *Greater financial independence.* No one's breathing down your neck about balancing the checkbook or treating yourself to a set of Columbo tapes.

• *Protection from spouse's creditors.* If one spouse has serious credit problems or a recent bankruptcy, the other spouse should definitely maintain a separate account. This will both shelter the account holder from attachments by the other's creditors and enable the continued buildup of a positive credit history, which will help both spouses when it's time to get a mortgage or a car loan.

• *Better escape hatch.* Should disaster strike—divorce, abandonment, etc.—a separate account will leave its owner in better position to pick up the pieces.

JOINT

• *Potentially lower fees.* Most banks beat up on the little guy with high minimum balances and exorbitant transaction costs for smaller accounts. If each spouse or partner normally carries a balance of $600 and the bank charges high fees for accounts under $1,000, combining your accounts will save both of you money.

• *Less accounting hassle.* A joint account can help eliminate the hassle of deciding which partner pays which bill. And there's half the mail and half the paperwork at the end of the month.

• *Connubial solidarity.* Just as there's something freeing about maintaining separate accounts, there's something sanguine about surrendering control of individual finances to a whole that's hopefully greater than the sum of its parts.

A hybrid of joint and separate is another option. Three accounts—known as the "his, hers and ours" method (or the "his, his and ours" or "hers, hers and ours"—we're talking finance here, not lifestyle)—offer many of the best features of both joint and separate by mixing independence with the ability to pay jointly for big purchases or agreed-upon recurring expenses. But the paperwork factor and the need to maintain three different minimum balances render this option awkward for some.

If you opt for any multiaccount system (separate or hybrid), don't forget that in the world of personal finance, it never hurts to negotiate. Some banks may lower or waive minimums if you agree to keep several accounts there, or if you threaten to take your business elsewhere. Others may agree to tally the minimum by the total held in all your accounts, rather than holding each one to a strict set of conditions.

Finances have a way of bringing out the worst in a couple. Two fairly compatible spenders may soon find themselves assuming the roles of tightwad and spendthrift. Before you and your betrothed opt for joint or separate, take into account the likelihood that the method you choose will accommodate your personalities. And remember: no matter how outrageous your mate's spending patterns, you haven't even glimpsed expensive until you've been divorced.

Credit/Debt ('Til Debt Do Us Part)

Remember those kids from Wheaton, Illinois, who drove their parents, friends and town crazy by running away to establish perfect love? They probably commingled all their finances, too.

Some couples think that the best way to show their commitment is to combine every piece of their money lives into a joint financial identity. Others think that keeping things totally separate makes the heart grow fonder.

Where you and yours fall is a personal decision. But it's a good idea for each spouse to keep at least one reportable account—a credit card or loan—in his or her own name. In the event of a split or if one partner dies, it'll be easier to establish credit.

For married or engaged couples in which one partner has bad credit, it's a different story. If you co-sign a loan or open a joint credit account (or bank account), transactions will be registered on both your credit ratings.

If the one with the crappy credit ends up having to declare bankruptcy, the assets in both names may be eligible for seizure by creditors.

Prenuptial Agreements: Covering Your Assets

Prenuptial agreements are pessimistic by definition. By raising even the possibility of divorce and codifying the division of assets in that sad event, prenups tend to shackle some of the doe-eyed buzz of a wedding. On the other hand, if one spouse-to-be enters the marriage with significantly more assets than the other, prenups can actually enhance the romance by allaying concerns that the poorer one's in it for the money.

Generally, marital property consists of any assets accumulated by either spouse during the course of the marriage. Marital property may also include the increase in value of premarital property, as in the case of employment benefits (pensions, 401[k]s, and so on)—that occurs during marriage. In most cases, that marital property belongs to both spouses, depending upon the state in which the divorce occurs.

Prenuptial agreements are largely designed to protect assets obtained by one spouse either before or after the marriage, as well as limit alimony responsibilities. Thus, if prior to the marriage you inherited $100,000, you might not want the deadbeat spouse you divorce after thirty days to claim fifty large of granny's money. And you might not want to be liable for supporting the lavish lifestyle of your Thunderbird-swilling spouse after things go bad—especially if it's a lifestyle you made possible by your hard work during the marriage.

With the average age of first marriages trending higher, many soon-to-be-weds have already accumulated significant assets. Some of these who are chilled by the idea of a prenup would agree to a "partition agreement." This establishes who had what at the time of the marriage and recognizes that a large, discrete asset—an inheritance, say, or a block of stock—belongs to one spouse only and not to "the marriage." One caution, though: if the spouse with the protected assets commingles those assets with marital assets, a court may hold that the entire sum was marital property. Should you decide you need a prenup, consult a competent domestic relations attorney who can walk you through the issues germaine to the laws of your state.

Taxes

The big tax issue a married couple faces is whether to file jointly or separately. For all its talk about family values, Washington is not very friendly to married couples. Or at least the IRS isn't.

Married couples can file either as "married filing joint" or "married filing separate," but both methods often carry what's called a "marriage penalty"—a tax burden that's higher than the sum of the couple's taxes would be had they stayed single.

The whole idea of taxing couples as a unit was started to reward marriages. And it still works that way—but only if one of the spouses makes substantially more than the other and neither makes a whole lot. With the single-earner household quickly going the way of the spotted owl, it's a system that ends up punishing more couples than it helps.

In general, if the spouses' earnings are split more evenly than 70-30, they can expect to suffer a marriage penalty, with the difference increasing as the salaries of the spouses grows more equal. Let's look at a couple of examples fairly typical of what a young couple earning a total taxable income of $70,000 might face.

Couple 1

Male has taxable income of $35,000
Female has taxable income of $35,000

Married Filing Joint: $14,244
Married Filing Separate: $7,122 each, $14,244 total
Single: $6,596 each, $13,192 total

The single couple pays over *$1,000 less* than the married couple with the same taxable income.

Couple 2

Male has taxable income of $20,000
Female has taxable income of $50,000

Married Filing Joint: $14,244
Married Filing Separate: $3,000 male, $11,328 female, $14,328 total
Single: $3,000 male, $10,796 female, $13,796 total

The gap is worse when the spouses earn equal amounts. But that's cold comfort to the married-filing-separate couple in scenario 2, whose $14,328 is our worst-case scenario. Because the 28 percent tax bracket for married-filing-separate filers ends at $49,800 (compared with $59,750 for single filers), the last $200 of the married-filing-separate female's income was taxed at a King George–like 31 percent.

Adding insult to injury for married filers is the gap in standard deductions, the amount a filer can knock off his gross income to lower his taxable income. Two single filers get a personal exemption of $4,150 each, or $8,300, compared with the married filers' total exemption of $6,900.

Given the above examples, why would anyone choose married filing separate? While it's true that married filing separate usually creates a tax penalty for a married couple, there are several instances where a couple should choose that option. One example occurs when one spouse has a substantial amount of expenses that are only partially deductible, such as educational expenses. There are a million exceptions, so you'll need to tread carefully, as you do whenever you itemize. But in general, these types of expenses are deductible only once they've exceeded 2 percent of your adjusted gross income. (Medical expenses work the same way, but the deduction doesn't kick in until 7.5 percent has been exceeded.)

Here's an example of a married couple who'd be helped by filing separately. Suppose your annual gross income (AGI) is $20,000 and your spouse's is $50,000. If you spent $5,000 last year on a graduate degree in a work-related field, you could deduct $3,600 of the cost if you file jointly, because that's the amount that exceeds 2 percent (2 percent of $70,000 is $1,400, so the amount of $5,000 over $1,400 is $3,600). And the remaining nondeductible $1,400 is all paid in the 28 percent bracket the couple is in because of its taxable income between $40,100 and $96,900.

But if you file separately you'd be able to deduct $4,600 (2 percent of $20,000 is $400), or $1,000 more in deductions than the joint filers. Plus, the $400 you still have to pay taxes on will be in the lowly 15 percent tax bracket.

There is a way around the marriage penalty. It's called not getting married. Some couples who face the highest penalties are opting out of marriage altogether because of the tax burden. And because the IRS allows couples to file as singles if they spend just one day of the year single (as long as that day is December 31, the day on which a person's status is decided), some couples actually marry and divorce each other every year. This is not a strategy I recommend, especially if the DJ at your annual wedding keeps playing "You Are So Beautiful."

Congress periodically makes noises about increasing the standard deduction, which would go a long way toward eliminating the penalty. But it'd be hard to do that without also giving those single-earner couples who already enjoy a marriage bonus an even juicier slice of the pie. Meantime, those contemplating marriage can at least take solace in the fact that they'll have someone to go broke with.

Insurance

Insurance is a contract between you and a big company in which you pay a periodic sum in exchange for the company's obligation to cover unexpected or catastrophic expenses that come your way. There are a million wrinkles and products designed to obscure that essential fact. But basically that's what it boils down to: you pay someone to assume risk.

Of course, risk can mean a lot of things, for the modern world is fraught with peril. You sprain your fender. You sprain your swear finger. Your computer becomes disabled or your ability to lift heavy stuff at work does. Your house is robbed clean or crumbles in an earthquake. And don't forget the really important stuff: your dependents are left without a provider when you shake this mortal coil before your time.

Actually, the insurance industry does an excellent job making sure you don't forget these ruinous disasters. They hound you with doomsday what-if scenarios, carefully making you feel like a selfish pig for not insuring against every conceivable contingency.

Insurance is among the most complicated areas of personal finance. And that's no accident. The insurance business is financed by the sales of an enormous army of agents. These agents earn commissions every time insurance is bought. The more insurance options a customer has, the more likely he is to purchase stuff he doesn't understand (or need) and fatten the wallet of the agent pushing it.

Luckily for the befuddled consumer, there are a few simple rules that should be followed when confronting any insurance decision. We'll cover the specific nuances of different types of insurance, but before you buy any kind of coverage—health, life, auto, whatever—consider these four issues.

1. THE DEGREE OF DOOM YOU FACE IF THE EVENT OCCURS

Insure yourself only against catastrophes—those events that would financially destroy you. Insurance is often sold to cover situations that would be merely inconvenient. These policies are nearly always overpriced and play more to a customer's fear than sense. Extended warranties, homeowner's warranties, credit card unemployment policies, credit protection and riders for little things on bigger policies all fall into this category.

2. TAKE THE HIGHEST DEDUCTIBLE POSSIBLE

A deductible is the damage amount over which the insurance kicks in to help cover your losses. If your deductible is $500, and you nick your car causing damage of $450, you're out of luck—the whole repair comes out of your pocket. If the damage is $2,000, you'll have to pay only $500 of it; your insurer will pick up the remaining $1,500.

For all types of insurance, the higher the deductible, the lower the premium out of your pocket and vice versa. That makes sense. When you have a low deductible, the insurer covers every little nick and scratch. You pay for that protection with a higher premium.

Beyond its lower premium, there's another good reason to take a high deductible. Low deductibles encourage the filing of claims. Since the buyer is paying through the nose for the extensive protection, he's darn well going to file a claim every time he can. Insurers don't like that. Sure, they're happy to collect the big premiums, but they're less psyched about dealing with customers prone to filing claims. One of the first questions an insurance applicant faces is "Have you filed a claim recently?" A reputation as an overeager filer can result in higher rates or even denial of coverage. And filing lots of claims may make a current insurer drop you—remember, the insurer is under no obligation to renew your insurance. If you get dumped, you might find yourself scrambling for another insurer and fighting a reputation as a prolific claims filer.

3. THE LIKELIHOOD OF THE DISASTER

Insurers are very sophisticated marketers. They know that no one would buy plane-crash coverage while sitting at home with a calculator and a checkbook. But put a little kiosk in an airport terminal and you can bet on some poor sap filling out the form as he shakes in his boots. Policies sold on emotional appeals are among the most profitable for insurers. But if you're making an insurance decision on a whim—whether insuring a package at the PO window or doubling your tornado coverage after renting *Twister*—chances are you're making a poor decision.

4. THE COMPATIBILITY AND SERVICE QUALITY OF THE INSURER

Young people tend to buy insurance in one of two ways: they either use the same agent/company their parents use or they buy the absolute cheapest coverage they can find. Both are bad ways to shop for insurance. All types of insurance should be custom-fitted to the buyer. Your dad probably buys insurance from some guy he golfs with and treats the transaction as a social obligation. You need to find an insurer who offers policies—and prices— suitable to your situation. In the life insurance section, we'll talk more about when and if you even need an agent, but for all situations, make sure you're comfortable with the insurer's grasp of your situation and ability to offer products that make sense for you.

At the other extreme is the insurance customer who buys the absolute cheapest policy available. Young insurance consumers are often so strapped for cash that they consistently are pound foolish with insurance. Insurance is not a "get what you pay for" business. It is definitely possible to find a low-cost policy that protects you better than an expensive one. But because you rely on insurance only in times of emergency, it's important to deal with a company that can be counted on to provide the customer service and hand-holding you'll need in times of great stress. The last thing you need when your apartment's on fire or your arm's falling off is a busy signal at the claims department or a nickel-and-dime hassle over your request for compensation.

Talk to people with similar insurance situations and ask how they've been treated by their insurer. Have they been threatened with cancellation simply for filing a claim? Have claims been handled with speed, completeness, politeness and compassion? Are questions answered thoroughly and correctly on the first try? These sound obvious. But because insurance is the one product that's best if never needed, it's easy to avoid thinking about it until it's too late.

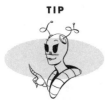

TIP

This Is Only a Test . . .

Before you buy a policy from an agent, ask what the procedure would be for filing a claim. Ideally, your insurer has a twenty-four-hour toll-free number. Call it and see what awaits—whether you're greeted by a know-nothing answering service or a claims representative who would be able to assist you in an actual emergency.

Automobile

LIABILITY

This is the most basic level of protection. If you cause an accident, you're responsible for the damages to the other car, property and people involved. Liability coverage handles damage you cause to others, but not to yourself or your car. Many states require liability coverage, but even drivers in those states that do not have it should. Not only is paying for damage you cause the right thing to do, but causing extensive damage you can't pay for is one of the worst financial jams a person can have. A judgment for a $100,000 broken limb can haunt an uninsured motorist for the rest of his days.

Even if your state requires less, look for a liability policy with at least 100/300/50 minimums—which means $100,000 maximum to each person injured, a total of $300,000 for all people injured and $50,000 for property damage.

Taking an Insurer's Financial Pulse

Apart from an insurer's intangible qualities are basic questions about its health as a business. When an insurer goes bankrupt, you risk losing the ability to collect on claims and any money you might have accumulated in a cash-value policy (more on those in the life insurance section). It's fairly uncommon for insurers to go broke, especially well-known big ones, and government agencies intervene in those that do to help policyholders recover their losses. But a few years of answering letters from people who have undergone this headache have convinced me it's one you need to avoid. Before you buy or renew any policy, investigate its solvency.

There are several agencies that rate the financial viability of insurance companies. Each uses its own letter-grading system (see chart). The insurer will tell you its grade but it might volunteer only its best marks, so check with the graders themselves for a particular company's rating. The raters use different criteria, with A.M. Best being a notoriously easy grader and Weiss Research more closely resembling Mr. Hand from *Fast Times at Ridgemont High*.

COLLISION

This covers your car in an accident, regardless of who causes the damage. If the crash is another driver's fault, then your collision policy will pay you and try to collect from the other guy's insurer, if he has one.

COMPREHENSIVE

This covers damage to your car from fire, theft and vandalism. The standard deductible is $500, but as with any deductible, the higher you go, the lower the premium and vice versa.

Insurance Rating Categories

		S&P	Moody's	A.M. Best	DCR	Weiss
Best *(Stable)*	1	AAA, AAAq	Aaa	A++	AAA	A+
	2	AA+	Aa1	A+	AA+	A
	3	AA,AAq	Aa2	A	AA	A-
	4	AA-	Aa3	A-	AA-	B+
	5	A+	A1	B++	A+	B
	6	A, Aq	A2	B+	A	B-
	7	A-	A3	B	A-	C+
	8	BBB+	Baa1	B-	BBB+	C
	9	BBB, BBBq	Baa2	C++	BBB	C-
	10	BBB-BB+	Baa3	C+	BBB-	D+
	11	BB,BBq	Ba1	C	BB+	D
	12	BB-	Ba2	C-	BB	D-
	13	B+	Ba3	D	BB-	E+
	14	B, Bq	B1	E	B+	E
	15	B-	B2	F	B	E-
	16	CCC, CCCq	B3	—	B-	F
	17	R	Caa	—	CCC	—
Worst *(Shaky)*	18	—	Ca	—	DD	—
	19	—	C	—	—	—

MISCONCEPTION Don't allow collision and comprehensive insurance to linger after the worth of your car no longer justifies them. These policies make sense only when the car is worth a lot more than the deductible. Cancel these policies on any car older than five years.

UNINSURED MOTORIST (AKA UNDERINSURED MOTORIST)

As insurance gets ever pricier, more and more schmucks are tooling around without liability coverage, or with too little. If you're hit by one of these dillweeds, or by a hit-and-run driver, your own damages—to your car and your pretty face—could easily put you in the poorhouse. You don't need uninsured motorist coverage if your car and person are already covered by other policies. But remember, your health care coverage won't cover others in your car when you're hit by an uninsured or underinsured motorist. That's not your financial problem, but keep it in mind as you refresh your defensive driving skills.

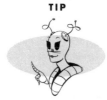

TIP

No-fault insurance is one of those ideas that's so sensible, so obviously right that it's little wonder it's had such a hard time catching on. One of the reasons auto insurance costs so much is that litigation adds a ton to the insurer's cost. Deciding who's at fault and the extent of the damages in court means greater costs for everybody and a bigger portion of the insurer's payout winding up in the pockets of lawyers rather than the injured. With no-fault insurance, litigation is entirely removed and there's no need to worry about uninsured motorists. This means drivers can pay less for insurance while still leaving more money on the table to be paid out to claimants. Don't even get me started—I'm known to go Polonius about no-fault, which is supported even by *Consumer Reports.* But if you're looking for a brilliant dissection of no-fault, its supporters and the extraordinary lengths to which its opponents (mainly trial lawyers) have gone to defeat it, dig up a copy of Andy Tobias's firsthand account of the battle in California (*Worth,* October 1996).

WARNING! Stay away from add-on policies, such as glass protection, towing insurance and riders that waive the deductible in certain circumstances.

25 Is a Magic Number

It's pretty arbitrary, but being twenty-five and being married will cut your auto insurance rates, and being female's not a bad idea either.

Expect your automobile insurance rates to drop dramatically when you hit twenty-five. Actuarial tables have deduced that twenty-five is the age when kids stop fiddling with the radio and putting on makeup to concentrate on the serious task of keeping a car between the white lines. Same thing applies to rental cars—many companies won't even rent to drivers under twenty-five.

In my case, I logged some 150,000 accident-free miles by the time I traded in the car lifestyle for Manhattan from ages twenty-three to twenty-six. By the time I resumed driving at age twenty-seven, I'd practically forgotten how to drive—luckily for me and my neighbors, my rates are now low enough that I can afford more insurance.

WHERE TO GET IT

Sometimes you can save money by purchasing two or more types of insurance from the same insurer—say, homeowner's and auto. But don't let the convenience of one-stop shopping seduce you into taking coverage that's not right for you.

Auto insurance, which had been spiraling in cost for years, is actually getting less expensive in some places, as political pressure is being brought to bear. Check with discounter Geico for prices (888-464-4111), and also with a local agent once you have quotes you can ask him to beat. *Consumer Reports* operates the Auto Insurance Price Service (800-999-6700), available to residents of California, Florida, Illinois, New Jersey, New York, Ohio, Pennsylvania and Washington. For $12 you can get quotes on up to twenty-five policies for your car, including *CR*'s rating of the companies.

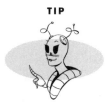

TIP Auto insurers consult a database called Comprehensive Loss Underwriting Exchange (CLUE) for info on prospective customers. This is kind of a driving credit record, with information about your claims history and driving record; a spotty report can cost you plenty in premiums or may result in your being denied coverage. Just as with credit reports, this database is far from perfect; mistakes occur and similarly named or numbered drivers may get a bad rap. If you've been turned down for coverage or quoted a price that reflects a driver with a worse record than your own, get a copy of your CLUE report. Write to the National Consumer Service Center, PO Box 105108, Atlanta, GA 30348-5108; 800-456-6004. Copies are free if insurance has been denied; otherwise, $8 (less in a couple states).

Life Insurance

Before we go any further, here are two rules about life insurance you can carry in your pocket for the rest of your days:

1. Don't buy life insurance if no one besides you depends on your income.

2. If you do need life insurance, buy only term insurance. Avoid cash-value policies—whole, universal, variable and all the other cash-value insurance.

Let's talk.

If you die, life insurance pays your survivor (or survivors) a set amount. That amount is called the death benefit, and the survivor you designate is called the beneficiary. You pay the life insurance company a premium every year not only for the death benefit, but for the security while you are alive of knowing that your loved ones will be taken care of when you croak.

Cash-value life insurance combines the death benefit and premium payment structure with a savings/investment program. A portion of your premium goes into a special account that grows over time and can be redeemed after many years, but while the insured is still living. The money in this "account" grows tax deferred and can be borrowed against at low rates.

Term life insurance is undiluted insurance. You pay a premium every year for a set number of years. If you die during that period, or "term," your beneficiary gets the death benefit set when you bought the policy. If you don't die during the period, your premiums are gone and you buy some more term insurance if there are still people depending on your income. There is no accumulation of savings, no tax advantages, no investment angle, no borrowing against it—as with auto or health insurance, there's only a benefit if calamity strikes.

So why would anyone choose term over whole, which has all those benefits? As insurance, term is a hell of a lot cheaper. For the same amount of coverage, cash-value (aka whole, universal, variable) insurance premiums are four to eight times higher than term insurance premiums. Any term buyer with the smallest amount of discipline can use the money saved on premiums to outperform the savings and investment benefits of cash-value policies.

The great majority of life insurance sold in America is whole life (and other cash-value policies), despite the shortcomings. Why? To quote an old saw, life insurance is sold, not bought. There is an army of insurance agents out there pushing whole life insurance. When you buy a whole life policy, between 50 to 100 percent of your first year's premium goes into the pocket of the agent. He deserves it—it's hard work selling an inferior product that costs more.

The reasons given for buying cash-value policies instead of term are bogus. Here's why:

• True, cash-value is paid in full after a certain number of years, while term requires payment as long as you want coverage. But that's no different from paying $100,000 over twenty years versus $50,000 over forty—sure, it'd be nice to be done paying after ten years, but not if you have to pay twice as much (more, actually, since the surplus money you keep in your pocket can be invested).

• True, you can borrow against the cash-value policy at low interest. That's mighty big of the insurer—letting you borrow your own money. If you'd put that same money into a lowly savings account, you could "borrow" it at no interest simply by withdrawing it.

• True, term life gets more expensive as you age while cash-value policies generally charge the same premium the whole time. But that's the opposite of how most people earn. Young people tend to earn more as they age and can better afford increases in term life. Rather than tying up a huge chunk of scarce dollars when they're just starting out, they should be sinking any excess cash into investments that will outperform insurance's meager returns. By the time term life gets really expensive, the ratio of a person's financial assets to the neediness of dependents usually have grown to the point where he doesn't need much insurance.

There are a couple more reasons why cash-value life insurance is not a good idea, particularly for younger people.

• Life insurance premiums are calculated by determining the likelihood that the buyer will die during the term. An insurer selling a young person a twenty-year term policy has a decent shot at never paying a dime, so the rates are low. But whole life, as its name suggests, covers the person for his whole life. The chances that a customer will die sometime during his lifetime are pretty good. So he pays more, over and above the commissions of the agent and the savings-account feature.

• The "savings-account" or investment feature of cash-value policies doesn't kick in until you've paid your premiums for several years. According to a 1997 study by the Consumer Federation of America that reviewed more than one hundred cash-value life policies, high commissions crush the returns early on in a policy's life. All told, the policies average a 13 percent loss over the first three years and only a 2.6 percent gain over ten years. It takes the average policy about fifteen years to get its return up over 5 percent. In the real world, a large percentage of people stop making payments on their insurance. Either they no longer need it (a divorce or the kids are all grown, or something else that eliminates need) or unforeseen hard times mean they can no longer afford it. With term, the worst that happens when you stop making premium payments is your insurance is canceled. With cash-value life, you can lose all the accumulated money—the feature that sold you on the idea in the first place.

 **WARNING!** To me, there's no better example of fearmongering in the cash-value life insurance business than those commercials that implore you to insure the life of your newborn or toddler. Usually there's a cute little rascal on a swing, while an ominous voiceover implies that not buying life insurance for your kid is the moral equivalent to wishing him dead. Not only is that a slimy

way to sell products, but it's bad financial advice. Yes, a person who loses a child will be plenty devastated, but not by the loss of the child's income. This talk about funeral expenses and such is nonsense—the ratio of expense to likelihood of occurrence is one of the highest in the insurance business.

Now that you're convinced you should stick with term, how much should you buy, what kind, where and how much should it cost?

HOW MUCH COVERAGE YOU NEED

Figuring out how much coverage you should have (i.e., how big the death benefit should be) is as much about peace of mind as hard-core financial considerations. Basically, it boils down to the particulars of your dependents. If you have a spouse who earns very little and two toddlers with no college savings, get enough insurance to replace your income for at least five years, and maybe ten, depending on the likelihood of your spouse being able to one day replace your income. If you have a spouse who earns the same as you and no children, you'll need far less insurance—perhaps just enough to cover the funeral expenses and a year's worth of grief over the loss of your charming companionship.

WHAT KIND OF TERM SHOULD YOU BUY?

Term insurance comes in policies of five, ten, fifteen and twenty years. A policy in which the yearly premium does not change (i.e., year one costs the same as year twenty) is called a *level premium*. There's less risk to the insurer that you'll give up the ghost in five years than in twenty, so the yearly premium is higher the longer you want to lock in the rate. Nevertheless, it's usually smart to take the longest term whose yearly premium you can afford—presuming you still expect to need the insurance at the end of the term. If you're thirty, it's worth scrounging for the first few years of a twenty-year term in order to avoid the higher premiums you'd face at thirty-five had you bought a five-year term. If you choose level premium insurance, make sure to ask if the level premiums are "fully guaranteed"— some supposedly level premiums increase after several years if circumstances change.

Another option is *annual renewable term* (ART) insurance. That means that you can renew your policy every year for an indefinite term. You won't face a new medical exam, and the rates are based on when you originally started the policy. The rates typically remain the same for the first five years of the policy, then are adjusted upward incrementally every year. This type of policy can be advantageous for three reasons.

First, the premiums are super-cheap for the first few years. Second, if you develop a serious or terminal medical condition, you can keep renewing every year. If you'd had a ten-year term policy and developed cancer that may kill you during year nine, you'd be hard-pressed to find anyone who'd insure you at all, let alone affordably. Third, it's a good idea to reassess your life insurance needs at certain critical times, such as when you have a child or take on your first mortgage. Annual renewable term allows the flexibility you'll need if you decide to up the amount of coverage or go to another insurer.

A young couple with a newborn will probably need insurance for at least twenty-two years, until the kid's out of college—longer if more kids are planned or if one spouse will continue to rely on the insured's income. I recommend ART insurance for anyone who fits either of the following three conditions: (1) is under thirty-five, or (2) has a kid less than three years old, or (3) may have another kid. You wouldn't want your twenty-year term policy to expire just as your youngest kid turned eighteen—it would be a lot more expensive to buy a new policy at that time than to renew an existing ART. But if some condition develops during the twenty years of the first policy, you might find yourself uninsurable just as your kids most need you to be covered.

When you first buy a life insurance policy, you usually need to pass a medical exam. That can be as simple as a "paramedical exam" (a nurse comes to your home or office to take your blood pressure and some pee) or a full physical. If you buy any sort of term insurance, make sure you have "guaranteed renewability," which means the insurer can't cancel your policy for health reasons before the term runs out.

WHERE TO GET IT

• USAA (800-531-8000) is a good place to shop for many types of insurance, including term life. Their sales force is uniformly helpful and they don't charge commissions. One product they offer is their annual-renewable term. The term is open-ended—the buyer can continue to renew every year without a physical until he or she is seventy. It's not a guaranteed-level, though; after the first five years, the yearly premium goes up each year you renew it.

• Several firms search for term life policies from a database that includes some four hundred insurance companies. Tell them the type of coverage you need, your age and smoking habits, and they'll check for rates, which they'll mail to you. As with a travel agency, the service is free for the user—if you buy a policy that they recommend, the insurer pays the search firm for the referral.

Quotesmith	800-556-9393
SelectQuote	800-343-1985
Termquote	800-444-8376

• Jack White & Co. (800-622-3699), a California-based discount brokerage, has an insurance division with the same no-frills, low-rate structure as its brokerage. Call them, give them your specifics and they'll send you the cheapest four quotes from companies they represent, all of which are rated A or better by A. M. Best.

• Several term-life companies have a presence on the Internet, including InstantQuote *(www.instantquote.com)* and Quotesmith *(www.quotesmith.com)*. You enter stuff like your date of birth, smoking status and amount of coverage and the sites immediately spit out several policies from several highly rated insurers.

WHAT IT COSTS

Term insurance is an incredibly competitive business. This helps the consumer—prices have actually dropped some 15 percent in the last five years. It also means that it pays to shop around.

Certain factors add or subtract to what a buyer can expect to pay: age, of course, but gender, smoking status, hazardous hobbies and occupation will also have an effect.

As a guideline, here are some sample quotes. Remember, it pays to shop around—don't assume that because you beat this quote, you've got a good deal.

For the USAA policy mentioned above ($250,000 term life, renewable annually), a twenty-eight-year-old nonsmoking male will pay $250 a year for the first five years. It'll go up to $252.50 for years six and seven. By year twenty, when the guy's forty-eight, it'll be $577 a year, and so on.

The same policy for a twenty-eight-year-old smoking female is $317.50 for the first five years; if she doesn't smoke, it'd be $222.50.

Under the same USAA plan, a nonsmoking twenty-six-year-old female who wanted only $100,000 of coverage would pay $119 a year for the first five years.

 **WARNING!** Smoking's expensive. Smokers can expect to pay about $100 more per year for $250,000 worth of coverage. If you quit, it'll take a full year without tobacco or tobacco substitutes (like nicotine patches or chewing gums) before you get nonsmoker rates. It's also not a good idea to lie about your smoking status, or any other health factor. If you die before your time, the insurer will be looking for reasons not to pay. Don't give them any.

 **WARNING!** Credit life insurance and mortgage insurance are both actually dressed-up life insurance policies. Each offers to take care of your obligation in the event that you die (credit life pays your credit card balances; mortgage insurance pays your mortgage). Both of them are rip-offs. A typical example will have someone paying about $7 a year for every $1,000 of credit card balance that the insurer will cover. But $1,000 of term life insurance usually costs a nonsmoker between $2 and $3 a year. If you're worried about dependents who will get stuck with your mortgage or bills should you meet an untimely demise, take that into consideration when buying regular term insurance.

Health Insurance

People too often can't afford or ignore health insurance. But it's actually the most important insurance there is. A health disaster that befalls an uncovered person can ruin a financial future. The last thing you want to be worrying about when you're down for the count healthwise is how you're going to pay for whatever treatment you need. Worse, those without health insurance tend not to seek the preventative care that helps stave off disaster before it starts.

Unfortunately, even with all the political noise, an amazing 40 million Americans do not have health insurance. This is one of America's greatest shames. But before I get all Hillary, let's talk about what you can do to get good, cheap health insurance.

Most large employers, and many small employers, offer health insurance to their employees through health maintenance organizations. These are basically Price Clubs for health care—HMOs keep costs down by buying physician time and medical supplies in bulk.

In general, HMOs are a great way to receive health care. There are a couple drawbacks—doctors usually must be chosen from the HMO's list, and trips to specialists usually must be approved in advance by that same doctor, who's called a primary-care physician. But those are minor hassles when you consider that many HMO plans charge just a $10 copayment for a visit and $5 for prescriptions. Obviously, the generosity of your company has a lot to do with the effectiveness and affordability of the plan. But even if you're pinched for a $100 per month or so by your employer, it's still a bargain compared with what you'd pay without coverage.

That leaves the millions of self-employed and unemployed people who don't have insurance and aren't eligible for Medicaid (the government's health insurance program for low-income Americans). The first thing an uncovered individual should do is try to obtain coverage as a member of a group. Check with every group that could conceivably count you as a member—your alma mater, professional societies, even your church, synagogue, mosque or monastery.

Failing that, you're going to have to pound the pavement as an individual. Get ready for a big expense, even if you're young and healthy. To keep costs down, get "major medical" coverage, which handles what you'd expect but leaves doctor's visits and prescriptions up to you. Take the highest deductible possible, and also the largest copayments available. You're likely going to have to take a medical exam of some sort to get health insurance, but make sure any policy you buy has guaranteed renewability, which entitles you to renew without taking a new physical every year.

Some HMOs allow individuals to join. It's typically more expensive than an employer would pay to have you in the same HMO, but less than you'd pay for non-HMO insurance—especially if you visit the doctor often.

If you're shopping for your own plan, choose one with a lifetime maximum benefit of at least $2 million. Also be sure that your policy covers at least 80 percent of the expenses above and beyond your deductible.

CAN THE GOVERNMENT HELP?

In the eighties Congress enacted the Consolidated Omnibus Budget Reconciliation Act (COBRA). For just 2 percent more than an institution had been paying for their health care, employees and students could extend their coverage for a year and a half after leaving whatever institution had been providing it. That was a lot less than it'd cost most people to get individual health care. But it did little for those with preexisting conditions or other things that made them difficult to insure, which resulted in their staying at jobs they hated simply for the medical coverage, while the companies in turn resented the employees whose special needs drove up health care costs.

When President Clinton signed the Kennedy-Kassebaum Bill in 1996, health insurers were restricted from barring applicants for a variety of preexisting conditions. Health insurance was also made more portable, so employees could take their old coverage to new jobs more easily. Critics claim the bill is filled with loopholes, and they're right. But it's a start.

CHANGING JOBS

Whenever an American changes jobs, the question of health insurance arises. Moving from a big company's HMO to self-employment—or unemployment—can create a health insurance vacuum. Even if moving from one large employer to another, there may be a gap before the new company's coverage kicks in. Be aware of this and either seek coverage under COBRA or temporary care from a regular insurer.

COBRAs Can Be Dangerous

If you leave a job, COBRA is a good stopgap until you find a new insurer. But waiting the maximum eighteen months COBRA allows until getting a new insurer isn't a good idea, even if it saves you money in premiums. If you were to develop some sort of condition, you might become uninsurable when your COBRA coverage runs out.

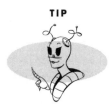

TIP

GIMME INDIE DOC

About one in three Americans goes to practitioners of alternative medicine every year. Health insurers are finally starting to wake up to this phenomenon as more and more treatments—from chiropractic to herbal remedies—are being covered by HMOs and other plans. Check with your provider for details on what's covered—HMOs, for example, usually require a referral from a primary-care physician. If you're into, or even interested in, alternative medicine, definitely consider a health plan's attitude toward it when selecting both a plan and a primary-care doctor.

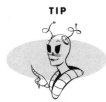

TIP

BIG BROTHER'S DOCTOR

Did you know that there's a big company keeping track of your maladies? The health insurance industry uses a database kept by the Medical Information Board to set prices when writing policies. If you're in excellent health but are denied coverage or offered rates very high compared with others of similar age and health, there may be an error in your MIB file. If you suspect there's a mistake, get a copy of your file by contacting the MIB at PO Box 105, Essex Station, Boston, MA 02112; 617-426-3660. It's free if you've been denied coverage, inexpensive if you just want to look.

Disability Insurance

Disability doesn't get much attention. When a product isn't sold very hard, however, it's often time to take a closer look. Life insurance, with its cash versus term wars, and health insurance, with its high political profile, get a lot more play. But an average young person is a lot more likely to lose his income for six months to disease or injury than he is to die. Even if he has enough health insurance to cover the medical costs, he's still looking at six months' living expenses that have to be paid.

With so many young people going into business for themselves or into start-ups with friends, disability insurance is particularly important. While many large corporations provide or offer it, a remarkable number of people simply don't buy it if their employer doesn't make it available.

Here's what to look for in disability coverage:

• A policy that pays you if you can't do work in your field, rather than one that pays only if you can't do any work. That's called "own-occupation" coverage. The last thing a Dilbert look-alike with broken wrists wants to hear from his insurer is that he could still be a tap dancer if he tried hard enough.

• A feature that allows you to collect partial benefits if your disability leaves you able to work, but not full-time.

• Guaranteed renewability, which means you won't need a new medical exam to renew your policy each year.

• Young people with low salaries that will soon be growing should consider a feature called "future insurability." This allows you to up your coverage without reapplying for coverage. Since your salary will soon be higher, you'll want to allow for the option to add to your coverage as your fortunes warrant. But if you're already making about what you're going to make in ten years, it's not worth it.

When you buy disability coverage, you'll choose the length of time after the disability occurs before the insurance starts making payments to you. This is known, somewhat ominously, as the "elimination period." Think of this as a different sort of deductible—the longer you can wait, the less you'll pay for the insurance and the less likely you'll have to file a claim. If you think you can manage it, select six months to a year. You'll also have options about what percentage of your salary you'll want replaced while you're down for the count. Again, the lower you choose, the lower the premium, so calculate what you'd be able to get by on rather than what would put you in the lap of luxury.

If you and two friends are in the market for disability, you may be able to pool your resources. Ask your agent to bill you together—a process called "list billing"—which will save you all about 15 percent.

WARNING! Don't count on Social Security to cover your disability. First, about three-quarters of applicants are rejected. Moreover, Social Security doesn't kick in until you've been disabled for more than five months, and then only if you're expected to be disabled for more than a year.

Worker's compensation only covers on-the-job accidents. Disability insurance protects you no matter where the disability occurs.

MISCONCEPTION

How Much?

Here are a couple real-life quotes of what someone might pay for disability insurance. As with life insurance, these are just guidelines—use them to get an idea of what someone with your income, risk and health might pay.

• A thirty-six-year-old nonsmoking healthy guy with a desk job making $55,000 a year can buy coverage that pays 60 percent of his former income ($2,750 a month) and kicks in after six months for about $665 per year. The yearly premium is guaranteed not to change, and the coverage is renewable every year until age sixty-seven without a physical.

• A twenty-eight-year-old nonsmoking woman making $40,000 can buy coverage that pays 60 percent of her former income ($2,000 a month) and kicks in after three months for about $740 a year.

Where to Get It

Unfortunately, individual disability insurance is not so easy to buy. The first place to look, of course, is your employer. Ask your human resources person if you're covered. Beyond that, however, your options are limited. Owing to the skyrocketing cost of claims and the lack of interest from buyers who don't appreciate its importance, disability coverage has been dropped by many firms that sold it until just a few years ago. Here are a few sellers who are still in the game, along with their caveats.

• Wholesale Insurance Network (800-808-5810) sells only the policies of Provident Life, which will insure only those with a yearly income above $47,000.

- USAA (800-531-8000) sells reasonable disability insurance but covers only a very limited amount of occupations, such as accountants and engineers. Dangerous vocations such as freelance writers and artists are excluded.
- Guardian Life Insurance writes affordable disability policies but cannot dispense quotes over the phone. Call 888-482-7342 to find an agent near you, but steel yourself for a tough sales pitch.

> "I would be loath to speak ill of any person who I do not know deserves it, but I am afraid he is an attorney."—Samuel Johnson

Capitalism doesn't work in a society unwilling to assume risk. The reason America has the most vital securities markets in the world, and the most entrepreneurial success, is that there have always been people willing to assume risk in exchange for the opportunity of reward.

Calling a long list of companies that once sold many different types of insurance but no longer do puts me in mind of the despicable lawyer ads running nonstop on daytime television. "Are you injured? Someone ought to pay." The notion that any misfortune must always result in financial compensation has done greater harm than clog our courts and make the word *justice* laughable. It has systematically removed our ability to distinguish right from wrong. We're left wondering not whether a decision is moral but only whether it is actionable.

It's not out of pity for fat cats that I so dislike the trend toward automatic lawsuits. It's not just philosophical opposition, either. The results of lawsuit mania trickle down to the average Joe in so many ways, and that's what really gets me. It's bad enough when the regular person has to pay three times as much for a ladder or have only one choice of football helmet because other manufacturers have been sued out of existence. What's happening now, though, is truly scary.

Because of legal costs, much of them from frivolous suits, vital services are being lost or priced so high that regular people go without. It's not the fat cats who don't have access to insurance. It's the blue-collar worker who can't afford disability, the freelance artist whose health no one will insure. That means that the people who can least afford it are assuming the most risk. The blame lies not just on lawyers who promote passing the buck, but on us all for refusing to acknowledge the simple fact that bad stuff sometimes simply happens.

OK, sermon over, you may now have two good Tam Tams and one good drink.

Other Insurance

Renter's insurance (homeowner's insurance is covered in the Home Buying section) protects apartment-dwellers from theft and fire. These policies make sense only if you've got a lot of expensive stuff in an apartment likely to be robbed. In general, the less insurance you need, the more you pay for a dollar of coverage (i.e., a $10,000 policy might cost $100, while a $50,000 policy costs $200). So a lot of times, the best form of insurance a renter can get is a couple of strong deadbolts.

UMBRELLA POLICIES

This is a liability policy over and beyond what your homeowner's and auto insurance would cover if a huge judgment was levied against you. Say your homeowner's policy gives you $200,000 of liability protection. A neighbor comes over for coffee, which she promptly spills in her lap. You're hit with a $500,000 judgment. Your homeowner's insurance would cover the first $200,000, but you'd need an umbrella policy to cover the rest. Because judgments over homeowner's liability ceilings are rare, umbrella coverage is pretty cheap: the first $1 million will cost about $200 a year, and each additional mil will run about $50—even less if you buy it from whoever sold you your homeowner's policy.

The federal government used to offer low-cost crime insurance, which would compensate policyholders who were victims of crime, but like a lot of sensible programs, this one recently bit the dust. A couple of states have made stabs at picking up where the feds left off, but the jury's out on their effectiveness.

Just about all other sorts of insurance are ill-advised. Remember, you're looking to protect against the big stuff. Little pocketbook expenses can be annoying, but it's almost always cheaper and easier to pay for them as they arise than to buy insurance for all of life's little irritants.

A Handy Guide to Insurance Wheat and Chaff

Coverage you should ALWAYS carry

- Health insurance
- Auto insurance (presuming you drive, smarty-pants)

Coverage you should SOMETIMES carry

- Life insurance (if anyone besides you depends on your income)
- Disability insurance (if you work for a company that does not already provide it)
- Homeowner's insurance (if you own your home)
- Umbrella liability insurance (if you have assets in excess of what your homeowner's and auto policies would cover should a judgment go against you)
- Natural disaster insurance (if you own a home in an area affected by floods and/or earthquakes, both of which are not typically covered by homeowner's policies)
- Private mortgage insurance (only if you have less than 20 percent equity in your house)

Coverage you should NEVER carry

- Home buyer's warranties
- Extended warranties on products
- Niggling little riders and add-ons to other policies
- Mortgage insurance (different from Private Mortgage Insurance)
- Credit life insurance
- Impulse insurance:
  - Mailing insurance
  - Moving insurance
  - Plane crash insurance

And Some Miscellaneous Protections . . .

Write a Will

About three quarters of Americans don't have a will. That's outrageous. Don't tell me you have nothing to bequeath. First, you probably have *something* whose ownership you'd like to specify, even if its value is purely sentimental. And there are other reasons to write a will. Most often overlooked is a parent's wishes for the care of a child. Even if you have no dependents, you may also want to specify to which cause or charity your assets go should you happen to expire. Without a will, the state will decide how to divvy your assets—you might not be thrilled by the idea of your detested aunt driving your beloved Beetle.

And don't try the old "I can't afford a lawyer" excuse. Virtually anyone can write a totally kosher will with the aid of a self-help book or one of the great software walk-through programs available. Unless your estate is particularly complicated, or you have assets substantial enough to trigger estate taxes ($600,000 if left to one person), you probably don't need a lawyer (though you shouldn't hesitate to contact one if you feel the need). Consult the following:

• *Nolo's Simple Will Book,* Denis Clifford, Esq. ($17.95), complete with forms to create a will valid in every state except Louisiana.

• *Nolo's WillMaker 6.0* (Macintosh or Windows, $29.97), a walk-through of your choice of many different forms, including a living will with instructions on heroic measures, do-not-resuscitate orders and other weighty issues featured on *ER.*

Social Security: Investigating Your Slice

You should occasionally check to see if they're recording your payments properly. Call the Social Security Administration (800-772-1213, Mon.–Fri., 7 A.M.–7 P.M.). The agency's a patience tester no matter what, but the shortest waits are before 9 A.M. and after 4 P.M., Wednesday through Friday. When a human being finally replaces the saxy Musak, ask for a copy of your earnings history. They'll send you a Personal Earnings and Benefits Statement. You'll fill it out and return it to them. And then you'll know whether all FICA donations—yours and those that your employer makes on your behalf—are being recorded correctly. You can also get the form online at the SS's tons-'o-fun website *(www.ssa.gov)*.

Add-on Warranties

Extended-service warranties on appliances, electronics and computers are a big profit booster for stores. So they're pushed aggressively, usually as the glow of making the purchase still lingers in the air. But they're a bad deal for consumers.

Extended warranty policies are essentially insurance products. The consumer pays a set amount in hopes of not having to pay a larger amount should disaster strike. But the first rule of buying any kind of insurance is to consider the degree of doom you face if the event occurs. A television blowing a picture tube on day 366 is a situation worthy of many swear words, but not a disaster. So it's not worth insuring against.

The companies selling them know that they'll end up taking in more money from the policies than they'll spend fixing and servicing what they insure. So any money over and above what they spend is profit for the warranty seller. Why give them extra profit on top of the profit they've made on the item they sold you? If the store is selling merchandise that breaks after the manufacturer's warranty expires, you should punish them by taking your business elsewhere, not reward them by buying an extended warranty.

Protect Yourself from Bogus Charities

Beware of come-ons from charities you've never heard of with quasi-legit names. These often crop up on the heels of natural disasters. There are four excellent watchdog organizations that provide information about the percentage of money collected by a charity that winds up spent on programs (rather than on advertising, administration and fund-raising) and can alert you to sham charities.

National Charities Information Bureau, 212-929-6300 or *http://www.give.org*

Council of Better Business Bureaus, 703-276-0100 or *http://www.bbb.org*

American Institute of Philanthropy, 314-454-3040

Evangelical Council for Financial Accountability, 800-323-9473 (for religious charities)

Also check out the Internet Nonprofit Center *(http://www.non-profits.org.)*. This has a searchable IRS database of all the nonprofits, so you can check whether the name of the group that just called you begging for cash is actually registered as a charity.

Claiming What's Yours: Lost and Forgotten Assets

Americans have more than $1 trillion in unclaimed assets. Abandoned bank accounts, unreturned electric company deposits, life insurance payouts that never found a beneficiary, inheritances that were never claimed—all of these wind up in the treasuries of the rightful recipient's last known home state.

Here's how to investigate whether you're among the one in ten Americans who has some found money coming, and how to retrieve it if you do. Contact the unclaimed property division, sometimes called "escheating division," of any state in which you or relatives who may have left something resided. You can find the address of all the states' unclaimed property divisions by contacting the National Association of Unclaimed Property Administrators (PO Box 1272, Jefferson City, MO 65102, or *http://www.intersurf.com/~naupa)*.

Avoid search firms, though, which tend to do exactly what you could easily do for free, then charge a percentage of any amount recovered.

What if you happen upon a long-forgotten stock certificate or a savings bond buried in an underwear drawer?

It's often difficult to determine the worth of abandoned stock certificates. Companies often go out of business, merge, are taken off the market by leveraged buyouts, etc., all of which makes the detective work on their old shares more complicated. Do-it-yourselfers might try the library, where the *Fisher Manual of Valuable and Worthless Securities* lists just about every stock there is in its fifteen volumes. Those who don't like to roll up their sleeves should consider using a search firm, which is different from random lost-property firms, because a stock certificate firm charges a flat fee rather than a percentage of recovery. Two that I recommend are R. M. Smythe and

Company (who publish the *Fisher Manual*) and a guy named Robert Fisher, who used to be the chief researcher at R. M. Smythe but now has his own business. Both charge around $50 to $75 for a search; unfortunately, it's been my experience that these shares often turn out to be worthless, so paying the cost of the search firm is something of a gamble.

- R. M. Smythe   800-622-1880
- Robert Fisher   201-945-0080

As for savings bonds, your average EE bond (the kind you probably got from your grandma for your birthday) matures after seventeen years (meaning it reaches face value) and stops earning interest after thirty. On the upper right corner of your bond will be a notation of what series your bond is (E, EE or H, in all likelihood). Beneath that will be a notation of its issue date so you'll know how long you've held it and how long it takes to reach final maturity.

So if you discover a bond older than thirty years (and any age if you're not interested in being invested in bonds), get thee to a bank to redeem at once. Savings bonds, unlike stocks or corporate bonds, can be replaced if they're lost, so long as you know the serial number. If that sounds like you, call the Bureau of Public Debt at 304-480-6112 and ask the Savings Bond Operations Office for Form 1048.

5. Enjoying It

Enjoying it? Wait a minute. You mean there's a point to all this counting, repaying, investing and protecting?

If you've got any money left to enjoy, you've almost certainly worked hard to get it. The point of all that hard work wasn't to stare at a big number on a brokerage statement, or walk barefoot through a pile of currency like Mr. Burns. You want—and deserve—to enjoy the fruits of all that discipline and austerity. Unfortunately, spending money smartly is sometimes even tougher than not spending much of it at all.

I don't believe in penny-pinching tips. Shortcuts that save a quarter but cost a dollar's worth of energy and aggravation are not my idea of smart money management. And the bulk of smart spending tips—thrift stores are cheaper than Saks, buying in bulk is cheaper than one-at-a-time—are pretty obvious. But there remain a lot of different financial challenges out there, each one waiting to gobble up money from those who confront them unawares. So here's hoping your dollars are working harder for you than you are for them.

Buying a Home

Nothing connotes the grown-up world more than home ownership. When I was a kid, I guess I assumed that somebody had just plopped my mom and dad into our house. The tremendous amount of effort and sweat and luck that go into the leap from renting to owning was invisible to me, and to most kids, I imagine.

By the time I was a teenager and started to understand how difficult even holding a fast-food job could be, I sort of gave up on the idea of owning a little chunk of America. There seemed to be something different about those who climbed the Everest of home ownership, a togetherness and élan even more foreign and imposing than other grown-up rituals, like marriage and babies and minivans.

That sense of unattainability is heightened by the fact that home ownership is such a powerful symbol of the American Dream. Americans are told in a thousand ways that owning one's home is the right thing to do. Some are subtle—television shows nearly always use a home to connote family and warmth (think of the afghan on Roseanne's couch or the thousands of viewers requesting the floor plans for the Brady's house). Apartments are for the projects *(Good Times)* or for sassy whippersnappers *(Friends, The Single Guy)*, while ownership is associated with stability even in urban living (do you suppose Mr. Drummond or the Jeffersons *rented* those righteous East Side cribs?).

Then there are the not-so-subtle hints of American bias in favor of ownership. The biggest kiss to homeowners comes courtesy of the Internal Revenue Service. It's called the mortgage-interest deduction (details to follow) and provides owners with a big financial edge over renters. At the local level, tenant-rights laws are slowly finding themselves extinct at the same time as owners become more adept at the politics of local boards and zoning codes.

Should I Stay or Should I Go Now (Buying vs. Renting)

Most people know that renting is a losing financial bet over the long haul. It doesn't take a genius to understand that paying rent for thirty years and ending up with nothing doesn't compare favorably with paying a mortgage for thirty years and ending up with a house. On the other hand, renters don't have to mow the lawn or pay the plumber when the toilet breaks. If the neighborhood turns into Beirut, renters can vanish scot-free while owners are stuck with a house that's hard to sell.

There are plusses and minuses to both methods of getting a roof over your head, many of which fall outside the realm of dollars and cents. There is no good way to calculate the precise point at which renting makes less sense than buying. It's tough to quantify the pride that accompanies ownership and you can't put a price tag on the feeling of freedom that renting offers. The decision has as much to do with individual personalities as it does with cut-and-dried finance.

Like a lot of dorky independent-minded kids, my post high school years were spent flitting from apartment to apartment. In ten years, I lived at fourteen addresses, most of which would have done the Munsters proud. One place was the first floor of a two-story house in a dicey hood on Chicago's North Side. The good news: I felt safe because of the five rottweilers that the ex-con landlord was breeding on the property. The bad news: too broke for real dog food, the landlord fed them scrap lettuce from the Heartland Cafe, resulting in a lawn that looked like a Jackson Pollack painting and could only be navigated with waders. Renters don't have much power to craft their surroundings to taste.

For freedom and mobility, it's tough to beat renting. If you're in a phase of your life where the option to pick up and leave every year is important to you, renting is probably still the best option. If you're strongly considering relocating to go to graduate school or a warmer climate, the skimpy binds of renting are probably preferable to the anchor of home ownership. Or if your career is one that requires frequent transfer, you may want to delay ownership until you've reached a point of greater stability.

Buying a home[3] triggers considerable transaction costs. There are dozens of one-time charges, ranging from lawyers to inspectors to points to wallpaper, all of which render the transaction a lot costlier than the actual price of the home. In addition, mortgages are structured so that the first several years of payment are dedicated almost exclusively to interest rather than principal. This stuff is covered in detail in the sections to come. Put simply, it's not smart to buy a house if you may move in a year or so. Unless you're committed to staying in the same location for at least three to five years, you're probably better off renting.

That doesn't mean you're trapped if you buy a place and end up hating it or suddenly needing to move. If you've made a mistake or your house is haunted, you can of course sell. But a house needs to appreciate about 10 to 15 percent to cover those initial costs, in addition to the costs of selling it. If you move before that appreciation has occurred, you'll end up eating those expenses.

Some more things to consider when weighing the buy versus rent question. Renters are at the yearly mercy of landlords. A dramatic rent increase or nonrenewal of your lease can mean a big headache. Renters also lack borrowing leverage, which means they can't borrow money using their home as collateral, as you can when you own. Finally, renters have both less incentive and less freedom to craft their surroundings to their liking. Everything from pets to painting is regulated to some degree by the land-

---

[3] By "home" I mean house, condo, co-unit or any dwelling that involves a mortgage and ownership.

Enemies: One Renter's Story

In the real world, it's almost as hard to evict a problem tenant as it is to bring a negligent landlord to task. Guerrilla renting stories are commonplace in any big city. One 'zine editor I know recently ended a year-long deadlock with his landlord. "I'd cut off my nose and ears to spite my face with this guy" was the perky way the tenant described his strategy. Indeed, he spent over a year with no hot water and no heat after a dispute about his noisiness could not be resolved. "I lived like an animal for a year, but I paid no rent. It cost my landlord thousands more in court appearances and lost rent from other tenants I chased away. Eventually, knowing that the marshal was coming soon, I decided to bolt. But first I broke everything in sight. I poured cement down the drain, glued the locks, and for the pièce de résistance, I bought two dozen West Indian cockroaches from the pet store. These things are big as a thumb and multiply instantly."

lord. And even if you find a landlord cool enough to allow prettifying your apartment, there's little point when you'll probably move shortly. Basically, you end up exchanging life in a place that's how you want it now for the freedom to move easily to another in the future.

How Homes Are Bought

It's understood that most homes aren't paid for with a suitcase full of cash. The overwhelming majority of homes in America are bought with a small amount of the buyer's money and a great big loan. The buyer's cash is called the down payment and the loan is called the mortgage.

Sounds pretty simple, right? But the exact procedure behind obtaining a mortgage—and even what a mortgage is—remains a mystery to many first-time home buyers.

WHAT THE HELL'S A MORTGAGE?

A mortgage is an agreement that pledges a piece of property to a lender as collateral until the debt is repaid. Obviously, in this case we're talking about borrowing from a bank or other institution to buy a home and pledging that home as the property that the bank can seize if the debt goes unpaid. Put more simply, a mortgage is the most money you've ever borrowed.

As with all debt that doesn't originate with your dad (and some that does, depending on your dad), mortgage lenders make money by charging you interest. Mortgages belong to a special kind of debt that's called "amortized." That means that the percentage of your monthly payment that is applied to repayment of the principal is predetermined by the length, or "term," of the loan (typically thirty years, sometimes fifteen). The percentage that's applied to interest is huge toward the beginning of the loan, but as the years go by, the monthly payment begins to apply more to the principal and the borrower begins building equity in the home more quickly.

Let's take a look at just how a real mortgage works. Say you buy a $115,900 home on January 1, 1999. For simplicity's sake, we'll presume you pay nothing down and borrow the entire amount at 8 percent interest.

Your monthly payment will be $850 (actually, it's $850.43, but rounding is divine). By December, you've paid one-thirtieth of the total loan. But that doesn't mean you now own one-thirtieth of the house. Because of the way amortized debt is stacked in favor of interest toward the beginning of the term, only $968 of the $10,200 you shelled out over the year is applied to principal, with the remainder going in the bank's pocket ($850/month = $10,200 for the year). So you actually own less than one-one hundredth of the house.

Before you despair, however, remember that the money you spend on mortgage interest is fully tax-deductible. The $9,232 deduction in this case will reduce the tax bill of most people substantially. As the years pass, a greater percentage of that $10,200 is applied toward the principal. Ten years hence, in 2008, that same $10,200 is divided about $^{80}/_{20}$ with $8,220

Here's a detailed look at how equity builds over time.
For 1999, here's how it breaks down:

	Principal	Interest	Balance
January	$77.77	$772.67	$115,822.23
February	$78.28	$772.15	$115,743.95
March	$78.81	$771.63	$115,665.14
April	$79.33	$771.10	$115,585.81
May	$79.86	$770.57	$115,505.95
June	$80.39	$770.04	$115,425.56
July	$80.93	$769.50	$115,344.63
August	$81.47	$768.96	$115,263.16
September	$82.01	$768.42	$115,181.14
October	$82.56	$767.87	$115,098.59
November	$83.11	$767.32	$115,015.48
December	$83.66	$766.77	$114,931.81

So for the whole year, here's how it looks:
Principal = $968.19 Interest = $9,237.01 Balance = $114,931.81

And here's how the remaining 29 years work out:

Year	Principal	Interest	Balance
2000	$1,048.55	$9,156.65	$113,883.27
2001	$1,135.57	$9,069.62	$112,747.69
2002	$1,229.83	$8,975.37	$111,517.87
2003	$1,331.90	$8,873.30	$110,185.96
2004	$1,442.45	$8,762.75	$108,743.51
2005	$1,562.17	$8,643.03	$107,181.34
2006	$1,691.83	$8,513.37	$105,489.51
2007	$1,832.25	$8,372.95	$103,657.26
2008	$1,984.33	$8,220.87	$101,672.93
2009	$2,149.03	$8,056.17	$99,523.91
2010	$2,327.39	$7,877.80	$97,196.51
2011	$2,520.57	$7,684.63	$94,675.94
2012	$2,729.77	$7,475.42	$91,946.17
2013	$2,956.34	$7,248.85	$88,989.83
2014	$3,201.72	$7,003.48	$85,788.11
2015	$3,467.46	$6,737.74	$82,320.65
2016	$3,755.26	$6,449.94	$78,565.39
2017	$4,066.94	$6,138.26	$74,498.45
2018	$4,404.49	$5,800.70	$70,093.96
2019	$4,770.07	$5,435.13	$65,323.89
2020	$5,165.98	$5,039.22	$60,157.91
2021	$5,594.75	$4,610.45	$54,563.16
2022	$6,059.11	$4,146.08	$48,504.05
2023	$6,562.02	$3,643.18	$41,942.03
2024	$7,106.66	$3,098.54	$34,835.37
2025	$7,696.51	$2,508.69	$27,138.86
2026	$8,335.32	$1,869.88	$18,803.54
2027	$9,027.15	$1,178.05	$9,776.39
2028	$9,776.39	$428.80	$0 (Woo-Hoo!)

Total Interest paid: $190,255.93

toward interest and $1,984 toward principal. By 2018, it's nearly fifty-fifty (interest, $5,800/principal, $4,404). By 2028, the last year of the loan, nearly the full $10,200 goes to the bricks and toilets of the principal—just $429 goes to the bank.

A mortgage, like all debt, is a compound interest problem in reverse. Consider the above-mentioned $115,900 thirty-year loan at 8 percent. By the time you're done paying it, you'll have laid down a total of $306,156. In other words, $190,256 on top of the original loan is paid in interest— nearly twice as much as the principal.

MORTGAGE PREPAYMENT

One way to raise the ratio of principal to interest is to pay more than the required monthly payment. Prepayments are credited entirely to the principal of the loan so they can really speed the building of equity. Because mortgages use compound interest over a long time horizon, the effects of even small payments can be striking.

Let's use the example of the $115,900 home from above to see how contributing an extra $100 a month saves a borrower. That extra $100 will shave almost nine years off the length of the loan, saving the borrower a total of $66,356—a pretty good return on an investment of just over $25,000.

A slightly different form of mortgage prepayment comes in the form of bi-weekly payments, which functions just like it sounds and can end up saving the borrower plenty.

Whether to prepay or not relies in large part on the interest rate of the mortgage and the rate that would be achieved were the money invested elsewhere. A borrower with a mortgage at 7 percent will likely be better off sticking that extra $100 in a mutual fund, especially if he has access to tax-deferred investment opportunities, such as an IRA. On the other hand, someone borrowing at 10.5 percent would likely benefit from applying that hundred bones toward a prepayment. Those who have a tough time finding the will to invest can think of prepayments as an easy way to force an investment program. You're already writing the check—adding a couple bucks nets a guaranteed return of whatever the rate of your mortgage. As always when weighing investment versus debt repayment, the rate's the thing that'll catch the king.

THE BASKIN-ROBBINS OF BORROWING

Mortgages come in a dizzying array of flavors. The two basic types are *fixed* and *adjustable.* Fixed-rate mortgages are easy. The interest rate and monthly payments stay the same for the entire length of the loan.

Adjustable-rate mortgages, or ARMs, have an interest rate that changes along with a widely followed benchmark. All ARMs operate the same way: Index + Margin = Rate. The bank will use an index—the one-year Treasury bill, or the cost-of-funds index of the 11th district (called a COFI loan—pronounced like *coffee*). Then they add an agreed-upon margin, say 3 percent, to determine the rate a borrower pays. That means that the rate is essentially set by where interest rates are going.

The reason ARMs exist is that banks get burned when rates go higher and they can't raise the rates on all the fixed-rate money they've got out there. Borrowers can often refinance if rates drop, but lenders are stuck with their pants down when interest rates rise—they can't just jack up the rates on all those fixed-rate loans they've written. ARMs were created so that borrowers shoulder some of that risk.

In exchange for assuming that risk, consumers often get a better initial rate on an ARM than they'd get on a fixed rate. But we've already seen how small changes in rates can have big consequences in a borrower's monthly payment. A 1 percent jump on a $200,000 loan means an additional $142 per month, so you can imagine how the rate swings of the late seventies and early eighties were whipsawing homeowners with ARMs.

To smooth some of the bumps, ARMs are required to have *caps.* These control the amount that the rate can change in any one adjustment period (usually a year, sometimes monthly) as well as how much they can change over the life of the loan.

Because ARMs come in such wide variety, comparing offers between two lenders is extremely aggravating. One bank's COFI ARM with a margin of 3 percent that's fixed for three years may or may not be a better deal than another bank's six-month T-bill ARM with a margin of 3.5 percent that's fixed for seven years. The comparison is based not only on a prediction of the direction (not the direction, really, so much as the intensity) of those two indexes and knowledge of where they're at today, but also an analysis of how likely the borrower is to stay in the home long enough to outlast the initial fixed portion.

Don't beat yourself up if all this confusion sends you scurrying for the relative comprehensibility of fixed-rate loans. At a time of relatively low historical rates, ARMs are aggressively pushed by lenders. That alone is often a good reason to buy something else.

Tease, Tease

ARMs often lure borrowers with super-low rates good for the first few years of the loan. These are especially attractive to young borrowers, who figure their ships will

MISCONCEPTION

have come in by the time the rate is ratcheted up. But unless a borrower has a real strong reason to suspect that she'd soon be able to afford the high end of the range, she's better off borrowing less with a fixed rate or getting an ARM with a higher initial rate but a lower margin.

Balloon Mortgages

These function like regular fixed-rate mortgages, charging regular payments that are weighted toward interest

at front. Except with balloon mortgages, the entire balance becomes due on an agreed-upon date, usually after only five to ten years. Because the lender is gambling on the direction of interest rates only for a short time, it can afford to offer lower rates than most fixed loans. Don't be seduced by that low rate—the lender knows a certain percentage of balloon borrowers won't make the final payment and will have to forfeit the house. Unless you're absolutely positive that you'll have the balloon payment when it comes due, these are best avoided.

How Much House Can You Afford?

Once you've decided to take the ownership plunge, the first thing you should establish is how much you can spend on a home. Unfortunately, there is no simple recipe for determining exactly what amount suits your income, assets, obligations and spending habits. Luckily, the lenders of America think there is.

I PITI THE FOOL

When you buy a home, lenders will make assumptions about what you can afford. They don't want you borrowing more than you realistically can repay. So they've come up with a formula for establishing a ballpark figure.

Every month, a mortgage holder pays these home-related expenses:

- mortgage payment, which consists of principal and interest
- property taxes
- homeowner's insurance (and sometimes private mortgage insurance)

Together, these expenses are known as PITI—Principal + Interest + Tax + Insurance (condo, co-op and townhouse buyers should include association and maintenance fees). You're in good shape if your monthly PITI is less than 28 percent of your monthly income before taxes.

Another benchmark is if your total monthly debt payments (PITI + other loans, like car, credit cards, student loans, etc.) are less than 36 percent of your monthly income.

Remember, these are just rules of thumb. Solid credit history, a higher down payment, length of employment and intangible "solid citizen" stuff all help. And, of course, the opposites of the above hurt.

What does all this mean? Let's look at the numbers in home #1 from the sidebar, the "Horse of a Different Color" (page 228). Its selling price is $115,900, and the loan amount (80 percent) is $92,720. Realistic monthly expenses are $680 for the mortgage payment, $193 in property taxes and $48 in homeowner's insurance. So that's a total PITI of $921. A lender will look favorably on an applicant with a monthly income of $3,289 ($921 is 28 percent of $3,289), or about $40,000 a year.

Home buyers with lots of other debt might want to consider the other benchmark. Suppose a couple looking at the house in the example above have a car loan that costs $250 a month, student loans of $150 a month and credit bills of about $200 a month. That $600 plus the PITI of $921

How to Estimate a Monthly Mortgage Payment

Rate	Monthly Payment per $10,000 Borrowed (30-year mortgage)
6.0%	$60.00
6.5%	$63.20
7.0%	$66.50
7.5%	$69.90
8.0%	$73.40
8.5%	$76.90
9.0%	$80.50
9.5%	$84.10
10.0%	$87.80

Example: Borrowing $100.000 at 8 percent would mean a monthly mortgage payment of $734.

means a total debt load of $1,521. The couple's combined pretax income should be about $4,225 ($50,700 a year) to look good on a mortgage application.

The Down Payment

The biggest obstacle for most first-time home buyers is amassing the mountain of cash known as the down payment. So the first thing to do when contemplating a home purchase is to assess what kind of down payment you can put together.

Time was, people without 20 percent of the purchase price would get kicked out of the bank without a Dum-Dum. Lenders are much more flexible these days. Borrowing 90 percent or even 95 percent of a home's price is common, and borrowing the entire purchase price (i.e., putting no money down) is no longer impossible. In fact, about half of the 5 million or so homes sold in America each year are now purchased by buyers who borrow more than 80 percent of their home's purchase price. Many pro-

Mortgage Interest:
The Last Great Tax Shelter

The buyer about to pile on debt that would sink a small nation can take solace in the last great tax break for the little guy: the mortgage interest deduction.

The borrower in the $115,900 home example we used above would pay $9,232 in interest in his first year of home ownership. That entire amount is tax deductible. Suppose a young married couple with a combined adjustable gross income of $55,000 owned that house. Subtracting $9,232 from $55,000 means the couple pays taxes on an AGI of only $45,768. Since they're in the 28 percent tax bracket, they'd shave a whopping $2,585 off their tax bill.

The significance of the mortgage interest deduction, nifty as it is, is somewhat oversold (mostly by banks and mortgage brokers). It sometimes doesn't help those homeowners who arguably need it most. Like any tax deduction, it comes into play only if the taxpayer is itemizing deductions and has deductions greater than the standard deduction to which every filer is entitled. Second, the less a homeowner earns, the less it helps because the tax bracket structure puts poorer people in lower brackets. Nevertheless, the mortgage interest deduction is a big trump card for ownership.

grams are geared specifically toward the first-time home buyer with a bright future but limited means.

• State housing agencies are an excellent source of financing for low-down-payment first-time buyers. There are usually ceilings on the income level and purchase price for borrowers (they're not about to grease the wheels for a whippersnapper millionaire's mansion). But many programs arrange for loans to borrowers with as little as 3 percent down, with interest rates as much as a point lower than the going market rate. Those buying in hard-hit urban areas are sometimes rewarded with extra incentives.

What If I Don't Need a Mortgage?

Say you just inherited $200,000 and the house you've been eyeing costs exactly that. Is it smart to forgo a mortgage altogether and simply pay cash for the whole thing?

It depends. If your personality is such that any sort of debt gives you the willies, plunking down the purchase price is an option. Not an entirely unattractive option either: not having to pay 8 percent in interest is the same as getting a guaranteed 8 percent return on an investment—not bad. (It's not exactly the same, actually; since mortgage interest is tax deductible, avoiding a mortgage actually produces slightly lower gains than the percentage the loan would be at. The precise amount lower depends on the borrower's tax bracket.)

Assuming you're not opposed to debt on moral (or even religious) grounds, however, I don't recommend paying more than 30 percent down on a first home, at least not while interest rates are in the 8 percent range. There're simply too many opportunities out there to do better than that, and a young person can and usually should avail herself of greater risk in hopes of greater reward.

There's also a lot of uncertainty, which doesn't favor having all your dough locked up in an illiquid investment like a house. You may be flush now, but you might need that money for an emergency or opportunity. Yes, a home equity loan is always a possibility, but borrowing when you're desperate is seldom cheaper than using your own money.

It's true that paying entirely in cash eliminates the grueling mortgage-approval process. But putting down 30 percent of the purchase price will greatly ease the process, even if your credit isn't spotless. It will also leave you 70 percent to do with as you choose. Of course, if "what you choose" are low-yielding fixed-income investments, it probably doesn't make sense to pay a mortgage at 8 percent while collecting 5 percent.

Remember, when you own your home, it's not just your shelter, it's a substantial investment. So think of it this way: using your capital on a house is a lot like investing in a real estate investment trust that has only one property and you as investment manager. Unless that sounds like an investment you'd make, you're probably better off with the bulk of your money in conventional investments rather than putting it all into the bricks and shingles that surround you.

Those who find mortgages ominous and suffocating might not be surprised that the term comes from the French words *mort* and *gage*—"dead" and "pledge."

Examples: Illinois offers a Springboard Mortgage Program that permits qualified first-time buyers to borrow with only 2 percent down, and provides up to $5,000 in closing cost assistance. California arranges for first-timers to secure ARMs with margins at bargain-basement levels. Call your state's housing agency or finance authority for details.

• The Federal National Mortgage Association is a true friend to the hard-up first-time home buyer. Also known as Fannie Mae, this quasi-government lending agency offers a variety of programs that make it possible to buy a home with little up-front capital.

Three Fannie Mae programs to consider:

1. If your income is less than the average for the city in which you hope to buy, special loans are available that require only a 3 percent down payment.

2. One loan they offer has a down payment of 5 percent and allows the borrower to make initial monthly payments below the normal payments for the first two years. This method builds equity even slower than usual, of course, but it's suitable for those with low-but-growing current incomes.

3. The three-two loan, a 5 percent-down loan in which a parent contributes two fifths of the down payment and the grateful, vegetable-finishing kid puts down the remaining three fifths.

Many mortgage lenders have their own Fannie Mae–associated pro-

So What's a House Really Cost?

Calculating whether home ownership is within reach can be complicated. A look at some real-life scenarios provides a window on what it actually costs.

Here are three different homes from real newspaper ads. For the sake of this exercise, I've built in a set of assumptions. They're realistic—conservative, even—but different circumstances will impact your ability to afford similarly priced homes.

Assumptions:

- You bought the house for 95 percent of the price listed in the ad
- Property taxes: 2 percent of purchase price
- Mortgage: thirty-year fixed with three points at 8 percent (7.5 percent for the fifteen-year mortgage scenario)
- Homeowner's insurance: .5 percent of purchase price per year
- Down payment: 20 percent (for home #1, there's also a scenario for a 10 percent down payment; for that one, the mortgage crept up to 8.25 percent and private mortgage insurance added another .5 percent of the loan amount to the yearly cost)

HORSE OF A DIFFERENT COLOR

Entirely different from any other Townhouse, this modern structure has a large, appealing kitchen, finished basement and a huge master bedroom. Skylights show off the recent redecorating and pretty oak floors. **$122,900.**

Home 1

Advertised Price: $122,900
Purchase Price: $115,900
Loan Amount: $92,720 (8 percent 30-year fixed)
Down Payment (20 percent): $23,180
Points: $2,782
Mortgage payment: $680

Property tax: $2,318/year; $193/month
Homeowner's Insurance: $579/year; $48/month
Total monthly cost (PITI): $921

With a 10 percent down payment . . .
Advertised Price: $122,900
Purchase Price: $115,900
Loan Amount: $104,310 (8.25 percent 30-year fixed)
Down Payment (10 percent): $11,590
Points: $2,782
Mortgage payment: $784
Property tax: $2,318/year; $193/month
Homeowner's Insurance: $579/year; $48/month
Private Mortgage Insurance: $528/year; $44/month
Total monthly cost (PITI): $1,069

With a 15-year mortgage . . .
Advertised Price: $122,900
Purchase Price: $115,900
Loan Amount: $92,720 (7.5 percent 15-year fixed)
Down Payment (20 percent): $23,180
Points: $2,782
Mortgage Payment: $860
Property Tax: $2,318/year; $193/month
Homeowner's Insurance: $579/year; $48/month
Total monthly cost (PITI): $1,101

NO PLACE LIKE HOME

High ceilings and parquet floors dominate this
renovated pre-war condo. Also featuring pocket
doors and huge bay windows. Closets a-plenty, a
marvelous eat-in kitchen and a "jacuzzi" bath
are also included in this 2br dream apartment.
$155,000.

Home 2

Advertised Price: $155,000
Purchase Price: $147,250

Loan Amount: $117,800 (8 percent 30-year fixed)
Down Payment (20 percent): $29,450
Points: $3,534
Mortgage Payment: $864
Property Tax: $2,945/year; $245/month
Homeowner's Insurance: $736/year; $61/month
Total monthly cost (PITI): $1,170

LUCKY THIRTEEN!

You can beat the odds and buy a quality home in a great location for under $200,000. Delightful 3br Colonial on a quiet street near schools and trans. Lots of extras, including first-floor powder room, ceiling fans, modern kitchen, new roof. **$199,000.**

Home 3

Advertised Price: $199,000
Purchase Price: $189,050
Loan Amount: $151,240 (8 percent 30-year fixed)
Down Payment (20 percent): $37,810
Points: $4,537
Mortgage Payment: $864
Property Tax: $3,025/year; $252/month
Homeowner's Insurance: $945/year; $87/month
Total monthly cost (PITI): $1,203

These models were built with the help of an elegant little website designed by Hugh Chou:
http://www.mikron.com/mort.htm.

grams, which go under a variety of brand names. When you're shopping for a mortgage, ask the loan officer about any Fannie Mae loans they offer. You might also inquire about loans associated with Fannie Mae's competitor, Freddie Mac (Federal Home Loan Mortgage Corporation), which offers several small-down-payment loans of their own. One caveat: both agencies are sticklers for good credit records, so get your affairs in order.

• *PNC Mortgage.* A national lender with offices all over the country, PNC's conventional loans require just 5 percent down. They also arrange for Federal Housing Authority–backed loans for first-timers that require even less down. Call 800-665-1082 for an office near you.

• *Gifts and "gifts."* If someone gives you a substantial chunk of money to apply toward a down payment, you'll have to get the giver to sign a notarized letter stating that the money was given free and clear. This is so that the lender can accurately judge just how deeply in debt you are when assessing whether you can afford the payments on the loan. But because most gifts of that size involve parents or other relatives, it's pretty easy to get them to sign such a letter even if the money is actually a loan. I'm not necessarily recommending this method. Lenders have those guidelines for a reason and if they say a borrower is too deeply in debt, there's a good chance they're right. But loans masquerading as gifts happen all the time, so the maneuver bears mentioning.

• *Borrow from your 401(k) plan.* Many plans offer penalty-free loans if the money is applied to a down payment. This counts as a loan, so it'll affect that 36 percent total indebtedness figure banks consider. But because you're making the payments to yourself when you borrow from your own retirement plan, it's less painful than borrowing from an outside source. Like any raid on your 401(k), this is a good choice only if you're real certain of staying in that job until the loan's repaid.

Closing Costs

Buying a house triggers a flurry of one-time expenses known as closing costs. These include fees for the application, credit checks (that the borrower has to pay for these when they're intended to protect the lender irks me), appraisal of the land, a "commitment" fee, flood certification and tax service fees. There are also the inspection fee, the lawyer's bill, points (explained later) and a million other niggling little fees that crop up. When calculating how much house you can afford and how big a down payment you can muster, factor in closing costs of at least 4 to 6 percent of the home's purchase price.

Homeowner's Insurance

If your house were destroyed, chances are you wouldn't stick around for thirty years to keep making payments. So most lenders require borrowers to prove they have insurance that will cover them in the event of theft or destruction. Homeowner's insurance costs about .5 percent of your home's value per year—more or less based on a variety of weirdo factors such as whether the house has a buried oil tank on the property, bite history of certain dogs, proximity to tidal waters, number of smoke detectors, quality of locks and presence of a burglar alarm. As with all insurance, lower your costs by getting the highest possible deductible. But don't skimp by going with a disreputable company—the last thing you need when your house is in ashes is an insurer that can't be reached.

Even if it weren't required by lenders, homeowner's insurance is a good idea. A homeowner's policy protects three separate things:

• The home itself, if damaged by fire or a tree falling on it or whatever (though not floods and earthquakes, as we'll see later on)

• The stuff in the home, if stolen or destroyed

• Damage you, your family and pets do to others at your home, or in many cases outside your home

Here are some things to keep in mind about each of the three protections.

In the event of total destruction, some homeowner's policies cover only what it would cost to buy a similar home. You're better off with a policy that offers "guaranteed replacement cost." Say your beloved bungalow was completely destroyed by lightning. A regular policy might pay you the $100,000 that similar houses would sell for on the open market. But "replacement cost" means that if it cost $150,000 to rebuild your house from scratch, the insurer would cover it.

The typical homeowner's policy assumes that the contents of the house are worth half of the house itself. This is usually plenty, but make sure your coverage is for the "replacement value" of your stuff, not the value of an item at the time it was destroyed or stolen. If you have lots of valuable furniture or equipment, you should up the value of the contents part of the policy, which is relatively inexpensive. Some contents, notably expensive jewelry and furs (not that you'd ever have furs—as if!), often need to be insured separately, with a policy called a rider. Ask whoever sells you the policy to specify things that are not included in the policy and avoid companies that exclude from the main policy a lot of stuff you own. Be prepared to document any losses from a robbery—the insurer doesn't have to take your word for it. One simple method is to walk a camcorder through your house, taping all your groovy gear. But don't leave the tape in the camera—it'll probably be among the dear departed.

A homeowner's policy also features liability insurance. If you're accused or held liable for something, your insurer will provide a lawyer to defend you and pay judgments against you. This covers judgments against you from lawsuits by those injured on your property, or if your dog bites a neighbor off your property, or if you accidentally knock someone over while jogging in the park. Check to make sure your liability coverage is as broad as possible, protecting you from as many of these scenarios as you can imagine. If the liability coverage on the policy you like only covers the value of 100 percent of your financial assets (including your house), ask how much it'll cost to up that figure to 150 percent or even 200 percent. It's usually not much extra, and can be well worth it—especially if you tend to host toga parties or leave upturned rakes on your lawn.

An American Liability Story

My dad used to shock and amaze his easily shocked and amazed kids by telling the perhaps apocryphal story of the burglar who stole a guy's ladder. Using the ladder to break into the guy's house, the burglar fell and injured himself. You had to see my dad's expressive round face twist with outrage as he reported that the thieving scoundrel prevailed in a lawsuit against the man whose broken ladder injured him.

Don't confuse homeowner's insurance, which pays for your stuff if it's ruined, with mortgage repayment insurance, which pays off your mortgage if something happens to you. The former's a must-have, the latter's a rip-off.

WARNING! Oddly enough, the disaster that most often ruins houses, flooding, is typically not covered by homeowner's insurance. Those at risk (which means anybody who's ever heard of the Mississippi River) can find out where to get a flood insurance rider through the government's flood insurance program (800-638-6620).

Mortgage Shopping

This is the most frustrating part of the home buying process. While shopping for a house is difficult, there's at least the fun of picturing yourself in all these different places, imagining what you'd do with the metallic wallpaper and poison ivy. With a mortgage, it's pure stress. It's also humiliating. Get ready to explain—and prove—why you were thirty days late with a credit-card payment four years ago, moved five times in five years, and how a big one-time deposit you just put in your bank account was from a book advance and not a gas station stick-up.

We've already discussed what a mortgage is and how they work. Now we'll cover how to find one that makes sense for you.

The first thing to do is to fish out the pertinent documents from the shoe box in which you've been storing all your records. Here's a list of what you'll need:

- Bank statements for all accounts—savings, checking
- Credit card statements (preferably showing a zero balance)
- Brokerage statements, including IRA and 401(k) summations
- Student loan account statements. If you've paid off one or more of them, bring the paid-in-full statement that the loan servicer sends.
- Tax returns for the last two years
- Several recent pay stubs

- A copy of your marriage certificate (if you're married, duh)
- Several months worth of utility bills (to show that you pay on time—not all utilities report late payments to credit ratings bureaus)
- Auto loan statement; year and make of any car you own or lease
- Cash-value life insurance policies (whole, universal, variable, etc.)
- Proof of expected income from other sources (contracts for freelance jobs, for example)
- Canceled rent checks, as many as you can find (to demonstrate timely payments)

Ask around. People you know who are satisfied with the deal they got can point you in the right direction. Just about everyone in your new neighborhood will have advice about mortgages. It's not always easy to ask people about this stuff. But it's just too important to let bashfulness force you into choosing a lender that might not be best for you. Ask your realtor for some recommendations, but be wary of using someone your realtor "always works with." Interview at least three different lenders and feel free to walk away any time you feel uncomfortable with the sales tactics.

Writing mortgages is an incredibly competitive business. That means that shopping around can uncover big differences in rates—as much as a full point. As with investing, small differences can add up fast. On a loan of $150,000, a loan at 8 percent means a monthly payment of $1,100. At 9 percent, it's $1,207. Over the life of the loan that's a difference of $38,520. That's more than enough to cover the sedatives you'll need after shopping for a mortgage.

The most important factor of a mortgage is the rate. But signing a mortgage puts you in a long-term relationship with the lender. Good service and patience for questions are critical.

Mortgage Brokers

Mortgage brokers are just like a mortgage shoe store: they buy mortgages from several different lenders and sell them to you at a markup.

The advantage is that the broker has a sense of what loan's right for a borrower and where a borrower's credentials need beefing up. Mortgage brokers are particularly useful for first-time home buyers because they're usually less skittish about borrowers with sketchy credit or skimpy down payments.

Find a broker by recommendation, not by picking a name out of the phone book. While the right one can offer far more options than you'd discover by shopping yourself, a lazy or overly aggressive mortgage broker can cost you thousands of dollars or steer you into a loan that's a better deal for him than for you. At the very least, ask the broker for referrals. And make sure the broker deals with at least five to ten lenders—fewer than that, you could do the work yourself.

Some brokers are paid by the lender, some charge the borrower a fee, some do both. The method doesn't really matter, but if you have reasonable credit, your total cost should be no more than 2 percent of the loan amount. Get the broker to specify the amount he's paid in advance.

• All but eight states license mortgage brokers. You can call a state's banking agency to make sure your broker is licensed and hasn't been hit with any disciplinary actions.

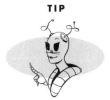

TIP Like everything else, the appraisal that the mortgage lender performs on your house is going high-tech. Many banks now offer a service that judges whether your house is roughly worth what you're paying simply by checking a database that lists recent selling prices in your neighborhood. Not only can this shave a week or so off your closing, it usually costs about $75 less. Ask your lender if they offer this service and use it as the deciding factor between two otherwise equal lenders.

What the Hell's a Point?

A point is 1 percent of the loan amount. Used primarily as sales commissions, points are paid by the borrower to the lender at the time of the loan. A $100,000 loan with three points will cost the borrower $3,000 up front. So why would anyone agree to pay points? There's a relationship between points and interest rates. In general, the more points a borrower pays, the lower the interest rate the bank will offer. They're also tax-deductible.

Points are negotiable and should be paid reluctantly, especially by those who may not stay in a house longer than ten years. Lenders are required by the Truth in Lending Act to include points when representing interest rates to customers. (That's why you sometimes see an ad trumpeting 7.5 percent rates, then mention of an 8 percent annual percentage rate right next to it.)

Private Mortgage Insurance

To me, the initials PMI will always stand for Phyllis's Musical Inn, a dive on Division Street like something out of Nelson Algren. But in the world of home buying, they're an insidious irritant. Borrowers who pony up less than 20 percent are usually required by lenders to carry private mortgage insurance, which takes over the loan should the borrower vanish or go bankrupt. It'll add another .5 percent of the cost of the home to the yearly PITI. When the buyer's equity reaches 20 percent, either by making payments or if the property's value appreciates, PMI can be removed. The bank doesn't make the removal process very easy, sometimes requiring that the policy be kept for a certain length of time regardless of equity, and we've already seen how long it takes regular payments to build equity. Removal of PMI has recently gotten a lot easier, however—Congress has ordered banks to alert borrowers to the fact that their equity has reached 20 percent.

Picking a Neighborhood

The world of real estate is packed with nearly as many clichés as the stock market, and a lot of them have just as little meaning. But one of them— "buy the neighborhood"—is actually a great place to begin. This old saw is particularly appropriate for first-timers. First-timers have to be careful not to buy into an area that's plummeting so quickly that the house will be tough to sell if they choose to relocate as kids and careers warrant. And that goes double if one doesn't relocate.

This brings us to another good real estate saw: buy the worst house on the best block. Buying a house with potential is particularly appropriate for first-timers. With the best house, there's nowhere to go but out. A fixer-upper leaves room for improvement as your family and paycheck grow.

First, there are dozens of practical questions, some of which can be used to eliminate some areas right off the bat. If you commute to a job, you'll need access to transportation. That means bearable traffic, well-maintained roads if you drive or safe, nearby stations if you use public transportation. Usually, but not always, homes become more affordable as they move farther from the center of a city. Think about how long you're willing to spend traveling to and from work each day. Do you really want to endure three hours in a train in order to afford a house you'll seldom see because you're stuck commuting?

You're going to be living in this place for at least a few years. If you're like a lot of young hipsters, you probably haven't lived at the same address for five years since you left the parental nest. There's no formula for the gut-level questions you'll have to ask yourself as you search for a place to call your own. But that doesn't mean the way a neighborhood "feels" isn't every bit as important as its property taxes and proximity to transportation.

Buying a first house is an incredibly emotional situation. Whether you're squatting in a tenement near Tompkins Square or stretching to buy a bungalow in 90210, where you live says a lot about you—your values, your style, your taste. So the choice carries tremendous emotional baggage. And because you're also going to be dealing with tons of numbers and terms that are unfamiliar to you, these emotions are swirling just at the time you most need your rational, analytical faculties to be functioning at their sharpest.

As you begin to zero in on different areas that appeal to you, prepare yourself for some touchy-feely questions. It's easy to get swept up in the romance and beaten down by the complexity of first-time buying. Which makes it that much more important to be honest with yourself about what you need from a home and from a neighborhood. Some of these factors are obvious. Some people can't think without quiet solitude and others find it spooky. Other factors might require a little deeper soul-searching. Some people want to live and breed in areas of mixed class and race. Others like to look out their windows and see what they see when they look in their mirrors.

Once you've narrowed it down to three or four neighborhoods, spend at least a full day in each. Walk around, eat at local restaurants, go where people shop, go to the park, get a beer. And talk to people everywhere. Ask them how they like it, what's swell about the town and what sucks.

On the way home, it's time for more questions for yourself (and, of course, if you're buying the house with a spouse or friend or lover, the trip home is a good time to discuss these). How does the neighborhood feel to you? Are the flags people hang from their porches endearing or nauseating? Do the guys loitering outside the 7-Eleven seem to add local color or fodder for the crime blotter? Are you comfortable there? Does the town seem friendly to pets? Maybe too friendly? What does the town remind you of? Does it bring forth warm associations? Don't be afraid to cross a town off your list for reasons that are difficult to explain. If you discover an affordable neighborhood with great schools and a beautiful mountain view, don't think twice about disqualifying it if you get the creeps when you walk around in it. Remember, Stepford had pretty lawns, too.

Once you've narrowed your search to a neighborhood you love, start digging deeper. Go to the town library to investigate the schools and the local politics. If you're home shopping in the summer, look for lawn signs that indicate your neighbors are doing work on their home. If people are spending money to paint, add rooms or otherwise spruce up their homes, it usually means they like the neighborhood and prefer to pretty up or enlarge their current home rather than move to a pricier hood. Talk to neighbors and be blunt. Is the street usually this noisy? Any crime problems? Does that house with the "Don't Tread on Me" flag belong to a patriot or a militiaman?

Find out how long it has been taking for houses to sell. Get a couple dozen recent "sell sheets" from your realtor and also get a few from a year and two years ago. These will give you some insight into the kind of discount you can expect from the list price. If owners routinely sell for 80 percent of what they're asking, you'll know that there's room to bargain. If the houses sold for 95 percent or more of their original listing prices, it's a good indicator of a brisk housing market.

The New People in Your Life

The characters a home buyer comes to rely on resemble the cast of a David Lynch movie. Whenever possible, resist the temptation to work with one because of a recommendation from another. For a variety of reasons, these guys have incentive to rub each other's back so it's best to get independent referrals whenever possible.

Meet the players:

THE REALTOR

By far, the most important hire you'll make is the person who represents you in finding and purchasing your home. A good realtor is equal parts teacher, consigliere, priest, friend and diplomat.

You should feel absolutely comfortable asking any question, and absolutely positive that the realtor knows the answer or will find out quickly. This is too important a relationship to allow a reluctance to confront someone stop you from canning an agent who doesn't merit 100 percent confidence. Here are some other things to think about:

• Hire someone who does real estate full-time. Not only do you want someone with as much time for you as possible, but you want someone with an extra incentive to do what it takes to satisfy customers in a business that lives and dies on referrals.

• Find a realtor who's worked with a lot of clients in your price range. You don't want to be a small fry who gets no attention or a high-spending guinea pig.

• Don't be overly impressed with "million-dollar club" and other awards that indicate a realtor does a lot of deals. Sure, you want someone who can get your name on the bottom line, but not if it means he favors sales volume over patience and service.

• Don't overlook local one-office real estate agencies. Oftentimes, the most knowledgeable and experienced agents work at the quirky little offices that have been around the town forever.

Don't Go It Alone

Some financial books advise buyers to try to save a few bucks by going it without a realtor. Don't do it. Your agent's commission will eventually come out of the 6 percent that the seller pays. But the right agent will earn her fee several times over by bringing experience and negotiating prowess that you don't have. Perhaps a buyer who's been around the block a few times can fly solo, but a first-timer needs a lot of hand-holding and expertise.

Ask the realtor to fax you appropriate new homes the instant they come on the market. What she selects to show you will provide an idea of how closely your ideas about style and price range are in synch with the realtor's. When you go to look at houses, always let the realtor drive so you can look around. But when you revisit a house you like, ask her to take you a different route to get a more complete picture of the neighborhood and reduce the primrose path syndrome (and hopefully, you'll visit more times by yourself before you're ready to make an offer).

THE LAWYER

After you've negotiated with the seller and agreed on the price and inclusions, your lawyer will get the contract with both signatures. In many states, there's a "lawyer review" period of three days, which means you can back out no questions asked, even after the contract is signed. Closing a house is fairly mundane work for a lawyer, so you'll usually face a flat fee. Don't let the lawyer treat you like just another closing, though. The advantage of a flat fee is that you can ask a million questions without the meter running—take advantage of it to clear up anything you don't understand.

THE INSPECTOR

Once the contract has been approved by both sides' lawyers, you need to get a home inspection. In some states, like New Jersey, you usually have ten days to do this, but get started right away, because some tests, like the one for radon, take four days. Sign up an inspector as soon as you've narrowed the search to an area. The realtor will be more than happy to recommend an inspector, which is akin to a wolf recommending a shepherd. Remember, the realtor doesn't get paid unless a house gets sold, so she's got an interest in recommending an inspector who goes easy on the house, which he in turn is willing to do in exchange for more referrals from the realtor. Instead, get recommendations from homeowners in the neighborhood.

Insist on accompanying the inspector through the house and make clear that you want him to be brutally frank about things that look iffy, even if they're not serious enough defects to warrant reimbursement from the seller or backing out of the deal. After enduring the search and negotiation process, it can be a drag to hear an inspector diss your dream home's every little flaw. But the more he finds wrong with it, the better your bargaining position. Remember, though, inspection is not an exact science. Don't be surprised when annoying little problems creep up after you've bought a house that sailed through inspection.

Touring the house with the inspector is also a great way to become intimate with a house—you may not see the water shut-off valve or supplementary fuse box again until you're deep into a jam. Also, don't allow the seller to walk through the inspection with you—the inspector might sugarcoat the flaws and the seller may even argue that things aren't as bad as the inspector thinks. It's weird to tell someone not to walk through his own house with you. That's why you get your realtor to tell him.

Home Buyer's Warranties

These are bought by the seller as an added lure to the buyer, especially for older houses. They protect the buyer should anything go wrong with the house for one year after the sale, including stuff like the dishwasher breaking or the toilet springing a leak. Unfortunately, these policies are usually worth about what the buyer pays for them—nothing.

The main problem with these policies is that the buyer has to prove that the defect was not there when the house was bought, but was also not created by something the buyer did wrong. Here's how it works.

The oven in your new house suddenly stops working. You call the warranty company. They tell you who they'll send to fix it. (That you have to use their repair person is another irritant—it's like a plumber/electrician HMO). The repairer shows up and determines what's wrong. You show your home inspection report to prove that the oven worked when the inspector tested it. Then the repair person calls the warranty company, explains the situation and estimates what it'll cost to fix it. They either give their approval or deny it.

But even when they approve it, you still have to pay a deductible, usually $75. On a $500 repair, that's no big deal—you'll have saved $425. But if the repair is $100, you've only saved $25, while losing the ability to choose your own repair person. That might not sound like a big sacrifice. But when you move to a new area, it's important to start building relationships with local plumbers, electricians, etc. If the warranty company sends someone from an hour away, you don't get the benefit of throwing some dollars around locally. When the warranty runs out, you'll start the relationship-building process from scratch. Plus the repair person can be counted on to be grumpy because he's had to travel and because it takes a while to get paid by the warranty company. He also has little incentive to do a first-rate repair job because he knows you won't be hiring him once the warranty expires—since he operates an hour away, he wouldn't even want you to hire him.

Home buyer's warranties don't cost the buyer anything, so there's no reason to avoid them. But don't let a seller tout its value as a bargaining chip.

 **WARNING!** First-time home buyers should prepare for accounting hassles when they make their first few mortgage payments. The very nature of the escrow system—the borrower pays into a pool of money from which the lender makes property tax payments—is inherently confusing because a giant bank navigates the deadlines and assessments of all the local towns in which its borrowers live. But mortgage lenders depend on precise calculation and enormous data flow for their livelihood. So it's a mystery why so many of them consistently screw up the servicing of loan accounts. But they do, and wrongly crediting your payments or not sending correct bills can add to your bill and your blood pressure.

Here's how to fight back:

• Keep careful track of mortgage payments. Computer money-management software like Quicken provide terrific amortization schedules that track payments and can account for prepayments and taxes.

• Be sure that the statements you receive from your lender properly credit all payments you've made. Be especially vigilant the first few cycles, until both you and the lender have the hang of it.

• Alert the lender the instant you receive a delinquent payment notice from your new town. Assuming you've paid your mortgage bill, it's the

Home Buying Info Numbers

Good information is crucial to the entire home buying process. Your realtor and lender, while indispensable, are in the business of getting you into a house. That means you should do your best to obtain independent information. You don't need to second-guess the professionals—you're paying them to know the answers. But more information equals better questions and less anxiety. Some places to start:

Mortgage rates:

• HSH Associates, 800-873-2837/201-838-3330. Has info on two thousand lenders in lots of areas in more than thirty states.
• Gary Myers and Associates, 800-873-6463/312-642-9000. Issues weekly mortgage-rate reports on about a dozen big cities.

Free booklets:

How to Shop for a Mortgage, Mortgage Bankers Association of America, 1125 15th St. NW, Washington, DC 20005; include SASE
Maintaining Your Home, ASHI, 85 W. Algonquin Rd., Ste. 360, Arlington Heights, IL 60005-4423; include SASE. A good checklist from American Society of Home Inspectors
Consumer Handbook on Adjustable Rate Mortgages (ARMs), 202-452-3000

Co-ops:

National Association of Housing Co-operatives, 703-549-5201. Call for information specific to co-ops

Building Inspectors:

- National Association of Property Inspectors 800-486-3676
- American Society of Home Inspectors 708-290-1919
- American Real Property Inspection 800-947-2774

Appraisal:

- National Association of Master Appraisers, 210-271-0781/ 800-229-NAMA
- The Appraisal Institute, 312-335-4100

Property Tax

About one in three American homes are assessed at more than they're worth, which means their owners are paying too much in property taxes. But about half the people who challenge the assessment win a tax reduction. If you feel like your taxes are unfairly high, send $2 to *How to Fight Property Taxes,* National Taxpayers Union, 108 N. Alfred St., Alexandria, VA 22314.

lender's responsibility to pay the taxes and also the late fees, if there are any.

- There's no law that forces home buyers to pay into an escrow account. The bank likes to make buyers do it that way so it can make sure the taxes are paid and the insurance doesn't lapse—it's mostly their house, after all. But if they consistently goof up the escrow system, tell the lender you wish to make your own property tax and/or homeowner's insurance payments.

I'm in Love with My Car

(Or, "Please Let Me Die Without Seeing Another Car-Buying Chapter Titled 'How to Buy a Car Without Being Taken for a Ride' ")

Buying a car is like report card day: some look forward to it with giddy anticipation, others dread it with glum resignation. It's both frightening and exciting, especially for those buying a car for the first time. Whether you're combing the paper for a rusty relic or scouring the dealerships for a cherry chariot, a little homework goes a long way.

The main factor in driving away with a bargain is good information. Until recently, that information was in the hands of the sellers. Buyers without the intelligence-gathering tools of the Mossad were largely at the mercy of dealerships. Along with everything else in the information age, the process of buying a car has changed dramatically in just the past few years. I don't really care what make or model tickles your fancy (though I'll confess to a soft spot for mid-seventies International Scouts, if anyone's got one to sell), but I do want you to get the best deal. Whether you buy or lease, go used or new, here are some strategies that'll come in handy.

New Cars

Every gleaming, tantalizing, irresistible new car has a magic number. It's called the dealer's cost. If you can figure out what the dealer paid for a car, you stand a good chance of walking out with the car for just a few bucks more.

Unless the car you want is in extremely high or low demand, the price you pay will be between the dealer's cost and the manufacturer's suggested retail price. The salesman will try to focus on the latter. Ignore it. The dealer's cost should be the jumping off point for your negotiation. If you go in armed with that price, you're in a position of strength. It'll be up to the salesman to inch you up bit by bit rather than you having to shave a few dollars off his price.

The dealer's cost simply means what the dealer paid for the car, including options like factory air and fuzzy dice, plus destination charges. You can learn that number from the resources listed below. Once you've got it, show up at the dealership, announce your intention to pay no more than that price and get ready for some outraged expressions.

It's tough not to feel bad when the salesman starts moaning that you're taking food off his kid's plate and not paying a fair price. First-time buyers are especially vulnerable to these tactics, so steel yourself before you even begin negotiating. Don't forget that you can *always* walk away, at any point of the deal, no matter how much work you and the salesman have invested in getting to that point. Keep in mind, however, that the more time the salesman has spent with you, the less likely he is to walk away without a sale. Remember also that car salesmen are professional negotiators. They're trained in the art of the pitch, down to the intervals they let you stew while "considering" your offer and scripts to tug at your heartstrings. They're not going to let you rob them, so don't let them guilt you into anything. And if you still feel bad, know that the dealer often gets a "holdback" from the manufacturer of about 3 percent of the MSRP, which covers the dealer's advertising and other overhead.

Sometimes, a dealer will let a car go out the door for as little as $100 above his cost, especially if that model is a slow seller or end-of-the-month sales targets are nearing. More often, expect a hard-nosed negotiation to result in a final price about $200 to $500 above the dealer's cost.

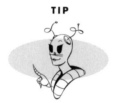

TIP When selecting a new car, don't lose sight of total cost. Two cars that are priced similarly may depreciate differently. A lush sedan loses about half its value in the first three years while a Jeep with the same retail price can retain as much as 75 percent of its value. And if the model you've got your eye on costs a lot more to repair and fuel, it's not as economical as a similarly priced tank that seldom breaks down and gets better mileage. Look to *Consumer Reports* and other ratings for clues; knowing the cost of owning a car is as important as paying the right price.

Some negotiation no-no's

• Never let a salesman know your "maximum price" or what you "planned on spending." If you do, you'll end up paying it, for sure.

• Never mention the method you plan to use for financing the car until you agree on price. The dealer may try to substitute "favorable financing terms" for the lowest price you could otherwise get.

• If you plan to trade in your current car, don't mention it until the price of the car you're buying is settled. A miserly offer on the trade-in might make you decide to sell it elsewhere, so you don't want to mingle the two negotiations.

WARNING! Many aggressively sold (i.e., highly profitable) options are a waste of money, particularly when included in option "packs." Paint sealing, fabric protection and extended-service warranties are generally wasteful. Dealer-applied rustproofing is actually worse than wasteful—it often traps moisture inside a car's body and creates more rust than it prevents.

Used Cars

A smart used car purchase brings a ton of advantages. Obviously, the purchase price is lower. You also are likely to pay far less to insure a used car. And the booming popularity of leasing has flooded the market with three-year-old models that are cream puffs because they've been driven under strict "excess wear and tear" restrictions.

Buying used can also bring plenty of indigestion. Mechanical defects can quickly turn that terrific bargain into a nightmare of garage visits and throwing good money after bad. Researching a car's reliability history is always a good idea. But no matter how careful your research, lemons come in all makes and models. So don't hesitate to pony up the $50 to $100 it'll take to get a good mechanic to give the car the once-over before you make an offer.

If buying a used car from a dealer, use the same basic tactics as when buying new. One wrinkle: it's impossible to know what the dealer paid for the car. The "Blue Book price"—learnable at Kelley's website (*http://www.kbb.com*) or any bank that does auto loans—will give you a ballpark figure of what cars of a certain year, condition and mileage are going for. Arriving armed with information about the car and options you like is critical. Use the sources listed here to get an idea but do as much comparison shopping as you can.

Financing a Car Purchase

As with houses, most new automobiles (and a lot of used ones) are bought with a small down payment and a lot of borrowed money. An auto loan is typically provided by a bank or the dealership that sells the car, and it's secured by the car itself, which means the lender can repossess it if you fail to make the payments. Unlike credit cards, which are *revolving loans* (meaning there's no set time limit or amount to the borrowing, so long as you make your minimum payments and stay under your credit limit), an auto loan is an *installment loan.* That means there's a fixed amount of time until the loan's paid off, and the payments, or installments, are of fixed amounts.

Car dealers sell their financing deals as aggressively as their automobiles, so shopping for a loan can be as important as choosing the car itself. And as with any loan, the interest rate is key.

A sixty-month $15,000 loan at 9 percent will mean a monthly payment of $311. The same loan at 6 percent will cost only $290. That's more than $1,260 over the life of the loan.

Shopping for a good rate might enable you to take a shorter-term loan, too. Let's say you need to borrow $20,000 to buy the Land Cruiser you simply can't live without. Suppose the most you can afford to pay on a monthly basis is $400. A loan at 7 percent will need a payment of $396 to be paid off in five years. At 10 percent, however, the $425 monthly payment breaks the budget. In order to get the payment under $400, you'll have to take a longer-term loan.

Like all loans, a longer term means more in total interest costs by the time the loan is paid in full. Unlike a house, however, a car usually gets less valuable over time. So even though a longer term will lower the monthly payments, it's usually better to go with the shortest term loan and the biggest down payment you can afford.

Sometimes, dealers offer attractive financing in order to jump-start sales. These deals can save you plenty, but don't let the tail wag the dog: buy the car, not the financing. If you're not going for one of those highly promoted dealer-financed loans, it's best to arrange for financing before you even go to the dealership. Rates from lenders can vary pretty widely, so it's worth shopping around. Credit unions often offer the best rates on auto loans, so it might be a good time to think about joining one, if you haven't done so already.

 **WARNING!** Leasing used cars is becoming more popular, but like many trends, this one will come to be regretted by those who embrace it. The primary advantage of leasing is getting your bottom in a new car for less up front than buying, so leasing a used car misses on that score. What's worse is that if you lease a lemon, you're stuck with the thing for the duration of the lease. If you buy a lemon, you can at least try to sell it to someone even more oblivious to the pool of tranny fluid beneath it than yourself.

Resources: Car Pricing and Info

New Cars

• The best car-pricing service is operated by *Consumer Reports,* the "shopping can be intensely pleasurable" magazine. For $12, their New Car Price Service (800-933-7700) will provide a printout of the invoice and list price of just about any model car, as well as a list of available options and their prices. Included are any available rebates or financing deals.

• *Edmund's New Cars: Prices & Reviews* is available at most bookstores for about $7; it's free on the Internet *(http://www.edmunds.com)* and regularly updated. *Edmund's* reviews and comparisons of used cars are excellent as well.

• *Consumer Reports Cars: The Essential Guide* is available on CD-ROM and covers new and used cars, ranking and reviewing a dizzying array of vehicles. It's about $20; 800-331-1369, ext. 173.

USED CARS

• Kelley Blue Books are the standard—those plain books of lists that'll tell you what a car's worth when you look up the year, condition, mileage and options. Their website *(http://www.kbb.com)* is also excellent. You plug in your car's every detail and the site spits out the fair-market price, fast and free. Another excellent feature allows you to check the title history of a car you're considering buying. For $12.95, you can also check out a used car's title history. Having a hard time believing the ten-year-old cream puff you're looking at only has forty thousand miles on it? A quick look at the title history may show that the car had twice that mileage when the seller bought it last year.

• *Consumer Reports'* Used Car Price Service (900-988-3333) can give you the trade-in value of your car or price that ancient Mustang you've been eyeing. It's $1.75 a minute, so have the information you need at the ready.

• Edmund's website *(http://www.edmunds.com)* features an incredible assortment of used car data. Included are its own ratings, in categories such as "safety," "reliability" and "fun to drive." Particularly useful to the used car buyer is the way that options are listed with dollar amounts. If you're looking at two different cars of the same model, you can gauge the relative value of the one's aluminum wheels and cruise control against the other's sunroof and spoiler. Also noted are recall info and features that were added in that model year.

CAR BUYING SERVICES

These are for buyers with hard-core aversions to bargaining, but who want cars from dealers who don't offer "no-haggle" pricing. These services will actually do all the shopping for you. Your involvement ranges from choosing among actual "best offers" from local dealers to soup-to-nuts car buying—you just show up at a dealer and pick up your car, with the color and options you ordered. Though they supposedly offer "guaranteed lowest prices," an individual willing to go to war with a local dealer will usually do better. And be sure you know exactly what model, options and color you want.

Leasing vs. Buying

Uncommon just a few years ago, leasing will account for a whopping one third of new cars this year. Some of the plusses and minuses are as follows.

Leasing advantages:

- Avoids the hassles and expense of aging cars
- Keeps you in the newest safety features
- Easier to walk away at the end of the relationship

No selling or trading in means no ads in newspapers, no insultingly low trade-in offers from dealers, and no psychos coming over to your house to test drive your car like your neighborhood was on the Autobahn.

I once advertised a beloved Nissan Stanza for $1,000. Four gang members, none of whom could drive stick, showed up for a test spin. We piled in and they went through the clutch plate like a Doberman through tenderloin. They offered $800, all in hundreds. I demurred. They made what might be called a counteroffer. I thanked them for the $800.

Leasing disadvantages:

- Breeding ground for shifty salesmen
- Bizarre terminology makes comparing deals difficult
- Restrictions make you feel like a permanent borrower of your brother's car—skimpy mileage allowances, "wear and tear" clauses, etc.
- Locked into a term—premature termination of the lease can cost thousands of dollars.

But all this is beside the point. The main reason people lease cars is because it's cheap—at least at first. Indeed, it's often the cheapest route to that new ride that's been burning rubber in your imagination—the down payment and monthly payments are lower than those if you bought the car with a loan. That's because at the end of the lease, you return the car, which the owner—either the dealer or a finance company—can sell.

Leasing has a well-deserved reputation as nirvana for fast-talking car salesmen. Aside from utilizing a terminology that's unfamiliar to most car shoppers, the deals are so complicated they're almost impossible to compare with one another.

Even if you walk into the dealership intending to lease a car, approach the deal as though you were buying. Cut the best deal you can and the final price will be your "capitalized cost." The "capitalized cost reduction" just means your down payment. Multiply the "money factor" by 2,400 to find the approximate interest rate the lease is costing you (i.e., if the money factor, or "lease charge," is .004, your interest rate is about 9.6 percent).

You want a closed-end lease, which means you can walk away at the end of the term. You should also get GAP insurance, which covers the difference between your auto insurance and any penalties if the car is stolen or ruined. Because of these awkward terms and phrases, it's always a good idea to take a lease home for a night or two to consider it. Don't cave in to sales pressure to "sign now." Remember, once your name's on that dotted line, it's difficult and expensive to get out.

• Get the free buy versus lease pamphlet "Driving a Bargain" by sending a SASE to "Driving a Bargain," PO Box 12099, Washington, DC 20005. It's as informative as its title is clever.

• Nationwide Auto Brokers (800-521-7257) will send you a sheet that lists the dealer's invoice and all available options on any car you wish. You can use the sheet just for information or go ahead and have them buy you the car; $11.95 for one car, $9.95 for subsequent quotes, and the price is refunded if you use the service.

• Auto Advisor (800-326-1976) is a high-end service with a high-end price. For $359, the company handles the whole process, including trade-ins and negotiating with local dealers.

Other Resources

• *Don't Get Taken Every Time: The Insider's Guide to Buying or Leasing Your Next Car or Truck* by Remar Sutton is a thorough analysis of every aspect of the car buying process, particularly good on financing and debunking various sales pitches.

• *How To Buy Your New Car for a Rock-Bottom Price* by Dr. Leslie R. Sachs. A tip-laden do-it-cheap guide, with good advice on buying with a small down payment and managing the actual negotiation process.

Problems and Advice

• The Better Business Bureau runs Autoline, a service that arbitrates disputes between customers and car dealers. Call 800-955-5100 for info.

• The BBB also offers a bunch of useful brochures for free. "Tips on Buying a Used Car" and "Tips on Buying a New Car" can be had by calling 703-276-0100.

• "The Official Used Car Guide" is published by the National Automobile Dealers Association (aka NADA, which hopefully doesn't refer to the value of their advice). To buy that, or to get the free brochure "Your Money, Your Car," call them at 800-252-6232 or visit the website at *http://www.nadanet.com.*

• The Federal Trade Commission (202-326-2222) has a free brochure entitled "A Consumer Guide to Vehicle Leasing."

Traveling: Anywhere but Here

What better way to enjoy your money than to see new places, taste new foods, walk on roads that never felt your feet before? This section doesn't point you toward cheap destinations or bargain cruise packages. Travel is too personal and individual, and particular deals change so frequently that specific details are better researched elsewhere (and a couple places to start looking are listed at the end of this chapter).

Nevertheless, there's a ton of overlooked advice and clever little strategies, many of which go unmentioned because it's in no one's interest to mention them.

Flying

You probably already know a bunch of ways to save money on airfare. Keeping an eye open for good sales and fare wars, booking your flight as far in advance as possible, including a Saturday night stay, and flying during off-peak times, such as Tuesday, Wednesday and Thursday afternoons, or real early or late in the day.

Here are some other strategies that'll stretch your flying coin.

• Investigate the prices of flying from a nearby city. Depending on the fierceness of competition at different airports, you might save enough to offset the hassle.

• Nothing's more frustrating than buying something that goes on sale soon after. If you buy an airline ticket and one of those fare wars breaks out, ask for a refund. The airline is under no obligation to grant one. But if you paid $500 for something that they're now saying is worth $300, you can often press your case successfully, especially if you bought through a travel agent, with whom the airline presumably would like to maintain a good relationship.

• Don't sweat the "nonrefundable" language of a lot of discount tickets, even if your plans aren't absolutely firm. True, you won't be able to get your money back for the ticket. But ticket *changes* can usually be made for a $50 penalty, and if you don't use the ticket at all, you can usually apply its cost (minus the penalty) toward a new ticket.

WARNING! Some nifty money-saving strategies may not be so smart:

• Hidden cities. You want to fly from, say, New York

to St. Louis. A round-trip ticket for that trip costs $300. But you can get a round-trip to Kansas City with a stopover in St. Louis for $250. So you simply get off in St. Louis and pull a Dr. Livingston. Then you return by boarding in St. Louis on the same flight you were going to be on had you started in K.C.

• Back-to-back. My friend flies from her home in Chicago to Los Angeles once a month to work from Monday to Friday. If she spends a Saturday night in L.A., her round-trip fare is $300. But if she wants to spend her weekends at home, the ticket soars to $650. Let's say she buys *two* round-trip tickets, one from Chicago to L.A. and back, the other from L.A. to Chicago and back to L.A. Then she uses the departure half of each ticket for her first month's trip and the return half of each ticket for her second trip. This gives both round-trips a qualifying Saturday night stay, which saves $350 each trip—$700 total.

Both of these strategies violate the "passenger contract" you enter into by simply buying the ticket. While the screening process for who is and is not on a plane clearly has plenty of holes in it, your ticket could be invalidated for using either of these schemes. So be sure not to employ these methods if you don't have the means to bail yourself out when you're far from home.

Tread Carefully with Super-cheap Fares

Consolidators have produced a lot of good bargains, but should be approached with caution. Consolidators buy a bunch of airline tickets at "wholesale," then sell them one by one to travel agents or directly to consumers. This often results in excellent prices, particularly for travelers who are flexible about airline and traveling dates. Unfortunately, there are often drawbacks beyond that. Many tickets bought from consolidators are not eligible for frequent flyer mileage, and some are actually tickets for charter flights, which are booked for specific trips and have notoriously unreliable schedules. Worse, consolidators have occasionally vanished without a trace, leaving would-be passengers holding worthless tickets.

If you decide to go with a consolidator, take steps to protect yourself.

• Before you've paid for the ticket, contact the airline to confirm the availability of the seat. The consolidator should have reserved the space—if not the exact seat. Sometimes, a consolidator will have purchased a standby seat, which is available only if there's enough room. Confirm with the airline that the seat the consolidator is offering is a regular confirmed seat on a specific flight. If there's a problem, ask the consolidator for a record locator number, then call the airline. If they still can't confirm the seat, don't buy the ticket.

• Even though you may face a surcharge, buy your ticket with a credit card. That gives you the ability to dispute the charge if the ticket comes up snake eyes.

• If you have a travel agent you trust, ask about consolidators. Some travel agents have histories with consolidators and can buy tickets for you more reliably than you could yourself.

• If you've chosen to ignore the horror stories you've heard about charter companies disappearing with your cash, at least write to the U.S. Department of Transportation for their fact sheet about charter flights: US DoT, Aviation Consumer Protection Division, 400 7th St. SW, C-75, Washington, DC 20590.

Hotels

People go ape over their frequent flyer miles, celebrating every free trip with an enthusiasm unseen since Senior Ditch Day. After scrimping and angling for every money break in the sky, however, most people just plop themselves down in the first hotel with a fancy sign.

Hotels, like airplanes, are businesses that make money only when they're near capacity. It costs almost as much to fly an empty plane as a full one, and an empty hotel still has to pay its taxes, electric bill, employees and other fixed costs. So the earlier you book your room (or your flight), the more you're worth to the hotel, in the form of one room they don't have to worry about. Be sure to use that leverage when you're booking early—demand the "best rate" and be ready to shop around. Other advice:

• Even if you use a chain's 800 number to find a hotel, don't make a reservation with it. Call the hotel directly. The manager will have more authority and incentive to offer a discount.

• Consider using a consolidator, which can save you 25 to 50 percent off the listed rates. Like their airfare counterparts, hotel consolidators buy up a bunch of rooms at a discount, then resell them to the public at thin markups. They also share the drawbacks of the airfare guys, so be sure you confirm any arrangements with the hotel itself.

Some consolidators:

• Accommodations Express, 800-444-7666, *http://www.accommodationsxpress.com*

Sample cities: Atlanta, Atlantic City, Boston, Chicago, Ft. Lauderdale, Las Vegas, Miami Beach, New Orleans, New York, Philadelphia, Washington, D.C.

Payment: Prepaid voucher with credit card charged day of arrival

Additional services: Airline packages available

• Central Reservations Service, 800-950-0232, *http://www.reservation-services.com*

Sample cities: Ft. Lauderdale, Los Angeles, Miami, New York, Orlando, San Francisco

Payment: Pay the hotel directly

Additional services: Car rentals

• Hotel Reservations Network, 800-964-6835, *http://www.hoteldiscount.com*

Sample cities: Boston, Chicago, Las Vegas, Los Angeles, Miami, New Orleans, New York, Orlando, San Diego, San Francisco, Washington, D.C.

Payment: Prepaid voucher

• Rmc Travel Center, 800-245-5738, 800-782-2674

Sample cities: Atlanta, Boston, Chicago, Montreal, New York, Philadelphia, Phoenix, San Diego, Seattle, Vancouver

Payment: Prepaid voucher by credit card

Additional services: Lots of resort packages, including Carmel, Myrtle Beach, Sun Valley, Tahoe; some overseas locations, including London and Paris

Traveling Abroad

RENTAL CARS

Make all arrangements, including payment, before you leave the States. Be prepared to drive stick or to pay extra for a wimpy automatic, and book way in advance. As with a domestic rental, ask about all late penalties, gas charges and discounts in advance.

Definitely make sure you're covered for collision and theft. Protection from these are offered by the car rental agency in the form of a collision damage waiver. Many credit cards provide this coverage, particularly gold cards and American Express, but they're getting pickier about the countries in which they provide it. Car-theft-ridden Italy, for example, has been removed from many issuers' cards, as have Israel and Ireland. If you don't have other coverage, you'll have to buy it from the rental agency, which will run you about $10 a day on top of the rental cost. Contact your card company before you travel to see if you're covered:

- American Express   800-338-1670
- Visa   800-847-2911
- MasterCard   800-622-7747

PAYING FOR IT OVERSEAS

Whenever possible, it's a good idea to arrange for a couple different options to pay for things. Some places that don't take credit cards do take traveler's checks, and vice versa.

- Credit/charge cards

Charge everything you possibly can when you're traveling abroad. Credit card purchases are made at the interbank exchange rate, which is the best currency trade the little guy can get. Plus you get all the normal conveniences of credit, like the ability to cancel immediately and a record of all charges. Visa and MasterCard are more widely accepted than American Express, but AmEx holders get other travel plums, like mail holding at AmEx offices and a round-the-clock hotline for all sorts of emergencies.

- Traveler's checks

The two big benefits to traveler's checks is that they're accepted just about everywhere in the world and can be replaced if lost or stolen. They also usually result in more favorable exchange rates than cash.

If you go with traveler's checks, stick with American Express. Their acceptance and replaceability consistently outdo that of rivals in tests by travel magazines, and market share is a big factor when you're talking about traveling to strange places.

Whatever brand you buy, be sure to make a list of the check numbers. Keep the list separate from the checks and cross off the ones you've used. Then if you lose them, you'll be able to replace 'em lickety-split.

Traveler's checks can usually be had for about 1 to 2 percent in commissions, meaning it'll cost you about $102 to buy a hundred dollars worth. Ask in advance and don't pay more than 3 percent. Certain organizations, like the AAA motor club, give their members breaks on traveler's checks, while banks sometimes waive the commissions for good customers—doesn't hurt to ask. Don't be surprised if some places charge you a few dollars to use the checks, which is particularly irritating since you've already paid for the things.

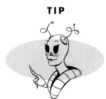

TIP

Best of Both Worlds?

There are now hybrid cards specifically designed to ease the hassles of getting cash overseas. Visa's TravelMoney card, for example, can be bought in any denomination up to $10,000 before the trip. It can be bought by phone if your local bank doesn't offer it (try First Bank, 800-444-1244) and cost from 1.5 percent to 3 percent of the value of the card. Then you can use it abroad at any of the 350,000 Visa-logoed ATMs all over the world. The good news is that, aside from the purchase price, the transaction costs are very low compared with overseas ATM transactions and the card can usually be replaced within twenty-four hours, even far from the USA. Plus, because it's a form of credit card, you're only on the hook for $50 if the card gets stolen or if your PIN is cracked.

CALLING FROM OVERSEAS

Rates from abroad to the U.S. can be absurdly high. In general, never make a call from your hotel room unless absolutely necessary. Surcharges of up to $4 a call can kill a travel budget. If you have a calling card, call your long-distance provider before you leave for access numbers for the countries you're going to. Some foreign hotels block access to calling cards. You can usually buy prepaid phone cards but expect to pay about four bits a minute. (That's 50¢, I think.)

You can also use a callback service. You get a number from the service and then call in from wherever you're staying. After it answers, you hang up and the service calls you back with a dial tone. This'll give you American rates, and can handle faxes and Internet stuff; callback services are great, but better used if you plan to make a lot of calls.

Some callback companies:

America Tele-fone	800-321-5817
International Telephone	800-638-5558
Prime Call	800-698-1232
Telegroup	800-338-0225

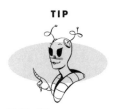

TIP

It'd be a drag to face a passport snafu on your way to Istanbul, Kuala Lumpur, Quito or Cannes. Renew your passport through the mail—it's easy, fast and will save you the $30 hit you'll take if you wait till the last minute. Here's what you do: get a DSP-82 form at the PO. Have two passport photos taken. Fill out the form and send it to the address on the back of it, along with the photos, your current passport and a $55 check. The National Passport Information Center recommends that you send the whole thing via Express Mail and that you include a self-addressed Express Mail envelope for the return package. If you have any questions, call them at 888-362-8668—for $4.95, they're glad to help.

Last Digs: A Few Final Financial Thoughts

Wring Your Benefits

Remember that big book you got on the first day at your job? When was the last time you opened it? It's under the short leg of your card table, you say? Let the table wobble and crack that book. It's called your company benefit book and beneath its turgid prose lie a treasure of underused and little-known prizes just waiting for you to claim.

Most people have a general idea about some of the big benefits their employer bestows upon them. But does every Apple Computer employee know that the computer maker offers assistance and benefits to employees who adopt children? Has every Coors driver scheduled a free appointment with the staff nutritionist to discuss working off some of the pounds brought on by the free afterwork beer? Is everyone at W. B. Fuller aware that the enviro-friendly glue maker not only gives ten-year employees extra vacation time, but spending money to boot? Does every stitcher at Levi Strauss & Co. know that the apparel maker offers high school equivalency courses on company time at the company's expense?

Benefits are a neat little part of one's overall financial health. Consider your perks part of your compensation—if your company gives you $30 a month in subway money or offers pretax legal assistance, that's tax-free income, worth more than if the company had paid the same amount in salary. Companies are also getting more creative in how they offer these perks. Flexible benefits, for example, gives the employee the opportunity to choose what benefits suits her situation—extra vacation days, a fatter health insurance deal or additional 401(k) contributions. Someone whose family has health insurance through another source might rake in the extra 401(k) dollars while a person with a side career could better use the extra vacation days.

It Pays to Shop Around

In the Middle East it's considered insulting not to bargain for a better price from a merchant. Well, I'm from the Middle West, and I think it's time for that adorable custom to go international.

It's always puzzled me why some situations seem to lend themselves to negotiation and others do not. Americans would never bring a load of groceries to the counter and start haggling over the price. But pay list price at Guitar Center and they'll hang a "sucker" sign around your neck. Other situations demand bargaining, such as car dealerships and, of course, home buying. So why should it end there?

What really burns me about the state of bargaining in America is the way in which it's treated as something unseemly. Not bargaining almost always works to the advantage of the seller. In other words, people who already have goods and services have managed to convince many of those who do not that there's something gross about not handing over more money than is necessary.

One good example is the recent popularity of Saturn-style fixed-price, no-haggling deals. These work out better for the company than the consumer. There's something vaguely sexist about them, too. These pricing strategies are heavily marketed to women. "You poor tender flower," sniffs the pitch. "Buy from us and no one will accost you with undignified— *egad*—selling." The result: the markup on the average Saturn is about twice what it is at a traditional dealership.

In fact, many things are negotiable. The key is competition. Any service or product that faces a lot of rivals puts the consumer—you—in the driver's seat.

• Professionals

When you hire a lawyer, accountant or other paid-by-the-hour professional, the rate will be agreed on in advance. There is absolutely nothing wrong with asking for a better rate or a more favorable payment plan. And try bartering. My mother-in-law, an attorney, routinely accepts payment in services from clients—a remodeling job here, some landscaping there.

• Telephone rates

A favored ruse of the long-distance slugfest is to offer promotions that promise a reward for switching from one's current carrier. Even if you're satisfied with your current company, there's no reason to miss out on the fifty bucks or so that these offers typically promise. Call your long-distance provider to see if they'll match the deal. Chances are good they will, shrewdly spreading the rebate over five months to ensure your continued devotion.

Here are the toll-free numbers of the five largest long-distance carriers.

AT&T	800-222-0300
MCI	800-444-3333
Sprint	800-877-4646

Working Assets   800-788-0898
Worldcom   800-844-0100

Representatives of the big three are available and chipper twenty-four hours a day (those curious about Worldcom must call between 7 A.M. and 7 P.M.) and will provide an instant price for an example call. And don't forget about upstarts like Excel and Working Assets. These companies rent their lines from Sprint and the others, so the quality is excellent, and the price is often as good or better than their better-known counterparts.

• Mutual fund minimums

Look, mutual fund companies are in the business of managing money. So even funds that require lots of money to open an account can usually be counted on to lower the bar. When you call for an account application, explain that you can't swing the $2,000 or whatever the minimum is. Often the company will lower it if you agree to a regular monthly direct deposit from your checking account. Even if the idea of an automatic contribution doesn't appeal to you, you can sign up that way, then cancel the direct deposit once you've got the account open. Don't worry, they won't kick you out of the fund. If the initial amount the fund requires is still outside your means, investigate opening an IRA account, which typically requires a lower minimum. That's a last resort, though, especially if you already have an IRA account elsewhere. IRAs are the investor equivalent to sliced bread, but paperwork is their defect. So keeping more than one account, while completely permissible, is not advisable.

• Credit card interest rates

This one's a gimme. It can save you a fortune, it's easy and it nearly always works. All's you do is call your credit card company. Tell them you need them to shave at least a couple points off your interest rate or you're going to have to cancel the card. Your odds are better if you've got a better offer in front of you, and a history of prompt payment helps, too.

• Trade commissions from full-service brokers

These guys face competition from all sides. Discount brokers, banks, ultra-cheap electronic brokers, the insurance industry, mutual funds—all are carving up the commission pie that used to belong to the full-service broker. If you make your trades through one of the big full-service houses—Merrill Lynch, PaineWebber, Smith Barney—ask your broker to lower his commission to be more competitive. He'll grumble, but usually come close to Schwab and Fidelity fees.

- Late fees (credit cards, utility bills, etc.)

If you've been paying on time, you can usually make a pretty good case for the service provider to cut you a break. Count on this one to work only once, though.

- Rent

No, really. If you're a good tenant with a reliable rent-payment history, there's no reason not to ask if the landlord will accept a lower monthly payment, or a smaller yearly increase. It costs a lot to find a responsible tenant. If you live in a city with a high vacancy rate, you stand a decent chance.

- Mileage limits on a lease

A dealer offering twelve thousand miles a year almost certainly won't lose a sale over another one thousand miles. At a typical 25¢ a mile, you might save yourself $500 on a two-year lease just by asking.

And Finally, a Walk-away Number: When It Pays to Walk Away, Even If Your Name's Not Renee

Regardless of the item or service being negotiated, it is crucial to go into any negotiation with a "walk-away" number. Good salespeople can smell your eagerness to buy whatever it is you're investigating, as well as your willingness to go elsewhere. You can bet that the amount you end up paying will be as close to the high end of that range as you let it be. So it's critical to set a cap on what you'll pay before the negotiation begins.

This is hard to do. Once a negotiation begins, a buyer is invested to some degree in obtaining whatever it is. You've already spent time shopping around, talking to the salesman, and you're this close to driving away or renting or moving into or whatever. So the temptation is not to let "a few bucks" keep you from sealing the deal. The problem with that thinking is that every number in the world is a few bucks higher than another number.

Say the car you've got your heart set on lists at $20,000. You've done your research (and read the car-buying section of this book) and you know the dealer has paid $16,000. You can pretty well figure the price you'll end up paying will be between those numbers, unless demand for the model is unusually high or low. If you enter the negotiation without a clear idea of exactly where your "not a dollar more" price is, you can bet you'll pay higher than you intended. Say the negotiation starts with the dealer offering the car for $19,500 and you countering at $16,500. Unless you have a clear idea of exactly what your cap is—say, $18,000—you can count on that price creeping higher and higher until you end up closer to the dealer's price than your own. A salesman who senses that you don't want to go home empty-handed will have an easy time making "what's another hundred dollars?" arguments—before you know it, you're closer to $19,500 than feared.

Remember, just as you've invested a lot of time in shopping for the car, choosing the options, talking to the salesman, test-driving, so too has the salesman invested a lot of time in showing you the car and talking up its virtues. He doesn't want to walk away without a sale any more than you want to ride home in the beater you've been driving since high school.

Appendix I:
Where to Go for More Info

It is painful to admit that there exists more financial knowledge than can be contained between these covers. Alas, it is true; here are some places to seek additional enlightenment.

Books

All good financial books resemble one another, but each crummy financial book is crummy in its own way. Here are some of those that bear yearly rereadings and a treasured place on your bookshelf.

Barbarians at the Gate, Bryan Burrough and John Helyar. A terrific story first and a smart dissection of a leveraged buyout second, *Barbarians* portrays the billionaire egos behind the fight for control of RJR-Nabisco, maker of Camel cigarettes and Oreos. Not a half-bad HBO movie either, with a believably nic-addicted James Garner as the head of RJR.

Barron's Dictionary of Finance and Investment Terms. Exactly as boring as the title sounds, but crystal in its mission and comprehensive in its coverage.

Den of Thieves, James Stewart. This account of eighties greed and insider trading is more than a straw-man condemnation of Ivan Boesky and Michael Milken (although it's that, too). It's also a well-told and fascinating look at how things work at the top levels of Wall Street, and why it's critical that small players believe there's a level playing field.

Liar's Poker, Michael Lewis. This account of the macho culture and fraternity atmosphere of Salomon's training program is well observed and sparklingly told. The training-room scenes are like *Raging Bull* for bond traders.

The Motley Fool Investment Guide. Few new media types do as effective a job at getting their mugs in magazines and TV (especially considering their big giggles at the uselessness of "old" media like magazines and TV), so you probably already know who the Fools are and what they do. But more than their trademark suspicion of the "rules" of wise investing and pretty decent history of betting on small companies that later click with the investing public, the Fools bring to the table something that many investment book writers cannot—a way with words. Perhaps not surprisingly from two guys who named their industry after a line from *As You Like It,* the brothers Gardner are more than good stock pickers—they're good writers.

The Only Investment Guide You'll Ever Need, Andrew Tobias. Tobias is, by quite a large margin, the personal finance writer who is most fun to read. His conversational and funny prose goes by so breezily that the reader almost doesn't notice that there's a ton of advice packed into it. He also recognizes that personal finance is just that—personal. Sample from the section on money-saving tips: "You will never find me eating a ketchup other than Heinz. But is it really worth 80 percent more to you to sneeze into a genuine Kleenex-brand 'kleenex'?" Not only is the thinking right on, but how 'bout that "eating a ketchup"—touché!

Personal Finance for Dummies, Eric Tyson. It'd be a mistake to dismiss this book simply because of its association with the annoying and insulting schtick of the "Dummies" series. While no subject gets the depth it deserves, this is a perfect midway point between a simple dictionary of financial terms and an exhaustive financial tour. Tyson also works in a surprising and refreshing amount of personal detail ("Don't eat meat!" pleads one sidebar), which enhances the trip through a pretty thorough guidebook. Strengths include its emphasis on budgeting, saving and insurance.

A Random Walk Down Wall Street, Burton Malkiel. A must-read historical look at markets and the seemingly unstoppable tendency of human beings to think they've beaten the system.

Wall Street, Doug Henwood. It's easy to forget that the world of investing is not always the benevolent opportunity and smooth-running system that the personal finance magazines and a seven-year bull market can make it appear to be. (Yes, I'll take responsibility for whatever portion of irrational exuberance my own enthusiasm has helped to generate.) This book does an admirable job of not only reminding that there's a ruthless side to Wall Street but also elegantly explaining some pretty sophisticated financial concepts.

American Splendor, Harvey Pekar's annual catalog of Chekhovian mundanities, isn't about personal finance. But it's still the best comic book in America.

Appendix II:
The Internet and Your Money

The number of financial websites is growing faster than a teenager in puberty. Every day, a new set of 1's and 0's cascades across the screen, promising faster quotes, more depth, greater riches. But that's the problem with information: too much is sometimes more dangerous than not enough.

That's especially true when it comes to investing. Most individual investors understand that the best way to make money over the long term is to buy quality stocks and hold them for a long time—known as the "buy-and-hold" approach. The Internet, with its instantaneous access to hordes of data, tends to emphasize short-term developments. Many stock-tracking sites seem to encourage this mind-set—some even have built-in "alarms" that notify the user by e-mail when a stock hits a certain price.

The Internet represents a great opportunity for investors. For the first time, many of the research capabilities formerly available only to brokers are now within reach of average Joes and Joannes. But with ordinarily prudent investors newly able—and seemingly willing—to trade securities at the click of a keyboard, it's important to identify those sites that actually provide meaningful insight.

Here are some sites for all things financial. But remember, no one's policing this stuff; it's up to you to do your own research and use your best judgment.

Business Practices

The Council of Better Business Bureaus operates a website *(www.bbb.org)* that lets users know how to file complaints and get information on companies. It's a spotty website, but the BBB does a thankless job and I'll bet you're as glad as I am that someone's doing it.

Cars

Kelley's website *(http://www.kbb.com)* publishes its venerable Blue Book prices for any car, once you enter its year, condition and mileage.

Edmund's new car prices and reviews are available free on the Internet *(http://www.edmunds.com),* where they're regularly updated. Helpful for used cars as well.

The National Automobile Dealers Association features advice about car buying on its website *(www.nadanet.com).*

Charity

National Charities Information Bureau *(www.give.org)* and the Internet Nonprofit Center *(www.nonprofits.org)* both provide lots of information on charities, including red flags for bogus do-gooders. The latter site has a searchable database of all the nonprofits registered with the IRS, so you can check whether a group is actually registered as a charity.

Credit Cards/Banking/Debt

Sponsored by Bank Rate Monitor *(www.bankrate.com;* on AOL, keyword: *bankrate),* this amazing site compares all rates nationally on many topics, including mortgages, savings, auto loans, home equity loans, credit cards, online banking, checking, ATM fees and credit union rates.

Check the Federal Deposit Insurance Corporation's website *(www.fdic.gov)* to make sure your bank is insured by the FDIC.

The RAM Research site *(www.ramresearch.com)* lets you check current rates and other credit card details from their extensive database.

Credit Reporting Agencies

Equifax *(www.equifax.com)* and Experian *(www.experian.com)* allow you to order a copy of your credit report directly from the site.

Trans Union *(www.tuc.com)* totally sucks; won't let you order a report or even print a form to do so.

Debt Counseling

Consumer Credit Counseling Service *(www.cccsedu.org)*.

Insurance

Several term-life companies have a presence on the Internet, including InstantQuote *(www.instantquote.com)* and Quotesmith *(www.quotesmith.com)*. Browsers can enter their particulars and the sites will proffer several policies from several highly rated insurers.

Investing

General Investing Advice

The venerable American Association of Individual Investors website *(www.aaii.org)* includes a wealth of articles aimed at the average investor, searchable by topic and packed with AAII's trademark rooting-for-the-little-guy style.

The Motley Fools *(www.fool.com;* also available on AOL at keyword: *mf)* have built a powerful brand name by blending sophisticated fundamental analysis with a writing style that, for a medium infamous for its illiteracy, is sharply articulate. What's really unique about their website (which started out as an AOL site) is the liveliness of its chat rooms. The Fools have come closer than any other investing site to achieving the "community" that Web hype has promised for years. Visitors still endure a lot of "This stock's great/No, it stinks" garbage, but the occasional unconventional insight is worth the wade. Founded by brothers Tom and David Gardner, the Fools' much-emulated portfolio has taken a bit of a beating this year, trailing the S&P 500 by about eight points through the first quarter. But after trouncing that average three years in a row, they were due for a slight comedown, and to their credit, they've stuck to their guns rather than dumping their holdings at the first sign of bad news.

Max's Investment World *(www.maxinvest.com)* is a clean, well-designed investing site for beginners. The commentary is clear and readable, while the "Chart Your Plan" feature offers a good tool for achieving a blend of investments suitable to an individual's taste.

TheStreet.com *(www.thestreet.com)* is the first real Internet-based Wall Street news operation. They do actual journalism here, not just slapping together a bunch of wire stories and retreads, and some of the reporting is giving the best of the "old media" a run for its money. Co-founder and storied investor James Cramer has a column "Wrong!" that's one of TheStreet's highlights—he names names and pulls no punches in his signature brand of ranting-reporting.

Brokers/Brokerages

Investigate a broker's disciplinary past and find tons more than you ever wanted to know about brokers in general at the website of the National Association of Securities Dealers, aka NASD *(www.nasdr.com)*.

Many discount and full-service brokers also offer electronic services. Here are the web addresses of various brokers:

ELECTRONIC BROKERS

E*Trade	*www.etrade.com*
PCFN	*www.pcfn.com* (also excellent for quotes and stuff, even for nonaccount holders)

DISCOUNT BROKERS

Charles Scwab	*www.schwab.com*
Fidelity	*personal.fidelity.com*
Jack White	*www.jackwhiteco.com*
J. B. Oxford	*www.jboxford.com*
Muriel Siebert	*www.msiebert.com*
Waterhouse Securities	*www.waterhouse.com*

FULL-SERVICE BROKERS

Dean Witter	*www.deanwitter.com*
Prudential	*www.prusec.com*
Merrill Lynch	*www.ml.com*
Smith Barney	*www.smithbarney.com*

Earnings Info

First Call *(www.firstcall.com;* on AOL, keyword: *firstcall)* is the authority on company earnings and analyst expectations for same.

Company Info

Hoover's *(www.hoovers.com;* also available on AOL at keyword: *Hoover's).* This is the electronic version of the venerable business biographer company from Austin, Texas. Company profiles, including history, principals and recent financials are free, but to access the really sophisticated stuff requires a subscription, which runs about $10 a month.

Mutual Funds

Mutual fund investors don't benefit quite as much from the speed of the Internet. Since funds can be bought only once per day, any order placed gets filled on the next day—even a low-tech phone order can handle that. But what might be missed in speed is more than made up for in information and convenience. Virtually all the major fund companies are now online. All offer downloadable prospectuses and applications and some even allow trading of their funds online.

MUTUAL FUNDS COMPANIES

Not surprisingly, these sites tend to emphasize retirement and IRA investing—both of which often include mutual funds. But don't dismiss these sites too quickly—many have more to offer than salesmanship. Fidelity's site, for example, has scooped traditional news sources by notifying investors of shifts in the closely followed portfolio of its behemoth Magellan fund.

Aim	*www.aimfunds.com*

American Century	*www.americancentury.com*
Fidelity	*www.fidelity.com*
Janus	*www.janusfunds.com*
Scudder	*funds.scudder.com*
Stein Roe	*funds.steinroe.com*
Strong	*funds.strong-funds.com*
T. Rowe Price	*www.troweprice.com*
Vanguard	*www.vanguard.com*

MUTUAL FUND RESEARCH

Morningstar *(www.morningstar.net)*. The site of the foremost mutual-fund-rating publication is a latecomer to the web, but well worth the wait. In addition to their trademark easy-to-follow report cards on almost eight thousand mutual funds, there's an up-to-the-day relative performance feature that allows comparison of an investor's mutual funds against like-minded funds. Investors can enter and track their own portfolios, with a daily percentage gain/loss tally providing a somewhat overeager play-by-play.

Mutual Funds Interactive *(www.brill.com)* is an exhaustive mutual fund listing service that doesn't really go the extra mile but is clearly presented and easy to navigate.

The Investment Company Institute is the trade group for the fund industry. So don't expect much muckraking from their mutual fund website *(www.ici.org),* which does include some good info on how funds work and legislative issues.

Small-Company Stocks

The Internet is notorious as a bastion for promoters of small companies trying to pump stocks to unsuitably high levels. One good place to sort the scams from the potential gems is the "Red Chip Review," the "Value Line of the small caps" *(www.redchip.com).* This site offers detailed, thorough scrutiny of companies you've never heard of, along with easy-to-follow letter-grade rankings. Subscribers to the newsletter get full access to the site, but regular stiffs can still read "Red Chip"'s analyst reviews of companies that might earn that most elusive title—"the next Microsoft."

Stock Exchanges

The three major stock exchanges all operate pretty extensive websites, though they lean toward promoting the companies listed on them.

American Stock Exchange *(www.amex.com)*
NASDAQ *(www.nasdaq.com)*
New York Stock Exchange *(www.nyse.com)*

Stock Tracking and Quotes

Microsoft Investor *(investor.msn.com)* is my kind of investor site: you store your info on *your* computer, not theirs. No passwords or logging in, and you can track multiple portfolios with as many as fifty stocks. Plus, their historical quote info will let you see what Coke was doing in the thirties or how many times Ford has split since the twenties. It also features "Jubak's Journal," electronic investing expert Jim Jubak's chatty investing column.

Quote.com is the gold standard for portfolio tracking. After entering her holdings, an investor can choose to view charts updated as frequently as she likes—every five minutes, fifteen minutes daily or weekly. This is great for comparing the portfolio one actually has against one that was being contemplated—say, an ultra-aggressive basket of stocks versus a safer, government-bond-laden mix. Piles of research are available right within quote.com, including Morningstar, S&P stock guides and analyst-rating clearinghouses Zack's and First Call. A thirty-day trial is free with registration, but the whole enchilada will run $9.95 and up, depending on complexity and number of portfolios tracked.

Stock Center *(www.stockcenter.com)* is a simpler but less feature-laden tracking site. It features quotes and easy-to-use, quick-loading charts measuring price and volume for the past one hundred days. News links to stories that affect the stocks are provided by Yahoo, which gives access to tons of hot links to stories from different sources.

Yahoo! Finance *(quote.yahoo.com)* is speedy and easy. From stocks to mutual funds to indexes and headlines, the info's quick and clearly presented.

Overseas: International Finance Corporation *(www.ifc.org)* comes as close as anyone to providing reliable stock data from markets as far afield as Ghana and the Philippines. Tread carefully, though—much of the info is out of date.

Socially Responsible Investing

GreenMoney Journal, the bible of so-called socially responsible investing, offers complete coverage of all aspects of business and investing that are earth-friendly, nonsmoking and tread lightly *(www.greenmoney.com).* The print version is available at 800-318-5725.

The Calvert Group, a socially responsible mutual fund company, operates Know What You Own *(www.calvertgroup.com),* a nifty little database that tattles on mutual funds investing in tobacco.

Figuring It Out

www.financenter.com: The many financial calculators of this site cover topics like credit, stocks and retirement. Included are simple plug-in scenarios that figure things like "What is my return if I sell today?" "Should I sell before or after one year?" "Should I lease or buy?" "Does it make sense to refinance?" and "How do exchange rates affect my foreign mutual fund?"

Jobs/Careers

Career Mosaic *(www.careermosaic.com)* is very pro, easily searchable.

Online Career Center *(www.occ.com)* is a bulletin board for corporate job fairs.

The Monster Board *(www.monsterboard.com)* is everything a job seeker could ever want, from a "personal job search agent" to profiles of progressive employers to a resume repository. There's even a sort-of cool "relocation service" that lists apartments and other stuff a new city would necessitate.

World Hire *(www.worldhire.com)* is a somewhat New Age-y career site; lots of emphasis on finding the career that's "right for you."

Mortgage/Home Buying

How sweet it is to come across those little Web gems built by a regular guy for the sheer fun of it. Hugh Chou's mortgage-related calculators *(www.ibc.wustl.edu/ibc/mort_links.html)* offer simple and elegant "what can I afford" scenarios, with special emphasis on home-buying stuff. Includes a Monthly Payment Calculator that can also figure biweekly payments, an Income Qualification Calculator and another that figures how much a given prepayment will shave off your total house cost.

Homebuyers's Fair *(www.homefair.com)* is another site full of calculators, including one about the relative cost of living in various cities.

There's a surplus of real estate websites that claim to offer lots of homes for sale in lots of areas. Most fail miserably, with the home listings either obsolete or sparse. Cyberhomes *(www.cyberhomes.com),* however, has an extensive database of homes in lots of areas, and also features a cool map function that puts a user a click away from a detailed street map of the home's neighborhood.

The official site of the National Association of Realtors *(www.realtor.com)* also operates a database of for-sale digs, thoroughly covering some areas and all but ignoring others. Then there's a site *(www.ired.com)* that works as a sort of clearinghouse to the myriad real estate sites out there, rating and organizing them.

Department of Housing and Urban Development *(www.hud.gov)* is packed with information on government property and downloadable pamphlets, lots of links.

Student Loans/Financial Aid

Sallie Mae, the company that ends up servicing the bulk of student loans, has a website *(www.salliemae.com)* that offers on-line access to your account status, a debt counselor and a repayment calculator.

Mark Kantrowitz, a grad student in Pittsburgh, has made a name for himself by knowing everything there is to know about financial aid, from phone numbers to common myths to special sources of aid. His Web page *(www.finaid.org)* is the authoritative source for info on scholarships, grants, government aid, and includes up-to-date warnings on the myriad scams and hucksters out there in the financial aid jungle.

Taxes

The IRS's website *(www.irs.ustreas.gov)* has downloadable forms and a blizzard of information. Don't expect a speedy experience around tax time, though.

The Social Security website *(www.ssa.gov)* has info on all sorts of stuff. Detail freaks can check that their contributions are being recorded properly, tattletales can report fraud and the plain old curious can explore the facts and figures of the government's largest program. *Habla español, tambien.*

Nettax *(www.nettax.com)* has terrific online calculators with easy interface and walks you through various tax scenarios (paying rent vs. taking a mortgage interest deduction, etc.). Good stuff for "special circumstance" taxpayers, like the self-employed.

Acknowledgments

My friend and partner, John Packel. In a world that rewards loudmouths and self-promoters (sometimes with book contracts), those with quiet dignity, steady competence and thoughtful natures don't always get the recognition they deserve.

The Jacobs, without whose rustic house as East as East gets, this book never woulda got wrote.

My agent, Flip Brophy, whose skill and sure-handedness with this project proved her worthy of that shortstop name.

Howard Patlis, Sue Feltman, and Lou Dobbs, who inexplicably put my questionable mug on TV a couple hundred times.

Everyone at Doubleday—Pat Mulcahy, Bruce Tracy, Eliza Truitt, Dennel Downum, Rob Robertson, Maria Carella, Suzy Zengo-Nolan, James Sinclair.

To my brother and sister, who have rooted for me since I was in knee pants; my beautiful mom, who knows how truly to enjoy life with or without money; and to my dad, whose wallet was crammed with every toll booth receipt he ever got. Hey, you never know. In-laws, too (Franny and Jack).

And finally, please know that I know how cheesy it sounds to thank "all of *Green*'s readers." But I do thank them, each and every one of them. When *Green*'s "get a free sample" 800-number rang, it rang where I live— literally and figuratively. So to all the people who sent in ten bucks for a subscription, wrote an "Ask Kenny" question, took the time to put some thought into a "Pollen Count" response, or simply enjoyed the magazine or found it useful, my Yankees cap is off to you.

Green Thumbs
These people have gone way beyond the call of duty for *Green:* Jay Pohl, hipster Parliamentarian, and Pat Redding, my friend and illustrator.

All these people have also contributed to *Green* in a big way: Eric Bluhm, Ivan Brunetti, Aaron Cohen, Jackie Day-Packel, Sara Eckel, Jack Frank, Sam Henderson, Chris Hull, Sarah Johnson, John Kerschbaum, Paul Kopacz, Peter Kuper, Andrew Lathrop, Louisa McCune, Harvey Pekar, Ted Rall and Polly Washburn.

To all the readers of chapters who lambasted my ignorance and made sure I didn't pass it along: Susan Lee, Ned Siegler, Tom Bauer, Charles Colson, Jonathan Butler.

Everyone at *Worth* who let me look over their shoulders and ask a million questions. All of these people taught me something about writing, reporting and finance: Monica Corcoran, Peter Edidin, Dan Ferrara, Tolman Geffs, Randy Jones, John Koten, Jim Jubak, Tom Nawrocki and Dean Robinson.

Lots of other people, for encouragement, good ideas or good advice: Lee Smith, Marisa Bowe, David Eggers, Sarah Gold, Michael Pollan, Margie Borschke, Randy Williams, James Grant, Andy Tobias, Ben Dickinson, Anita Leclerc, David Granger, Steven E. Landsburg, Mark Hulbert, Scott Raab, Jason Cohen, Jeff Lescher, Jim Michaels, Warren Cook, Marty Peretz, Diana Loevy, Robert Levy.

And finally, all the people who dug *Green* enough to bring it to others: Paul Lukas, who was first, David Rothschild, Mitch Slater, Jose Northover, Bill Bresnan, Sam Pratt, Ana Marie Cox, Seth Friedman, Ann Perry, David Brancaccio, Randy Williams and Josh Glenn at Tripod.com and everyone at CNNfn.

Where, When and How
Most of this book was written in New York, summer '97, in Chelsea and Montauk, but some of it was also written in Delaware, New Jersey, Utah, Illinois, Virginia and Washington State. I used a Macintosh Powerbook,

Nisus and Microsoft word processing products, Claris spreadsheets, America Online, Netscape, Nexis, Tetris Max and Maelstrom 1.4.

I watched a ton of baseball and basketball using Stats on AOL, sticking mostly to underdogs and high overs. (Thanks, Bowman Int'l.) No animals were eaten. I used Dean Markley strings, Zildjian cymbals and no Peavey equipment.

Index

About the Author

Ken Kurson is the founder and editor of *Green*, a critically acclaimed personal finance magazine for people in their twenties and thirties. Formerly a staff writer at *Worth* magazine, where he wrote "The Advocate" column, Kurson now covers finance for *Esquire* magazine. He has written for a wide range of publications and was named to TJFR's list of the best business journalists under the age of thirty, two years in a row. He has appeared on financial programs on CNBC, MSNBC, CNN, and is a regular guest on CNNfn. He lives outside New York City.